Comparative Psychology
for Clinical Psychologists and Therapists

of related interest

The Psychology of Ageing
An Introduction
5th edition
Ian Stuart-Hamilton
ISBN 978 1 84905 245 0
eISBN 978 0 85700 577 9

The Complete Guide to Asperger's Syndrome
Tony Attwood
ISBN 978 1 84310 669 2
eISBN 978 1 84642 559 2

Neuroscience for Counsellors
Practical Applications for Counsellors, Therapists
and Mental Health Practitioners
Rachal Zara Wilson
Illustrated by Pagan Tawhai
ISBN 978 1 84905 488 1
eISBN 978 0 85700 894 7

Self-Care for the Mental Health Practitioner
The Theory, Research, and Practice of Preventing and
Addressing the Occupational Hazards of the Profession
Alfred J. Malinowski
ISBN 978 1 84905 992 3
eISBN 978 0 85700 931 9

Ethical Maturity in the Helping Professions
Making Difficult Life and Work Decisions
Michael Carroll and Elisabeth Shaw
ISBN 978 1 84905 387 7
eISBN 978 0 85700 749 0

Comparative Psychology

for Clinical Psychologists and Therapists

*What Animal Behavior Can Tell Us
about Human Psychology*

DANIEL C. MARSTON AND TERRY L. MAPLE

Jessica Kingsley *Publishers*
London and Philadelphia

First published in 2016
by Jessica Kingsley Publishers
73 Collier Street
London N1 9BE, UK
and
400 Market Street, Suite 400
Philadelphia, PA 19106, USA

www.jkp.com

Library of Congress Cataloging in Publication Data
Names: Marston, Daniel C., author. | Maple, Terry L., author.
Title: Comparative psychology for clinical psychologists and therapists :
   what animal behavior can tell us about human psychology / Daniel C.
   Marston and Terry L. Maple.
Description: Philadelphia : Jessica Kingsley Publishers, 2016. | Includes
   bibliographical references and index.
Identifiers: LCCN 2015049921 | ISBN 9781849057431 (alk. paper)
Subjects: LCSH: Psychology, Comparative. | Comparative psychiatry. | Clinical
   psychology.
Classification: LCC BF671 .M275 2016 | DDC 156--dc23 LC record available at
http://lccn.loc.gov/2015049921

British Library Cataloguing in Publication Data
A CIP catalogue record for this book is available from the British Library

ISBN 978 1 84905 743 1
eISBN 978 1 78450 161 7

Printed and bound in Great Britain

CONTENTS

1. Introduction   7

2. Learning and Memory   25

3. Depression   51

4. Aggression   78

5. Substance Abuse   105

6. Gambling Problems.   128

7. Autism Spectrum Disorders.   151

8. Overeating and Obesity   181

9. How a Clinical Psychologist and a
    Comparative Psychologist See the World.   202

10. Conclusion   223

   SUBJECT INDEX   245

   AUTHOR INDEX   250

Chapter 1

INTRODUCTION

This is a book dedicated to helping mental health professionals learn more about behavior and behavior change from the perspective of comparative psychology, a field that is often neglected in clinical psychology programs. The book will address the contributions that comparative psychologists studying everything from pigeons to primates have made to our understanding of humans. Our aim is to provide clinicians with a more thorough understanding of the biological basis for human behavior through the lens of comparative psychology. We believe this will enable clinicians to have a more robust understanding of psychological conditions and effective ways of treating those conditions.

To understand the importance of the topics covered in this book, it is useful to start with questions about why mental health professionals do what they do. How is it that they know (or think they know) what may detract from our competence as clinicians? Where do they find the direction to determine what to say or what to do that can be helpful for another person? And why should they expect that what they are doing is more likely to be helpful than harmful to another person? These are questions that play significant roles in developing effective clinical professionals.

Knowing what to say and how to act as a mental health professional comes from a detailed understanding of the intricacies of behavior and behavioral change. This is the most important aspect setting psychological interventions apart from casual conversation. The very essence of psychological intervention involves conversing with the person but it involves a much deeper understanding of the human experience and how to incorporate behavioral changes.

Thus, clinicians need a solid understanding of what factors shape behaviors and an understanding of what is involved in eliciting change. All clinicians are looking to help people change and look to research for determining how to go about making that change.

Researching human behavior has been an essential strategy throughout the history of clinical psychology. If clinicians do not rely on research then they are not approaching their profession scientifically. It is only through the use of research that clinical interventions become anything more than just conversation. From early on during the development of clinical and counseling psychology, the emphasis has been on research to understand disorders. Clinicians have used their understanding of disorders, based on research, to decide what approaches were going to be most effective. Freud, for example, relied on his understanding of neurological disorders to develop a "talking cure" that helped to alleviate his patients' suffering. His approaches were not based on research but his understanding of what he was trying to treat was indeed based on research. Neurological research showed him the directions in which he wanted to go and he applied clinical approaches that he developed, or that he learned from others, to get him there.

In recent decades clinicians' emphasis has been more and more on "empirically supported psychotherapies" (Westen, Novotny, and Thompson-Brenner 2004). This term refers to therapeutic interventions that have been subjected to empirical research. Clinicians are asked to not only base their understanding of disorders on empirical research but also their understanding of what interventions work on empirical research. Although this approach provides clear support for interventions that work, it has been criticized for stifling clinical skills. Clinicians who rely on empirically supported therapies, some argue, limit themselves only to interventions tested on well-defined conditions and under well-controlled environments.

It is beyond the scope of this book to address whether relying only on empirically supported treatment is beneficial or not. But the discussion of empirically supported treatment shows the extent to which empirical conditions play an important role in clinical practice. Whether it was the early research on understanding behaviors or the later research on understanding what led to behavior change, the emphasis has been on studying humans as a way to help ourselves.

But studying humans has its limitations. For starters, we are an incredibly complex species. It is difficult to isolate and explain how a single experience influences our lives. In order to look at that level of detail, you would have to study a human from birth to death under intensely controlled environments. A single researcher would essentially have to devote their professional life to studying one subject. Not only would that be unethical, but also unfeasible. Instead, we have to study humans in experiments with relatively short durations. Since we cannot control for every aspect of the life history of those participants, those data are messy in all the same ways our lives are. Thus, in order to understand some of the mechanisms behind behaviors, we have to look for other ways to model similar phenomena. This is where comparative psychologists come in.

Many of the limitations inherent in human research can be overcome with the use of animal models. We are able to control many of the variables that make human data messy. We can control and manipulate factors such as rearing history, environment, and food intake. We can, more precisely than in humans, determine what behavioral changes result from slight environmental changes. We are also able, at least in some species, to study a single animal from birth to its natural death. This level of control enables comparative psychologists to be much more precise in what they are studying than psychologists who study humans. Please note that this is not a criticism of human research, as it is invaluable in understanding ourselves. However, to understand how we became human, we must look at other animal species.

Defining comparative psychology

Merriam-Webster's Dictionary defines "psychology" as the "science or study of the mind and behavior." It seems that most people interpret this definition to mean study of the human mind. In fact, the Oxford English Dictionary limits its definition to humans: "The scientific study of the human mind and its function." Comparative psychologists work to bridge that gap by studying how minds work in a variety of species. This is a worthwhile endeavor just to understand other animal species. However, by comparing and contrasting how minds work, including the human mind, comparative psychologists are able to offer a more comprehensive view of behavior and the causes of behavior change. Thus, we believe it is useful for clinicians to become more aware of the contributions of comparative psychology to the broader field.

One of the main goals of comparative psychologists is to document both similarities and variations in abilities (and traits and behaviors) across species. By doing this, we can then try and piece together the evolutionary pressures that made these abilities adaptive. The rationale for this is that if we understand how the processes evolve in nonhuman species, who are typically less complex than humans, this knowledge can impact on our understanding of how human abilities have evolved (MacLeon *et al.* 2012). Both similarities and differences between species can help to explain general characteristics of psychological constructs (Maestripieri and Roney 2006). If particular psychological traits serve similar functions in a variety of animal species, despite difference in how those functions develop, then the argument can be made that suggests they serve a similar function for humans as well. However, if humans exhibit a trait or behavior not seen in closely related species, that indicates a selective pressure acted on humans after the last common ancestor with those other species.

As Darwin (1871) noted, "the difference between humans and other species is generally one of degree and not of kind." Thus, understanding different species helps professionals understand humans better by expanding how we understand psychological constructs. We understand factors contributing to behaviors and behavior change in general regardless of the individual involved. What, for example, does it mean when a researcher says that something causes an individual to change? Does it mean that the researcher expects that the connection only applies for that one individual organism (whether human or nonhuman)? Usually the purpose of any research is to use the results to make general conclusions about the connection between different variables. This supposes that there are connections to be made. Comparative psychologists often base their research on the supposition that some connections can be made not only within species but also across species. Understanding behaviors and behavior change for one or more species can, therefore, provide information to understand behaviors and behavior change across species.

Comparative psychologists have also posited that understanding the simpler forms of learning in natural settings can help enhance our understanding of the impact of human culture (Claidiere and Whiten 2012; Laland and Galef 2009). Social psychologists often emphasize the importance of individuals' learning behaviors by witnessing those behaviors in others. This is one of the main categories of social influence. Social scientists and biological scientists have only recently started to investigate in detail the degree to which the social environmental factors impact behaviors and behavior change across species. Given the importance that the social environments have played in psychotherapy approaches throughout the history of clinical psychology (as reviewed in Ainsworth 1969), further research in this area will likely help expand our understanding of what factors influence psychotherapeutic effectiveness.

Despite the power of the comparative approach, there have long been people refuting that studying animals can aid our understanding of humans. Since Descartes declared that humans are thinking beings and all other animals are machines, there have been people touting the uniqueness of humans in the animal kingdom (Boesch 2007). However, it seems that whenever a claim is made about a uniquely human ability, studies showing at least the building blocks of those behaviors in other animals are inevitable. For example, both tool-use and culture were once thought to be the exclusive domain of humans, although modern research has shown these abilities in a variety of species (Boesch 2007). While it is true that humans engage in more pronounced versions of behaviors than other species, the same building blocks are present in other animals. For example, humans cooperate far more extensively with each other than any other species, even going so far as routinely cooperating with strangers (Highfield and Nowack 2011). We do not see cooperation on that scale in other species, but many nonhuman species do also cooperate routinely. Those that dismiss outright the contributions of comparative work often focus on the differences between species and ignore the similarities (see Daly and Wilson 1999 for a summary of these arguments).

Our position in this book is that studying different animal species can and does help to more fully understand psychological constructs. Specifically with regard to clinical applications, understanding behaviors and behavior change across different species can be useful for understanding how and why behaviors and behavior change function for humans. This is what makes studying comparative psychology important and useful for clinical practitioners. We will leave it to the interested reader to delve into more detail the authors who have argued strongly against this position. It would be reasonable to conclude that we would have not written this book if we fully agreed with their positions.

Comparative psychology at the beginnings of psychological science

In his article on animal research and its contributions for understanding personality, Gosling (2001) outlined some of the major areas of general psychology comparative psychologists have contributed to over the years. Names and findings that clinicians are likely familiar with emerged from this comparative approach. Pavlov, Tolman, and Skinner contributed significantly to understanding the mechanisms of learning. Thorndike and Kohler helped with understanding problem-solving and innovation. Harlow helped to understand attachment and the evolutionary basis of love. None of their significant contributions to psychology would have been possible without scientific studies of animal behavior. Their research highlighted commonalities across different species with similarly functioning psychological constructs.

A comprehensive look at comparative psychology needs to start at the very beginning of psychology as a science. Animal studies have been an important part of psychological science since its inception. There are two books that are the essential start of animal studies as part of psychological science. Charles Darwin paved the way for comparative psychology by acknowledging shared ancestry between species and formulating a mechanism, natural selection, for species to evolve in his seminal works *The Origin of Species by Means of Natural Selection of the Preservation of Favoured Races in the Struggle for Life* (1859) and *The Descent of Man and Selection in Relation to Sex* (1871). Pierre Flourens was the first author to use the term "comparative psychology" when he published his book *Psychologie Comparée* (1864). George John Romanes, a student of Charles Darwin, followed with his book *Animal Intelligence* in 1882. Both Flourens and Romanes proposed a science that would compare animal and human behavior.

Flourens and Romanes also helped found psychology as a science. But, the concept of understanding human behaviors through studying animals has been around for centuries. Aristotle is considered the "father of both biology and psychology" and wrote about the importance of considering both human and nonhuman species when studying behaviors and development. Plutarch, writing about 400 years after the time of Aristotle, thought that differences between humans and animals with regard to behaviors is often more of degree than of kind (Papini 2008), as did Darwin writing nearly 2000 years later.

In modern times, comparative psychology has been associated with clinical psychology since its inception. Lightner Witmer founded the first psychology clinic and is credited with first coining the term "clinical psychology." At the same time that he started his psychology clinic he also started a psychology laboratory. Witmer started the laboratory to assist children but also began conducting animal research. One of his most famous studies involved his conducting the same psychology tests on a chimpanzee that he conducted on children. Witmer concluded that the chimpanzee showed reasoning ability similar to children and could possibly be able to read or write under certain conditions.

In a history of Lightner Witmer, Thomas (2009) notes that there is no public record of the general response to Witmer's claim that he could teach a chimpanzee to talk or his comparisons of chimpanzees to children. He had also claimed to find the "missing link" that Darwin and other scientists had sought. There is also no public record about whether the scientific community gave this claim any credence. Thomas does note that there was at least one newspaper article from that time describing Witmer's foray into "monkey psychology" (as the newspaper described it) in a critical way. Thomas even speculated that this may have been a reason why psychology courses and texts have not covered much about Witmer's extensive contributions to the field. This is unfortunate given that there were other scientists in subsequent decades who gave serious consideration to the similarities between apes and children (Hayes and Hayes 1952).

Comparative psychology grew throughout the United States during the early part of the twentieth century. Ivan Pavlov and Edward Thorndike were two of the names who contributed to the field with their work on animal behavior. In Europe a closely related field called "ethology" grew during the early part of the twentieth century. Karl von Frisch, Konrad Lorenz, and Nikolaas Tinbergen were some of the most influential scientists in this field and shared a Nobel Prize for their studies of animal behavior (the Nobel Prize in Physiology or Medicine 1973). While comparative psychology engaged primarily in laboratory research, ethology emphasized the significance and importance of studying behaviors outside of the laboratory.

Comparative psychology and psychotherapy

In the twentieth century there was no broad field of psychology; rather, what we now call psychology was subdivided into several specialties. Psychological science and psychotherapy grew alongside each other but separately for the first half of the twentieth century. Clinical psychology was a distinct field that was limited to psychological assessment. Psychotherapy was primarily considered to be psychoanalysis during this time. Psychology as a science was centered in universities and was directed towards the understanding of behaviors and development. Animal studies contributed a great deal during this time to understanding behaviors. Psychologists studied behavior as it applied across different species and talked about behaviors both in a very general way (across species) and in a more specific way (between individuals). Universities focused on understanding behaviors and behavior change but not necessarily in terms of applying that understanding to the practicalities of changing behaviors.

Comparative psychologists started addressing issues important in psychiatry with articles on "experimental neuroses" or "conditioned neuroses" in the 1940s and 1950s. Ivan Pavlov spent a good deal of the last years of his life documenting how his research on conditioning in dogs could be applied to psychiatric disorders. In his 1943 book *Conditioned Reflexes and Psychiatry*, Pavlov chronicled how his research findings could help illuminate such psychiatric disorders as schizophrenia, hysteria, obsessions, and paranoia. Joseph Wolpe, famous for the systematic desensitization approach to treating phobias, built on Pavlov's writings and presented additional ways of understanding experimental neuroses (Wolpe 1952). His writings formed the basis for his now famous behavioral therapy approaches.

Considering the importance that evidence-based psychotherapy has in modern times it is interesting to note that this was not a major component of psychotherapy throughout the first half of the twentieth century. Psychotherapy was focused primarily on psychoanalytic treatment and this particular approach to treatment did not focus on empirical studies or on applying research to psychoanalytic treatment. Psychoanalysis was supported primarily through case studies and anecdotal research (Kazdin and Blase 2011) and was dominated by medical professionals. On the other hand, psychological research in the laboratories and universities was dominated by psychologists.

Following World War II, psychotherapy expanded as a form of treatment (Benjamin 2005). While psychoanalysis as a form of treatment expanded in the prior decades, much of the treatment was limited to those with high incomes and the well-educated. Partially due to the atrocities witnessed by soldiers and civilians during World War II, providing help for middle-class individuals became more of a priority.

As demand for psychotherapy increased, there was a shortage of medical professionals who could provide that service (Watson 1953). Psychologists were brought in to develop effective treatments that could be used for helping larger numbers of people. These psychologists came from the laboratories and universities where comparative psychology had flourished for decades. They understood what studies of animals offered in terms of understanding behaviors and behavior change and were able to use this information to develop effective treatments for humans.

During this time there was a demand not only for more professionals to provide mental health treatment but also for an understanding of what approaches were effective. Hans Eysenck, for example, called for an empirically based approach to psychotherapy (Kar 2013). However, empirical evidence of effectiveness in treating humans was lacking. Fortunately, there were decades of research on animal behaviors and behavioral change. Comparative psychologists and ethologists contributed a great deal to developing an empirically based approach to psychotherapy.

Comparative psychology and B.F. Skinner

Arguably the most prominent American psychologist was B.F. Skinner, whose career represented a convergence of comparative psychology and clinical psychology. He and his colleagues used rats and pigeons in most of their pioneering behavior-analytic research. They were comparative psychologists who used their research to develop the branch of psychology called "behaviorism." Behaviorism focused on quantifying and analyzing observable behaviors, while excluding internal motivations for those behaviors. Their work continued through the 1950s and 1960s in developing what has become one of the three major schools of psychological thought. And it was the direct application of this research to clinical settings that led to the development of "behavior therapy," "behavior modification," and "behavior analysis."

Skinner detailed his combining of clinical and comparative psychology in his definitive book *Science and Human Behavior* (1953). This book was the culmination of Skinner's work on addressing how behavioral principles, developed primarily through animal research in university laboratories, could be applied to understanding human behaviors. It was in this text that he specified how behavior analysis could be applied to understanding human behaviors and help facilitate behavior change. He covered many of the main topics associated with behavior analysis but also went into more complex human constructs, such as thinking and emotions.

Skinner also presented one of the earliest U.S. works in a scientific journal on the topic of how a human condition could be explained through analysis of animal behavior. In his 1948 article "'Superstition' in the Pigeon" (Skinner 1948a) he discussed how regular reinforcement of a pigeon's behaviors could be applied to understanding superstitious behaviors. He took a group of hungry pigeons and for a few minutes each day put them in front of a mechanism that fed them at regular intervals. Many of these pigeons developed behavioral habits that appeared to coincide with when they received food. Even though there was no actual connection between their behaviors and receiving food, these pigeons did show behavioral patterns suggesting that they had made such a connection.

Skinner's work was a major breakthrough in demonstrating how the work of a comparative psychologist could be used to more fully understand human behaviors. He not only addressed ways in which professionals could help humans but also went on to publish the book *Walden Two* (Skinner 1948b) which addressed how behavior analytic concepts could be used to make a utopian society. His work in behavior analysis was also called "radical behaviorism" because of his refusal to look into non-observable phenomena such as feelings (Schneider and Morris 1987) and this became one of the most prominent approaches to psychotherapy. He started his work in the laboratory with animals and then used that as a springboard into an approach for helping understand human behavior and behavior change.

Behavior analysis fitted well with comparative psychology because it was a reaction against the focus on introspection that had been such a large part of psychology throughout the first half of the twentieth century. The subject's verbal descriptions about sensations, private events, and feelings were identified as the primary focus of psychology. Behavior analysts worked against this focus and developed a scientific approach to understanding behaviors that focused on objective measures (Wolf 1978). Studies of animals fitted well as a vital source of data and research for this approach. It did not matter that the subjects could not talk and share their experiences verbally because the researchers were not interested in their subjective experiences.

In 1947 the first Conference on the Experimental Analysis of Behavior was held. Subsequent conferences gave rise to the Society for the Experimental Analysis of Behavior. This society is responsible for two journals that continue to provide important research for mental health professionals. The *Journal of the Experimental Analysis of Behavior* is primarily dedicated to behavioral research and the *Journal of Applied Behavior Analysis* is dedicated to the application of behavior analysis to clinical work (Edwards and Poling 2011). The first issue of the *Journal of the Experimental Analysis of Behavior* was published in 1958 and included articles on such topics as operant behaviors in children and behavioral extinction in rats. Both clinical and research articles were published in that journal until the late 1960s. This is when the society also created the *Journal of Applied Behavior Analysis* due to the large number of clinical articles that were being submitted to the *Journal of the Experimental Analysis of Behavior*.

Comparative psychology, ethology, and attachment theory

While behavior analysis grew as a significant part of clinical psychology in the United States throughout the latter part of the twentieth century, attachment theory grew as a significant part of clinical psychology in Europe. Attachment theory developed from ethological theory and was originally developed by British psychoanalyst John Bowlby. He posited that attachment behaviors such as crying and searching, that are common among mammals when separated from "attachment figures" (i.e. someone who provides support, protection, and care), are the result of an evolutionary process that played a major role in how human beings develop and function. This stood in stark contrast to other psychoanalysts who held that these expressions were manifestations of immature defense mechanisms that were operating to repress emotional pain.

Bowlby further (1958) posited that children are born pre-programmed to form attachments with others because of the survival advantages associated with those behaviors. Because manipulating variables such as not having an attachment figure would be highly unethical with children, animal models were needed. Harlow and Zimmerman (1958) studied rhesus monkeys to understand the attachment process and Lorenz studied geese to understand the genetically programmed process of imprinting as it relates to attachment (Lorenz and Wilson 2002). That research was essential in understanding the importance of attachment and its impact on future behaviors and behavior change.

Mary Ainsworth is another scientist associated with attachment theory. She conducted a large research project, called the Ganda Project, which addressed quality in mother–infant interactions. Her work was similar to Bowlby's work and the two collaborated on attachment theory for decades. One aspect of Ainsworth's work that is noteworthy here is that she presented her findings from the Ganda project at a meeting of the Tavistock Study Group, a series of influential meetings that included both infant researchers and animal researchers (Bretherton 1992). Proceedings from these meetings were subsequently published in a four-volume set called *Determinants of*

Infant Behavior published between 1961 and 1969 (Foss 1961, 1963, 1965, 1969).

Animal research played a critical role in both John Bowlby's and Mary Ainsworth's careers. Ainsworth used animal research to support, among other topics, the theory of a "critical period." This is the theory that if a mother is separated from her infant for a brief period of time postpartum she will often subsequently reject the infant. She used this theory to explain difficulties she observed in human mothers bonding with their infants if separated from them right after birth (Ainsworth 1985). Bowlby used animal research extensively throughout his career and found particular benefit from ethological research in supporting a Freudian instinct theory (Bowlby 2008).

Many introductory psychology texts present the concepts of attachment through the work of one of Bowlby's contemporaries, Konrad Lorenz. There often is an image of Lorenz with ducklings following him. These ducklings had "attached" themselves to Lorenz as he was the first individual they connected with following their birth (as their mothers had been removed from their environments). They were filmed and photographed following Lorenz around in a way indicating that they had clearly identified him as the "attachment figure." This is a rather basic example of how attachment works and the impact that attachment figures have on psychological development. However, the concept has played a major role in developing psychotherapy approaches.

There was a significant interchange between comparative psychology and ethology in the 1950s through 1975. Donald Dewsbury (1995) documents at least 84 North Americans who traveled to work in European ethological laboratories and at least 15 Europeans who relocated to North American laboratories. This exchange was instrumental in enabling ethological theory to have the success that it did in the United States. It allowed comparative psychology to reflect more and more of the complexities that were becoming evident through research advances. Interestingly, these advances in comparative psychology were occurring around the time that the "second wave" of behavior therapy, reflected in the development and increased prominence of cognitive-behavioral therapy, reflected advances in psychotherapeutic research and theory.

Dewsbury's work, culminating in 1975, is appropriate because this was during a period of time when Skinnerian theory was being modified by the work of ethologists. R.J. Hernstein's 1977 article in the *American Psychologist*, entitled "The evolution of behaviorism," summarizes this impact. For the prior 15 years or so behaviorism had focused on the operant conditions that included stimulus responses, reinforcers, and drive states. However, behaviorism could not explain all of the behaviors seen in humans and other animals. For example, behaviorism could not explain concepts such as a human forming a novel sentence (Chomsky 1959). As such, ethological research and concepts from the cognitive revolution that occurred in the 1950s were eventually woven into behavioral theory to allow room for internal states such as motivation, insight, and innovation. Hernstein addressed how the incorporation of motivational dynamics, due in large part to contributions by ethological researchers, allowed for a more practical and comprehensive approach to addressing behaviors and behavioral change.

Hernstein's article was not a criticism of Skinnerian theory but was a summary of how ethological research helped behavioral theory incorporate more of the complexities related to behaviors and behavioral change. Studying animal behaviors from a more naturalistic approach allowed more opportunities to see how motivations and other intrinsic factors likely played a role. This approach allowed for behaviors and behavioral change to be interpreted in a more complex manner. Thus, modern comparative psychologists have generally moved away from radically behaviorist interpretations of behavior. Because of this shift and the cognitive revolution of the 1950s (see Gardner 2008 for a history of that movement), comparative psychologists are now exploring the rich and exciting area of comparative cognition, a concept that Skinner would undoubtedly oppose.

Behavior analysis, particularly the radical behaviorism reflected throughout Skinner's work, continued to have a significant impact on psychotherapy over the next several decades and up to the present time. In the 1960s behavioral theory was combined with the growing cognitive theory movement. This grew into the field of "cognitive-behavior" therapy which is one of the three most prevalent general approaches to therapy today (psychoanalysis and humanistic therapy being the other two). Skinner was not supportive of this approach and strongly criticized the movement towards combining cognitive and behavior therapy approaches (Skinner 1977). Radical behaviorism, without being tethered to cognitive approaches, has continued to have a significant impact on psychotherapy (Hayes 2004). Two major psychotherapy approaches that continue to be prominent today and can be directly related to radical behaviorism are Functional Analytic Psychotherapy and Acceptance and Commitment Therapy (Kohlenberg, Hayes, and Tsai 1993).

Attachment theory has played a prominent role in recent decades for integrating different psychotherapy approaches (Liotti 2011). This theory offers a common developmental base from which psychotherapists can understand behavior and behavior change regardless of which clinical approach they are using. Disorganized attachments are also theorized to be a major factor in many psychiatric disorders and developmental psychopathologies. There have been recent treatments based on attachment theory developed for toddler–parent psychotherapy and parent–child psychotherapy. In addition, attachment theory has been a significant component in a number of major psychotherapy interventions, including Interpersonal Psychotherapy and Emotion-Focused Psychotherapy (Levy *et al.* 2011).

Summary

We have presented theories and works throughout this chapter written by some of the most famous psychologists. These names (e.g. Watson, Pavlov, Skinner, Lorenz), each of whom was a comparative psychologist, would be familiar to any student who ever took an introductory psychology course. They, along with many other comparative psychologists, laid the groundwork for what clinical professionals would offer to the mental health field when demands increased following World War II. And, as we have seen in our brief summaries of comparative and clinical psychology history, the work of comparative psychologists led directly into understanding major psychological constructs that impacted the clinical professions throughout its development. Two of those constructs, behavior analysis and attachment theory, continue to have very significant impacts on psychotherapeutic approaches.

This chapter outlined some major historical aspects of comparative psychology and clinical psychology. Our history here was very basic and made only the most general points about how these two fields have been related for more than 100 years, but it is clear that comparative psychology has contributed significantly to clinical psychology. In the rest of the book we provide considerably more detail about what comparative psychology offers for understanding the underlying conditions that clinicians treat and techniques that bring behavioral change.

References

Ainsworth, M.S. (1969) 'Object relations, dependence and attachment: a theoretical review of the infant–mother relationship.' *Child Development 40*, 969–1025.

Ainsworth, M.S. (1985) 'Attachments across the life span.' *Bulletin of the New York Academy of Medicine 61*, 9, 792–812.

Benjamin Jr, L.T. (2005) 'A history of clinical psychology as a profession in America (and a glimpse at its future).' *Annual Review of Clinical Psychology 1*, 1–30.

Boesch, C. (2007) 'What makes us human (*Homo sapiens*)? The challenge of cognitive cross-species comparison.' *Journal of Comparative Psychology 121*, 3, 227–240.

Bowlby, J. (1958) 'The nature of the child's tie to his mother.' *International Journal of Psychoanalysis 39*, 350–371.

Bowlby, J. (2008) 'Instinctive Behavior: An Alternative Model.' In *Attachment*, Volume I of *Attachment and Loss*. New York: Basic Books.

Bretherton, I. (1992) 'The origins of attachment theory: John Bowlby and Mary Ainsworth.' *Developmental Psychology 28*, 5, 759–775.

Chomsky, N. (1959) 'A review of B.F. Skinner's Verbal Behavior.' *Language 35*, 1, 26–58.

Claidiere, N. and Whiten, A. (2012) 'Integrating the study of conformity and culture in humans and nonhuman animals.' *Psychological Bulletin 138*, 1, 126–145.

Daly, M. and Wilson, M. (1999) 'Human evolutionary psychology and animal behavior.' *Animal Behavior 57*, 509–519.

Darwin, C. (1859/2003) *The Origin of Species by Means of Natural Selection of the Preservation of Favoured Races in the Struggle for Life.* New York: Signet Classic.

Darwin, C. (1871) *The Descent of Man and Selection in Relation to Sex.* London: John Murray.

Dewsbury, D.A. (1995) 'Americans in Europe: the role of travel in the spread of European ethology after World War II.' *Animal Behavior 49*, 6, 1649–1663.

Edwards, T.C. and Poling, A. (2011) 'Animal research in the *Journal of Applied Behavior Analysis.' Journal of Applied Behavior Analysis 44*, 2, 409–412.

Foss, B. (1961) *Determinants of Infant Behavior: Proceedings of the Tavistock Seminar of Mother-Child Interactions.* London: Methuen & Company Ltd.

Foss, B. (1963) *Determinants of Infant Behavior: Proceedings of the Tavistock Seminar of Mother-Child Interactions.* London: Methuen & Company Ltd.

Foss, B. (1965) *Determinants of Infant Behavior: Proceedings of the Tavistock Seminar of Mother-Child Interactions.* London: Methuen & Company Ltd.

Foss, B. (1969) *Determinants of Infant Behavior: Proceedings of the Tavistock Seminar of Mother-Child Interactions.* London: Methuen & Company Ltd.

Gardner, H. (2008) *The Mind's New Science: A History of the Cognitive Revolution.* New York: Basic Books.

Gosling, S. (2001) 'From mice to men: what can we learn about personality from animal research?' *Psychological Bulletin 127*, 1, 45–86.

Harlow, H.F. and Zimmerman, R.R. (1958) 'The development of affective responses in monkeys.' *Proceedings of the American Philosophical Society 102*, 5, 501–509.

Hayes, K.J. and Hayes, C. (1952) 'Imitation in a home-raised chimpanzee.' *Journal of Comparative and Physiological Psychology 45*, 5, 450–459.

Hayes, S.C. (2004) 'Acceptance and commitment therapy, relational frame therapy and the third wave of cognitive and behavioral therapies.' *Behavior Therapy 35*, 4, 639–665.

Hernstein, R.J. (1977) 'The evolution of behaviorism.' *American Psychologist 32*, 8, 593–603.

Highfield, R. and Nowak, M. (2011) *SuperCooperators: Evolution, Altruism and Human Behaviour (or Why We Need Each Other To Succeed).* Melbourne: Text Publishing.

Kar, S. (2013) 'Hans Eysenck – Contributions and controversies.' *Delhi Psychiatry Journal 16*, 1, 53–56.

Kazdin, A.E. and Blase, S.L. (2011) 'Rebooting psychotherapy research and practice to reduce the burden of mental illness.' *Perspectives on Psychological Science 6*, 1, 21–37.

Kohlenberg, R.J., Hayes, S.C., and Tsai, M. (1993) 'Radical behavioral psychology: two contemporary examples.' *Clinical Psychology Review 13*, 6, 579–592.

Laland, K.N. and Galef, B.G. (2009) *The Question of Animal Culture.* Cambridge, MA: Harvard University Press.

Levy, K.N., Meehan, K.B., Tenes, C.M., and Yeomans, F.E. (2011) 'Attachment Theory and Research: Implications for Psychodynamic Psychotherapy.' In R.A. Levy, J.S. Ablon, and H. Kächele, (eds) *Psychodynamic Psychotherapy Research.* New York: Springer Humana Press.

Liotti, G. (2011) 'Attachment disorganization and the controlling strategies: an illustration of the contribution of attachment theory and developmental psychopathology to psychotherapy integration.' *Journal of Psychotherapy Integration 21*, 3, 232–252.

Lorenz, K., and Wilson, M.K. (2002) *King Solomon's Ring: New Light on Animal Ways.* New York: Psychology Press.

MacLeon, E.L., Matthews, L.J., Hare, B.A., Nunn, L.L., *et al.* (2012) 'How does cognition evolve? Phylogenetic comparative psychology.' *Animal Cognition 15,* 2, 223–238.

Maestripieri, D. and Roney, J.R. (2006) 'Evolutionary developmental psychology: contributions from comparative research with nonhuman primates.' *Developmental Review 26,* 2, 120–131.

Papini, M. (2008) *Comparative Psychology: Evolution and Development of Behavior* (Second edition). New York: Psychology Press.

Pavlov, I.P. (1943) *Lectures of Conditioned Reflexes, Volume Two: Conditioned Reflexes and Psychiatry.* London: Lawrence and Wishart.

Schneider, S. and Morris, E. (1987) 'A history of radical behaviorism, from Watson to Skinner.' *Behavior Analysis 10,* 1, 27–39.

Skinner, B.F. (1948a) '"Superstition" in the pigeon.' *Journal of Experimental Psychology 38,* 2, 168–172.

Skinner, B.F. (1948b) *Walden Two.* New York: Macmillan.

Skinner, B.F. (1953) *Science and Human Behavior.* New York: The Free Press.

Skinner, B.F. (1977) 'Why I am not a cognitive psychologist.' *Behaviorism 5,* 2, 1–10.

The Nobel Prize in Physiology or Medicine 1973 (n.d.) Available at www.nobelprize. org/nobel_prizes/medicine/laureates/1973, accessed on 11 January 2016.

Thomas, H. (2009) 'Discovering Lightner Witmer: a forgotten hero of psychology.' *Journal of Scientific Psychology,* 3–13.

Watson, R.I. (1953) 'A brief history of clinical psychology.' *Psychological Bulletin 50,* 5, 321–346.

Westen, D., Novotny, C., and Thompson-Brenner, H. (2004) 'The empirical status of empirically supported psychotherapies: assumptions, findings and reports in controlled clinical trials.' *Psychological Bulletin 130,* 4, 631–663.

Wolf, M. (1978) 'How applied behavior analysis is finding its way.' *Journal of Applied Behavior Analysis 11,* 2, 203–214.

Wolpe, J. (1952) 'Experimental neuroses as learned behavior.' *British Journal of Psychology: General Section 43,* 4, 243–268.

Chapter 2

LEARNING AND MEMORY

Introduction

Learning and being able to remember what you have learned are two of the most ancient brain processes in animals. Learning not to do something that hurts is arguably one of the most adaptive responses in animal behavior. Even very simple organisms, such as earthworms, are capable of learning to avoid and escape aversive stimuli (Wilson *et al.* 2014). While there are obvious differences between humans and earthworms, studying the processes of learning and memory in nonhuman species has provided a tremendous amount of insight into how those processes work in the human brain and how they can shape human behavior. In this chapter, we look at learning and memory in ways that can be helpful for therapists and counselors. This involves not only addressing learning and memory in very general ways, but also delving into the specific types of learning and memory processes that are particularly important for creating behavioral changes.

Definitions

Learning

In his widely read textbook on learning and memory, Domjan (2015, p.14) provides a general definition of learning:

> Learning is an enduring change in the mechanism of behavior involving specific stimuli and/or responses that result from prior experiences with those or similar stimuli and responses.

Based on this definition, there are two main components of learning. First, learning must result in a relatively permanent change in behavior. If a college student crams for an exam and manages to pass, we do not consider that as learning since the material will likely be forgotten (McIntyre and Munson 2008). Second, learning is the result of past experience. That is, you must get some sort of new information before you can learn. This information could take many forms, including: failing at a task and learning from your mistakes; listening to a lecture or reading a book; watching someone else perform the task; or any number of other methods. But, you generally need some new knowledge or experience for learning to occur.

Additionally, this definition of learning relates to a change in the mechanism of behavior. This is subtly different than just acknowledging a change in behavior. What Domjan means here is that we need to ensure the change in behavior was due to learning rather than some other factor. For example, if a player misses an easy goal towards the end of a soccer match, we typically do not think that she has not learned to kick accurately. Rather, a more likely explanation is that her leg is fatigued and so her accuracy decreased. When we classify something as learning it is important to ensure we are really looking at learning, not at another mechanism that causes behavioral change.

Learning can be broken down into three types of learning: non-associative learning, associative learning, and social learning. Non-associative learning is learning that occurs without reinforcers. This includes habituation and sensitization. Habituation occurs when we get used to something in our environment and are then able to "tune it out." If you live next to a fire station, the sounds of fire engines become less intrusive over time. You become habituated to that sound and stop paying attention because it does not have a significant meaning for you. In contrast, someone who does not live next to a fire station may look out the window if they hear a siren. While that example may not seem particularly adaptive, habituation is actually quite a nice evolutionary trick. It frees your brain from having to process stimuli that are not relevant. If we did not habituate to certain stimuli, we would spend far too much time attending to irrelevant information.

Sensitization is almost the opposite of habituation. This is when some environmental stimuli have a very significant meaning, but can cause you to attend to similar, although irrelevant, stimuli.

Soldiers coming back from a war zone, for example, have often become sensitized to the sound of gunfire. If you are in a war zone, it may be a matter of life and death for you to pay attention to any sort of loud popping sounds, as they may indicate you are being attacked. However, when veterans return home, the sound of a car backfiring could trigger that sensitization, causing a physiological response similar to what they experienced during war.

Associative learning is when behaviors are changed because of their association with reinforcement. Many of the principles of associative learning apply across species (Rumbaugh and Pate 2014). These principles involve stimulus–response relationships and different species have shown remarkable similarities in how they respond to different schedules of reinforcement. Learning behavior is typically characterized, based on these stimulus–response relationships, as either a conditioned stimulus that is paired with an unconditioned stimulus (Pavlovian learning or classical conditioning) or a modification of an existing behavior that results from positive or negative consequences (Skinnerian learning or operant conditioning).

While the two types of conditioning are undoubtedly familiar to clinicians, we should briefly review those concepts here. The classical condition, as popularized by Pavlov and his salivating dogs, is when some meaningless stimulus, such as a light or a bell, is paired with a meaningful stimulus, such as food. Over time, as the meaningless stimulus and food are repeatedly paired together, the light or bell will come to elicit the same response as food. In Pavlov's famous experiment, the light itself elicited a salivary response in the dogs after it had been paired with food (Pavlov 1927). Note that we used the word "elicit" in reference to the dog's response. Conditioned stimuli elicit a response that is typically thought to be outside of the individual's control. That is, the dog does not decide whether or not to salivate at the sound of the bell, it just does. This sounds like a fairly simple principle, but people are just as susceptible to classical conditioning as dogs.

Operant conditioning is when a behavior is either increased or decreased due to reinforcement or punishment respectively. In other words, operant conditioning is basically training. However, in contrast to classical conditioning, the animal must first exhibit (or suppress) the behavior you want to increase (or decrease). That is, operant behaviors are not as automatic as classically conditioned responses because they are, to some degree, under the control of the individual in question. You can't reinforce a behavior if the individual never engages in that behavior, whereas salivating in the presence of food is automatic.

Most people are likely familiar with the concept of positive reinforcement, but the other three ways of operant conditioning tend to be less well known. Here, we give a brief overview of these concepts, but for a more in-depth discussion see Karen Pryor's seminal training book *Don't Shoot the Dog* (Pryor 1999). While this book is focused on animal training, it is filled with advice on how to apply the same concepts to people. For anyone interested in applying operant techniques in a clinical setting, it is well worth reading.

In operant conditioning the term reinforcement means increasing the likelihood that a behavior will be emitted. Punishment means decreasing the likelihood a behavior will be emitted. Positive means that you are adding something to the environment and negative means that you are removing something from the environment. Positive reinforcement, then, means providing a reinforcer (something good that the individual wants) after the individual engages in a behavior you would like to increase. If you have a dog at home, you are likely familiar with this procedure. If you are training your dog to sit on command, every time she sits when you say "sit" you give the dog a treat. This principle works exactly the way in humans. If your spouse cooks dinner one night, praise and thank him/her. It will likely increase the amount of dinners you get cooked for you.

But, positive reinforcement can be tricky because you have to take the perspective of the individual who is being reinforced. If a dad is at the grocery store with his daughter and the daughter starts crying, the dad may give her candy to keep her quiet. The dad may think that he is positively reinforcing her for being quiet. But, because being quiet occurred *after* she was given the candy, what she really may learn is that dad will give her candy if she cries. You have to use reinforcers immediately after the behavior you want to increase. Reinforcing a behavior before it occurs doesn't teach anyone anything.

Negative reinforcement also increases the likelihood of a behavior occurring in the future (reinforcement), but by removing an aversive stimulus from the environment (negative). If you have a headache and you take a pill that removes the aversive stimulus of the headache, that behavior has been negatively reinforced. Because the headache was removed, you are more likely to take a pill the next time you have a headache. Returning to the example of the father and daughter in the grocery store, the daughter actually negatively reinforced her dad. She removed the aversive stimulus of crying when her father gave her candy. This increases the likelihood that her father will resort to candy in the future. Again, negative in this context only means removing an aversive stimulus, not the more colloquial use of the word meaning "bad."

Punishment is also a rather misunderstood word. In the learning literature, punishment only means something that decreases the future likelihood of a behavior. Just as in reinforcement, punishment can be either positive or negative. Positive punishment is adding something aversive to the environment to decrease future behavior. Spanking is the classic example of positive punishment. By spanking a child, you are adding pain in an effort to reduce undesirable behaviors. Negative punishment is removing something pleasant from the environment in order to decrease a behavior. Sending a child to time out, for example, removes the child's access to toys in an attempt to decrease some behavior.

However, not all methods of operant conditioning are equal. Studies have demonstrated that the application of aversive stimuli produces aggression, an undesirable side effect. This is the empirical support that started the movement against capital punishment, supporting that aversive stimuli such as spanking could lead to increased aggression. Azrin, Hutchinson, and McLaughlin (1965) presented one of the earliest studies of this phenomenon. They studied squirrel monkeys who could produce an inanimate object by pulling a chain. They found that this chain-pulling occurred very little in the absence of any negative stimuli. But when a painful shock was administered these monkeys would increase their rate of chain-pulling significantly. They pulled the chain and then attacked the inanimate object that appeared. This response continued for as long as the inanimate object appeared and the shocks were administered. Punishment, the application of an aversive stimuli for a negative behavior, is shown here to be a more negative method of conditioning given the strong potential for aggressive responses.

The same goes for humans. Positive punishment is the least effective method for changing behavior. However, the person doing the punishment often *feels* like the punishment worked. If a mother spanked her child for throwing a tantrum, the tantrum may very well stop. This makes the mother *feel* like spanking was an effective method of behavioral control. However, positive punishment typically does not work in the long term. Instead, the child is likely to avoid throwing tantrums in front of his mother (but not stop throwing tantrums), harbor feelings of resentment towards the mother, or believe that aggression is an appropriate response for changing another person's behavior.

The final type of learning is social. Much of what we, and other social species, learn is learned by watching others. It is very possible to learn things on your own, but learning from others can save enormous amounts of time and effort. In the wild, animals are confronted by a huge variety of potentially edible things. But, the costs associated with eating something poisonous are very high. You may get sick, be more susceptible to predators, or die. Instead of trying and discovering for yourself which things are poisonous, it is much safer and more efficient to eat the same things that everyone else eats. In this way, the knowledge of more experienced individuals can be passed on from generation to generation. This is incredibly adaptive, particularly with more complicated skills such as tool use.

To test whether or not chimpanzees could socially learn, Horner and colleagues (2010) developed a puzzle box. The box could be opened by two different methods. In one group of chimpanzees, a "model" was trained to lift a door to open the puzzle box. In another group, the chimpanzee model was trained to slide the door open. Each model was then allowed to demonstrate opening the box for their group. If the chimpanzees were learning how to open the box by trial and error, half of them should have learned to lift and half to slide. But, they learned from each other. In the group with the lifting model, all the other chimps lifted. In the group with the sliding model, all the other chimps learned to slide.

However, not all models are created equal. In a follow-up study, the researchers trained a high-ranking and a low-ranking model to put something in two different buckets. Putting something in either bucket resulted in the chimps earning a piece of banana. If the chimps were indiscriminate in whom they learned from, half of the group should have exhibited the high-ranking behavior and half the low-ranking behavior. But, the chimps overwhelmingly preferred to do what the high-ranking individual did. They did this even when there was a fairly large amount of competition over the high-ranking bucket and the low-ranking bucket had no competition. In fact, one issue with running the study was that the low-ranking model wanted to switch to the high-ranking model's bucket. This tells us that, just like humans, chimps are choosy about who they copy.

Humans use social learning extensively. In fact, sometimes we do something another person has done even when that behavior doesn't make sense. Horner and Whiten created another puzzle box (Horner and Whiten 2005), with several holes and levers. They taught both chimps and human children a series of behaviors to do in order to "release" a reward. However, what the participants didn't know was that the series of behaviors she taught them were completely irrelevant for releasing the reward. They then made an exact replica of the box, but this time it was clear. The children and chimps could now see that their actions had no purpose. Chimps quickly skipped to the end and got their reward. Children, on the other hand, continued to perform the pointless series of actions. Thus, learning from those around us is such a powerful tool that we can rely on it to a fault. This is partially why social learning became so important in comparative psychology research (Nielsen *et al.* 2012).

Memory

Memory is an ability to represent past experiences and events (Spear and Miller 2014). This representation cannot be observed but its impact can. Recalling a memory is often the process by which an entity makes use of what it has learned. When an individual engages in a change in the mechanism of behavior it has "remembered" something that it "learned." As we will see later in this chapter, it is not necessary that the individual be conscious of what was learned in order for them to have remembered something. Thus, learning and memory are inextricably linked, as you can't learn from experiences if you don't recall them. Similarly, memories are not particularly useful if you don't learn how to adapt your behavior from them.

Animal and human research on memory and learning often appear very similar. Subjects (whether human or nonhuman) are presented with a task and given a number of trials to learn that task. Often the number of trials required is considered to be a measure of how quickly the individual subject is able to learn the task. Once the task is learned then the subject is allowed to engage in other activities. These activities are most often not related in any direct way to the task that was learned. This is important so as to keep any extraneous variables from impacting on the measure of how well the subject learned the material. After a certain period of time engaged in other activities, the subject is then prompted to again engage in the task that they learned earlier. How well a subject completes the task is usually the main measure for how well the subject recalled that task.

Most learning and memory research in humans and nonhumans follows the same process outlined in the previous paragraphs. There are, of course, many complex variations on how this process is followed across different experiences. Many different types of recall tasks and many different types of measures are used. One example of a method for studying memory that has been used with both humans and nonhumans is called Analysis of Receiver Operating Characteristics (ROC). This approach involves examining recognition memory by measuring the probability of endorsing an item as previously studied (also called "response bias"). For example, you may give humans a list of words to memorize. Then, have them do some math problems. After that, ask them if certain words were on the list they previously studied. Nonhumans lack the ability to display this skill verbally, but they can do it with visual imagery.

This method has been used for measuring free recall and recognition in humans and nonhumans. Studies support that the ROC method can be used to bridge the gap between memory studies across species. Koen and Yonelinas (2011), for example, found that speeding recognition responses leads to a reduction in recollection but not familiarity-based recognition. These authors found these results when using ROC for both rats and humans. Their results support that the method produced comparable results across species.

Similarities in learning and memory across species

Studying cognitive concepts in nonhumans has gained popularity over the past several decades as interest in human cognition has increased. There have been more attempts in recent years to develop large data sets across a diverse range of species. This type of research has shown general learning concepts common in studying different species. For example, research on twelve primate species on inhibitory control, the ability to resist a prepotent behavioral response, found that this ability is common among all the species but tends to follow different procedures across each of the different species (MacLean *et al.* 2012).

Learning and memory have traditionally been two of the main areas examined by using behavioral tests on animals. One consistent finding across this research is that the hippocampus is one of the most important brain structures in learning and memory for both humans and animals. But this research has also shown that the role of the hippocampus is complex since both human and animal research shows that learning can still occur even if the hippocampus is absent. This suggests other areas of the brain also play a significant role in learning and memory (Savage and Ma 2014).

Animal research helps show the complexity of learning and memory processes and also the purposes of these processes. There is ample reason to expect that the general processes associated with learning and memory would be similar, if not the same, across different species given the evolutionary benefits of these processes working well. An individual, whether human or nonhuman, cannot have any control over their environment if they do not have at least a basic ability to learn skills and recall what they have learned. Humans and nonhumans alike need to understand how to get food and how to get water if they are going to survive. There really is no reason to expect that the process by which this occurs would differ whether it related to learning and remembering how to get to the grocery store or where to find the nearest water buffalo. Depending a great deal on effective learning and memory is essential for surviving across all species.

Wystrach and Graham (2012) outlined the basics of learning and memory for solving tasks. They address the topic in their discussion of navigation among insects. Basics related to their review of navigation apply to learning and memory across species. This general process involves several more detailed cognitive processes. An animal must extract from its environment the information that will be necessary for navigation. The animal then robustly organizes this into memories. When navigating, it converts those memories into spatial decisions. Studying navigation provides a more direct way of studying these cognitive processes since the animal's behavioral goal (i.e. getting from Point A to Point B) is relatively clear. Other tasks (e.g. communication) would involve the same pattern of cognitive processes but the intentions of the parties might be less clear (e.g. intention of the signaler during communication may not be clear to an outside observer).

Studies of learning and memory across different species have shown similarities in some cognitive processes between humans and animals. Premack (2007) summarized some of the main human-like cognitive abilities shown by animals:

- Many animal species seem to teach. Animals such as cats and meerkats will not only show their young how to stalk and kill prey but also will adjust the frequency with which they disassemble the prey to the age of their young.

- Chimpanzee short-term memory is only slightly less than that of humans. Both remember no more than 5–7 items. They may differ in terms of the amount of information they can recall, primarily because of the human ability for recursive language and numbers.

- Many animals have the ability for "causal illusion" but not necessarily for "causal reasoning." "Causal illusion" is the mechanism by which an individual learns that goal-directed acts with which they are involved or that they witness produce desired items. "Causal reasoning" is the process by which an individual can learn that two events are causally related even if they do not occur near each other and even if the individual does not directly witness them (e.g. a light switch causes a light some distance away to turn on).

Neurobiological factors

Research on nonhuman species has helped our understanding of the individual variation in learning and memory abilities. Unsurprisingly, one consistent finding is that genetics play a significant role in learning and memory ability. Researchers artificially selected for learning and memory abilities over several generations of *Drosophila* flies and ended up with flies who exhibited heightened learning and memory abilities (Davis 2005; Mery and Kawecki 2002). The same is true for nematode worms (Wen *et al.* 1997). These findings demonstrate that genetics help shape an individual's abilities in these domains. However, it is unclear how much of these variations would occur in natural environments.

There are a large number of environmental factors that can mask the impact of genetics on learning and memory (van Praag, Kempermann, and Gage 2000). These factors include food availability and environmental stress. Improving environmental factors can help limit the impact of intrinsic factors, such as genetics, on learning and memory. Rampon *et al.* (2000), for example, found that housing mice in enriched environments can help overcome any limitations in learning and memory associated with genetics.

Animal research and subsequent human research support the impact that enriched environments can have on improving learning and memory. What this research shows is that improving environments is one significant way of helping to improve learning and memory. Given that this is a finding supported across research involving different species, there is strong evidence that this is a general aspect of learning and memory. Clinicians can apply this finding to help improve the therapeutic work of their patients. It is important for patients to have as much enrichment in their environment as possible in order to help them benefit from therapeutic work. This would include encouraging patients to get enough sleep and to eat properly if they are going to benefit from psychotherapeutic work. This is also important when helping patients from a lower socioeconomic household find ways of gaining support that can help to enrich their environment. This may seem like common sense, but it is not always the case that clinicians see the importance of helping their patients make good decisions regarding things such as diet and sleep. It is also not always the case that clinicians feel it is their role to help patients find the type of support services they need. Research into the impact of enriched environments on learning and memory across species support the conclusion that this is an important role for clinicians if they are going to help their patients benefit from therapy and counseling.

Animal studies and human studies have demonstrated that aerobic exercise helps improve a number of different cognitive abilities, including learning and memory (Hillman, Erikson, and Kramer 2008). This is an example of another type of finding that clinicians can use directly in their work with patients, encouraging them to engage in aerobic exercises to improve their learning and memory abilities and help them benefit even more from therapeutic and counseling interventions.

Comparative psychology studies over the years have helped improve our understanding of the neurological factors associated with learning and memory. Much of the research has supported that the hippocampus plays an important role in both learning and memory. This area of the brain has been identified as an essential part of learning and memory, but other research has also shown that its removal or damage is not necessarily something that causes learning or memory to stop or even be impaired significantly. There is a considerable amount of cooperation between the different parts of the brain and even damage to an area as essential to as the hippocampus can be compensated for by other areas of the brain taking over.

Studies involving human and nonhuman subjects show that memory is supported by multiple brain systems that differ in the types of memory they mediate. In a very general way, this distinction is most often made between memory systems that are located in the hippocampal area and those located elsewhere in the brain. Animal studies across different species show that many memory tasks involve activation of the hippocampal area along with other areas of the brain. There are clearly distinct memory systems that are anatomically and functionally distinct from each other. These systems function parallel and simultaneously with each other and do not likely operate completely separately from each other. There are times when the systems act in cooperation with each other and times when they act in competition with each other (Poldrack *et al.* 2001; Schwabe 2013;

Voermans *et al.* 2004). How these different memory systems are influenced by different physiological, environmental, and/or training factors is poorly understood (Poldrack and Packard 2003).

Research on animals shows the complexity of the brain and the different ways that the brain can compensate for damage. This research also shows what can be expected in terms of learning and memory for individuals who are older and individuals who are suffering from physical disease. This actually has quite a bit of relevance for clinical practitioners today. There are many populations receiving psychological services in modern times who would not have even been considered as possible candidates for therapy or counseling decades ago. This includes not only older individuals as such, but also older individuals who are in the process of developing dementia and other types of significant cognitive impairment. It also includes people who are suffering from significant physical disease and particularly individuals suffering from significant neurological disease. There are psychological interventions being used to help these individuals and it is noteworthy that comparative psychology research in the area of learning and memory supports that these individuals have the potential to benefit from therapy and counseling as much as individuals who are younger and/or not physiologically impaired.

Animal and human studies show that aging is not associated with a serious decrease in the rate at which the elderly acquire new skills, learn procedures, or form simple associations. A review of the literature in Foster, DeFazio, and Bizon (2012) shows that aging also does not have a negative impact on the long-term retention/performance of previously acquired skills or procedures. This is a finding supported across a number of different species. There is no evidence to suggest that aging itself would lead someone to not have the cognitive abilities to benefit from counseling and therapy interventions. This is a finding that helps support the use of counseling and therapeutic interventions for a specific population that decades ago would not have been considered appropriate candidates for therapy and counseling.

Even the onset of dementia does not impair learning and memory to the extent that an individual could not benefit from some types of interventions used in counseling and therapy. This again is a finding supported from both human and animal research. Humans with neurological disorders show intact learning and memory abilities. Areas affected by dementia most often include episodic memory, executive function, attention, and awareness of deficits (Irish *et al.* 2012) but memory for tasks and procedures is often unaffected/ unimpaired in individuals with mild dementia. Animals with similar disorders also show generally intact abilities. For example, rats with symptoms of Huntingdon's Disease showed generally intact procedural and memory for facts and details (Kirch *et al.* 2013). These results support that there are cognitive areas that can be targeted for psychological interventions even for individuals suffering significant neurological disorders.

And, finally, animal research has also shown that the impact of even significant dementia can be lessened by practitioners who take active steps to lessen the impact on learning and memory. Poor memory after brain damage (including that associated with dementia and neurological disorders) is usually considered to be the result of information being lost or rendered inaccessible. Rats with memory problems, such as those in amnesia and dementia, can relate to a tendency to treat novel experiences as familiar ones (McTighe *et al.* 2010). Memories of the impaired animals were improved simply by reducing incoming information prior to the test. This finding suggests that the type of impairment summarized in the research can be addressed with the use of approaches that help to decrease interference. These approaches can include keeping extraneous noise and activity out of the environments where the impaired individual is being helped, and focusing only on one type of intervention at a time so as to decrease the amount of novel material being presented.

Learning and memory in counseling and psychotherapy

In the previous paragraphs we covered the extent to which animal research has helped with our understanding of learning and memory. Comparative psychology research allows for studying general rules associated with these cognitive processes. Animal research laid the groundwork for topics that were subsequently addressed in human research. Cognitive systems studied across different species help to identify similarities between species. Taken together, these results provide an understanding of the general workings of learning and memory.

Learning and memory is a large subfield within comparative psychology research. A whole series of books could be written to summarize the research findings and their implications from this field. We certainly cannot undertake that endeavor, but we can look at very specific questions with regard to learning and memory topics relevant for the subject of this book. Namely, we can address questions about what types of learning and memory processes are most important for counseling and psychotherapy and how those processes work.

H.J. Eysenck (1966, p.353) provided a summary of the types of learning processes that are important for behavior therapy:

> From the point of view of learning theory, treatment is in essence a very simple process. In the case of surplus conditioned response, treatment should consist in the extinction of those responses; in the case of deficient conditioned responses, treatment should consist of building up the missing stimulus–response connections.

Eysenck's view of behavior therapy remains one that is still appropriate today. Behavior therapy approaches continue to focus either on the extinction of learned responses or on helping individuals learn responses that help build up stimulus–response connections. This is an essential part of understanding the role that learning plays in therapeutic interventions today. Examples of surplus conditioned responses being addressed can be seen in the use of relaxation techniques from treating phobias (decreasing anxiety level in feared situations). Examples of deficient conditioned responses can be seen in the use of bell ringing and special pads for night-time bed-wetting.

Behavior therapy interventions are very direct but are much more complicated than they might seem on the surface. This is something that therapists and counselors learn once they enter the "real world" of clinical interventions. The process of helping people learn new skills and put those skills into effect is not necessarily an easy one. Part of the reason for this is that the processes associated with classical and operant conditioning are much more complex than they often appear when summarized in textbooks. Understanding the complexities associated with the processes of classical and operant conditioning is one of the more significant contributions made by animal research.

The basics of operant and classical conditioning are considered hallmarks of comparative psychology research. Pavlov's work with dogs and Skinner's work with pigeons and rats show the very basics of learning that are familiar to any college student. But the descriptions covered in many introductory psychology texts make it seem like the process is very straightforward. Individuals either learn to engage in new behaviors because they are associated with food or something equally desirable or because certain behaviors are associated with certain reinforcers. And then the reversal of this process (i.e. the removal of reinforcers) leads to extinction of desired behaviors. These types of learning are often presented in introductory texts as very basic and this can often lead to an expectation that the behavioral interventions themselves need to be very basic.

Decades of animal research revealed that the whole process of learning new skills and extinguishing developed skills is very complex. Helping individuals (whether human or nonhuman) learn new skills depends on the type of reinforcement schedule that is used. It also depends on how much the reinforcement schedule is varied. It depends further on the type of environment where the new skills are taught and on how much the individual is motivated to make any changes. We will not go into specifics about these topics here as they will be addressed in subsequent chapters as they relate to specific psychological conditions. But what is important to realize here in a general discussion of learning and memory is that the whole process of learning new skills and extinguishing established skills is very complex and the complexities have been made evident through hundreds if not thousands of animal research studies.

In 1969, Leon Kamin made one of the most significant empirical discoveries in classical conditioning. He found that animals learn not only when a conditioned stimulus precedes an unconditioned stimulus but also when the conditioned stimulus predicts the unconditioned stimulus. This type of prediction depends on the strength of the unconditioned stimulus. In this way, associative learning does not depend on a critical number of pairings of conditioned stimulus and unconditioned stimulus but on the power of the conditioned stimulus to predict a biologically significant stimulus.

What Kamin's finding underscores is something experienced by any clinician who has tried to implement behavioral intervention.

And that is the fact that the effectiveness of that intervention depends not on whether there is a connection between a behavior and a stimulus but on the strength of that connection. There simply is no way to get a behavioral intervention to work if the conditioned stimulus does not predict a sufficiently desired stimulus. This is also the case for stimulus–reinforcer connections. A behavioral intervention using reinforcers simply will not work if those reinforcers are not desired enough by the individual. Clinicians can teach parents to offer computer time, toys, or even money as rewards for desired behaviors, but if those rewards are not desired enough by the child then there is simply no way that the intervention will work. This is a result of the need for the conditioned stimulus or reward to be powerful enough in order to motivate the individual to engage in a desired behavior.

Behavioral interventions depend on the strength of consequences, rewards, and conditions for their effectiveness. This is an important part of any interventions meant to help patients learn new skills and put those skills into effect. Cognitive-behavioral interventions also rely on what the patient sees as the potential benefit of interventions in order to determine whether they will put much effort into those interventions. Recognizing the power of the conditioned stimulus to predict a stimulus that is significant for the individual is important for clinicians trying to implement cognitive-behavioral approaches. Helping to identify the potential strength of whatever conditioned stimuli and reinforcers are used is an important step in the learning process associated with therapy and counseling.

Comparative psychology research has been important not only for understanding the learning process associated with therapy but also for understanding important aspects of memory relevant for therapy. What is interesting here is that, whereas learning is an essential part of cognitive and behavioral approaches, memory is equally important for cognitive-behavioral and psychodynamic approaches. Memory adds to the discussion of therapy and counseling in that at least part of the memory discussion involves a discussion of how to impact on nonconscious (or unconscious) processes.

Many of the recent advances in understanding animal cognition are ones that show the inadequacy of relying on observable stimulus–response models. Unconscious activity and thought is considered to be the typical state of functioning for animals and activities.

Additional activities, such as perception and thought, are needed to explain conscious activities (Terrace 2014).

Two memory processes essential for understanding unconscious mental processes are procedural (implicit) memory and declarative (explicit) memory (Kandel 1999). Procedural (implicit) memory involves learning skills that are evident only in performance rather than conscious recall. Declarative (explicit) memory is a conscious memory for people, objects, and places. Procedural and declarative memory are of particular importance for psychotherapy (Fuchs 2004). Procedural (implicit) memory encompasses all automatic performances and unconscious processes. Declarative memory records single experiences for lasting recall. Procedural memory is located primarily in the basal ganglia, cerebellum, and amygdala while declarative memory is located primarily in the temporal lobe, primarily the hippocampus. Lesions in the neonatal ventral hippocampus in rats lead to procedural memory deficits (Lecourtier *et al.* 2012).

Declarative memory and procedural memory are the two most important long-term memory systems in terms of function and areas served (Ullman 2012). Their roles have been studied extensively with both humans and nonhumans. Declarative memory is important for learning information about facts and events. Procedural memory underlies the nonconscious learning and processing of a variety of activities and functions. These two systems often interact with each other and there are a number of factors that determine which system is relied on more. Research in rats supports that there is more cooperation than competition between procedural and declarative memory systems (Cassel *et al.* 2012). There also is evidence that learning involving declarative memory may block the learning of similar knowledge in procedural memory. For example, research summarized in Lum *et al.* (2012) shows that procedural memory in animals and humans can be impeded by declarative memory.

Differences between declarative and procedural memory underscore some of the more important concepts emphasized in psychodynamic therapy. One example would be the emphasis on early developmental years and the importance of what was learned during that time. The fact that individuals are often impacted significantly by what happened during the first few years of life even though they cannot consciously remember what happened is explained through research on procedural and declarative memory. Infantile amnesia, the process by which few memories from early childhood are accessible to later recall, occurs in humans and animals, including rodents. Research suggests that this is likely due to the slow development of the declarative memory system (Clyman 1993). Notice here how a concept import to psychodynamic therapy gets research support from animal studies.

Improving learning and memory in therapy and counseling

Animal studies show that the learning of new skills often requires many trials every day (Curlik and Shors 2013). This research is consistent across multiple animal studies and also subsequent human studies. Individuals must exert sustained effort and/or concentration during the training session. During the early stage of training, performance is dependent on declarative memory but procedural memory becomes more dominant as the training progresses. This has been shown in research on rats (Chang and Gold 2003) and humans (Iaria *et al.* 2003). Multiple training keeps the cells alive that are initially developed by the training. There is a strong positive correlation between how well an animal learns a skill and the number of surviving cells in the brain. This supports the need for therapists and counselors to provide multiple training opportunities across therapy sessions if patients are going to effectively learn skills being addressed in the sessions. This also supports the use of homework assignments in counseling and therapy so as to make sure that the patient is continuing the training even outside of therapy sessions. There is a considerably lower likelihood that the patient will learn the new skills effectively if there are not multiple trials associated with the therapy process.

Animal research also shows better memory for emotional events than neutral events. Human memory research also has supported this conclusion. This is possibly because the amygdala enhances the function of the medial temporal lobe memory system (Dolcos, LeBar, and Cabeza 2004). This supports the emphasis on emotional material being addressed in therapy sessions along with interventions used to help the patient learn better skills. Bringing up emotional material can be difficult for patients even if it is that material which initially led them to therapy. Memory research supports that emphasizing emotional material in sessions can help patients benefit from sessions not necessarily because of catharsis (the process of releasing repressed emotions), although that could be a factor, but because it is more likely that the patient is going to effectively recall material covered in sessions if there is an emotional component to what is covered.

Two environmental factors that contribute to improvement in learning and memory are predictability and environmental stability (Mery 2013). Research across species has shown that learning and memory improve when there is more predictability and stability. For example, research conducted by Smid *et al.* (2007) showed that two species of larvae have significant differences in the number of trials required for them to modify their behaviors to find food on certain plants. One likely explanation for this difference was that the one species found food primarily on plants contained in the same area and the other found food on plants dispersed throughout different areas. Their differences in learning and memory are likely due in large part to the increased predictability and stability of where they find food for one species compared with the other.

Predictability and stability are important not only to larvae but also to many animal species, including humans. Counselors and therapists can help individual patients benefit from therapy sessions by making them feel comfortable by using the notions of predictability and stability. Some specific steps that therapists and counselors can take to maximize these factors include keeping the office layout consistent, keeping the same appointment time (or close to the same appointment time) for sessions, and keeping the general therapy process the same across sessions.

What we have seen throughout this chapter is that animal research and human research show that cognitive impairment does not necessarily prevent a patient from having a positive response to therapeutic interventions. Counselors and therapists should keep this in mind when deciding what sorts of interventions to use when helping someone who presents with cognitive impairment. For example, alterations in the environment or how interventions are implemented may be necessary to help maximize effectiveness, but therapy and counseling can still be effective for helping these individuals. For instance, people with mild cognitive impairments were able to improve their verbal memory scores and even increase their hippocampus activity through a cognitive training program (Rosen *et al.* 2011).

Cognitive rehabilitation offers more promise than cognitive therapy for individuals with significant cognitive impairment because it does not attempt to modify cognitive functioning but aims at developing and implementing in everyday life approaches that might help the person deal with day-to-day problems (Kurz *et al.* 2012). In addition, Aharonovich, Nunes, and Hasin (2003) studied cognitive-behavioral therapy treatment for cocaine abuse. They found that the individuals receiving this type of treatment were more likely to drop out early from treatment if they had significant cognitive impairments. Cognitive domains related to high drop-out rates were attention, mental reasoning, and spatial processing. These authors did not specify why the individuals dropped out.

One of the most promising approaches for using memory in psychotherapy was first developed based on animal studies. This process is called "memory reconsolidation." It is the process by which memories thought to be stable can re-enter an unstable state, be modified, and then stabilized again (Schwabe, Nader, and Pruessner 2014). This process was initially discovered through research on animals, including rodents and crabs, and has in recent years been studied for its more practical benefits involving humans.

There is actually not much known about what factors might influence memory reconsolidation. Much of the research has involved bringing up memories in situations similar to those where the memories were first formed. In animal research, this involves creating the same specific conditions where the memories were formed. But in a counseling setting, this process involves techniques used to help human patients focus on aspects of the situations where the memories were first formed. These processes could involve guided imagery and relaxation techniques helping the person focus without deterrents on aspects of the initial memories. Since much of the research on memory reconsolidation, both human and nonhuman, involves fearful situations this suggests that memory reconsolidation may be particularly helpful for healing trauma-related symptoms. Finnie and Nader (2012) summarized that the factors involved in memory consolidation are not very well known at this point and may very well change depending on the conditions where the memories were initially formed.

Summary

Comparative research across species demonstrates that learning and memory follow basic rules. These rules typically involve stimulus–response patterns for learning and involve extracting material from the environment (learning) and then recalling and applying that material when needed to help the individual exert some control over the environment. There are multiple types of memory that often work in conjunction with each other but also might work in competition with each other.

Research across different species, including humans, shows that learning occurs either as a new reflex develops through pairing with a conditioned stimulus (e.g. Pavlovian learning) or through modification of an existing behavior that results from positive or negative consequences (e.g. Skinnerian learning). All learning tends to involve some type of stimulus–response relationship. But there are a number of factors that add to the complexity of this process. Reinforcement schedules and strength of unconditioned stimulus are just two factors that enter into determining how likely it is that the individual will learn a new skill. In therapy and counseling, this translates into a need to focus on how often a reinforcer is provided and how motivating a stimulus is when deciding how likely it is that a behavioral intervention will be effective.

Declarative and procedural memory are the two types of memories most important for psychological therapy and counseling. Declarative memory is recall for conscious material while procedural memory is essentially recall for unconscious (or nonconscious) material. Procedural memory is located primarily in the basal ganglia and amygdala while declarative memory is located primarily in the hippocampus. Declarative memory would be the primary focus for cognitive-behavioral approaches that focus on skill development while procedural memory would be the focus for more psychodynamic approaches. Procedural memory, as understood from animal and human research, supports some of the concepts emphasized in psychodynamic therapy. This includes the importance of memories in the early developmental years and the emphasis on emotional material in therapeutic work.

Comparative psychology research supports a number of therapeutic interventions and guidelines that will likely help patients benefit from counseling and therapy. This includes the importance of emphasizing emotional material in session to help maximize the likelihood that the patient will remember what is covered in session. Use of homework assignments is also important given the need for multiple daily trials in order for individuals to effectively learn new skills. Emphasizing predictability and environmental stability is also important for helping patients learn and recall what is covered in sessions. Therapists and counselors should also keep in mind that individuals with cognitive impairment can benefit from therapeutic work but may often benefit more from a focus on skills-building. And memory reconsolidation is a therapeutic approach that, based on animal and human research, has a strong potential for patients suffering from traumatic events.

References

Aharonovich, E., Nunes, E., and Hasin, D. (2003) 'Cognitive impairment, retention and abstinence among cocaine abusers in cognitive-behavioral treatment.' *Drug and Alcohol Dependence 71*, 2, 207–211.

Azrin, N.H., Hutchinson, R.R., and McLaughlin, R. (1965) 'The opportunity for aggression as an operant reinforcer during aversive stimulation.' *Journal of the Experimental Analysis of Behavior 8*, 3, 171–180.

Cassel, R., Kelche, C., Lecourtier, L., and Cassel, J.C. (2012) 'The match/mismatch of visuo-spatial cues between acquisition and retrieval contexts influences the expression of response vs. place memory in rats.' *Behavioral Brain Research 230*, 2, 333–342.

Chang, Q. and Gold, P.E. (2003) 'Switching memory systems during learning: changes in patterns of brain acetylcholine release in the hippocampus and striatum in rats.' *Journal of Neuroscience 23*, 7, 3001–3005.

Clyman, R.B. (1993) 'The procedural organization of emotions: a contribution from cognitive science to the psychoanalytic theory of therapeutic action.' *Journal of the American Psychoanalytic Association 39*, 349–359.

Curlik, D.M. and Shors, T.J. (2013) 'Training your brains: do mental and physical (MAP) training enhance cognition through the process of neurogenesis in the hippocampus?' *Neuropharmacology 64*, 1, 506–514.

Davis, R.L. (2005) 'Olfactory memory formation in Drosophila: from molecular to systems neuroscience.' *Annual Review of Neuroscience 28*, 275–302.

Dolcos, F., LeBar, K., and Cabeza, R. (2004) 'Interaction between the amygdala and the medial temporal love memory system predicts better memory for emotional events.' *Neuron 42*, 5, 855–863.

Domjan, M. (2015) *The Principles of Learning and Behavior* (Seventh edition). Stanford, CT: Censage Learning.

Eysenck, H.J. (1966) 'Learning Theory and Behavior Therapy.' In R.D. Savage (ed.) *Readings in Clinical Psychology*. Oxford: Pergamon.

Finnie, P.S., and Nader, K. (2012) 'The role of metaplasticity mechanisms in regulating memory destabilization and reconsolidation.' *Neuroscience and Biobehavioral Reviews 36*, 7, 1667–1707.

Foster, T.C., DeFazio, R.A., and Bizon, J.L. (2012) 'Characterizing cognitive aging of spatial and contextual memory in animal models.' *Frontiers in Aging Neuroscience 4*, 12.

Fuchs, T. (2004) 'Neurobiology and psychotherapy: an emerging dialogue.' *Current Opinions in Psychiatry 17*, 6, 479–485.

Hillman, C.H., Erikson, K.I., and Kramer, A.F. (2008) 'Be smart, exercise your heart; exercise effects on brain and cognition.' *Nature Reviews: Neuroscience 9*, 58–65.

Horner, V. and Whiten, A. (2005) 'Causal knowledge and imitation/emulation switching in chimpanzees (Pan troglodytes) and children (Homo sapiens).' *Animal Cognition 8*, 3, 161–181.

Horner, V., Proctor, D., Bonnie, K.E., Whiten, A., and de Waal, F.B. (2010) 'Prestige affects cultural learning in chimpanzees.' *PLOS One*, May 19, 2010.

Iaria, G., Petrides, M., Dagher, A., Pike, B., and Bohbot, V. D. (2003) 'Cognitive strategies dependent on the hippocampus and caudate nucleus in human navigation: variability and change with practice.' *Journal of Neuroscience 23*, 13, 5945–5952.

Irish, M., Addis, D., Hodges, J., and Piavet, O. (2012) 'Considering the role of semantic memory in episodic future thinking: evidence from semantic dementia.' *Brain 135*, 7, 2178–2191.

Kamin, L.J. (1969) 'Predictability, Surprise, Attention, and Conditioning.' In B.A. Campbell and R.M. Church (eds) *Punishment and Aversive Behavior*. New York: Appleton.

Kandel, E. (1999) 'Biology and the future of psychoanalysis: a new intellectual framework for psychiatry revealed.' *American Journal of Psychiatry 156*, 4, 505–524.

Kirch, R.D., Meyer, P.T., Geisler, S., Braun, F., *et al.* (2013) 'Early deficits in declarative and procedural memory dependent behavioral function in a transgenic rat model of Huntingdon's disease.' *Brain Research 239*, 15–26.

Koen, J.D. and Yonelinas, A.P. (2011) 'From humans to rats and back again: bridging the divide between human and animal studies of recognition memory with receiving operating characteristics.' *Learning and Memory 18*, 8, 519–522.

Kurz, A., Thone-Otto, A., Cramer, B., Egert, S., *et al.* (2012) 'CORDIAL: cognitive rehabilitation and cognitive-behavioral treatment for early dementia in Alzheimer's Disease.' *Alzheimer's Disease and Associated Disorders 26*, 3, 246–253.

Lecourtier, L., Antal, M.C., Cosquer, B., Schumacher, A., *et al.* (2012) 'Intact neurobehavioral development and dramatic impairments of procedural-like memory following neonatal ventral hippocampal lesion in rats.' *Neuroscience 207*, 110–123.

Lum, J., Conti-Ramsden, G., Page, D., and Ullman, M.T. (2012) 'Working, declarative and procedural memory in specific language impairment.' *Cortex 48*, 9, 1138–1154.

MacLean, E.L., Matthews, L.J., Hare, B.A., Nunn, C.L., *et al.* (2012) 'How does cognition evolve? Phylogenetic comparative psychology.' *Animal Cognition 15*, 2, 223–238.

McIntyre, S.H. and Munson, J.M. (2008) 'Exploring cramming: student behaviours, beliefs, and learning retention in the principles of marketing course.' *Journal of Marketing Education 30*, 226–243.

McTighe, S.M., Cowell, R.A., Winters, B.D., Bussey, T.J., and Saksida, L.M. (2010) 'Paradoxical false memory after brain damage.' *Science 330*, 6009, 1408–1410.

Mery, F. (2013) 'Natural variation in learning and memory.' *Current Opinion in Neurobiology 23*, 1, 52–56.

Mery, F. and Kawecki, T.J. (2002) 'Experimental evolution of learning ability in fruit flies.' *Proceedings of the National Academy of Sciences 99*, 22, 14274–14279.

Nielsen, M., Subiaul, F., Galef, B., Zentall, T., and Whiten, A. (2012) 'Social learning in humans and nonhuman animals: theoretical and empirical dissections.' *Journal of Comparative Psychology 126*, 2, 109–113.

Pavlov, I.P. (1927) *Conditioned Reflexes*. New York: Oxford University Press.

Poldrack, R.A., and Packard, M.G. (2003) 'Competition among multiple memory systems: converging evidence from animal and human brain studies.' *Neuropsychologia 41*, 3, 245–251.

Poldrack, R.A., Clark, J., Pare-Blagoev, E.J., Shohamy, D., *et al.* (2001) 'Interactive memory systems in the human brain.' *Nature 414*, 6863, 546–550.

Premack, D. (2007) 'Human and animal cognition: continuity and discontinuity.' *Proceedings of the National Academy of Sciences of the United States of America 104*, 35, 13861–13867.

Pryor, K. (1999) *Don't Shoot the Dog*. New York: Bantam Books.

Rampon, C., Tang, Y.P., Goodhouse, J., Shimizu, E., Kyin, M., and Tsien, J.Z. (2000) 'Enrichment induces structural changes and recovery from nonspatial memory deficits in CA1 NMDAR1-knockout mice.' *Nature Neuroscience 3*, 3, 238–244.

Rosen, A.C., Sugiura, L., Kramer, J.H., Whitfield-Gabrielli, S., and Gabrielli, J.D. (2011) 'Cognitive training changes hippocampal functioning in mild cognitive impairment: a pilot study.' *Journal of Alzheimer's Disease 26*, Supp. 3, 349–357.

Rumbaugh, D.M., and Pate, J.L. (2014) 'Primates' Learning By Levels.' In G. Greenberg and E. Tobach (eds) *Behavioral Evolution and Integrative Levels: The T.C. Schneirla Conference Series* (Vol. 1). New York: Psychology Press.

Savage, S. and Ma, D. (2014) 'Animal behavior testing: memory.' *British Journal of Anaesthesia*, aeu014.

Schwabe, L. (2013) 'Stress and the engagement of multiple memory systems: integration of animal and human studies.' *Hippocampus 23*, 11, 1035–1043.

Schwabe, L., Nader, K., and Pruessner, J. C. (2014) 'Reconsolidation of human memory: brain mechanisms and clinical relevance.' *Biological Psychiatry 76*, 4, 274–280.

Smid, H.M., Wang, G., Bukovinszky, T., Steidle, J.L., *et al.* (2007) 'Species-specific acquisition and consolidation of long-term memory in parasitic wasps.' *Proceedings of the Royal Society B: Biological Sciences 274*, 1617, 1539–1546.

Spear, N.E. and Miller, R.R. (2014) 'Preface.' In N.E. Spear and R.R. Miller (eds) *Information Processing in Animals: Memory Mechanisms*. New York: Psychology Press.

Terrace, H.S. (2014) 'Animal Cognition.' In H.L. Roitblat, H.S. Terrace, and T.G. Bever (eds) *Animal Cognition*. New York: Psychology Press.

Ullman, M.T. (2012) 'The Declarative/Procedural Model.' In B. van Patten and J. Williams (eds) *Theories in Second Language Acquisition: An Introduction*. New York: Routledge.

Van Praag, H., Kempermann, G., and Gage, F.H. (2000) 'Neural consequences of environmental enrichment.' *Nature Reviews Neuroscience 1*, 3, 191–198.

Voermans, N.C., Petersson, K.M., Daudey, L., Weber, B., *et al.* (2004) 'Interaction between the human hippocampus and the caudate nucleus during route recognition.' *Neuron 43*, 3, 427–435.

Wen, J.Y., Kumar, N., Morrison, G., Rambaldini, G., *et al.* (1997) 'Mutations that prevent associative learning in C. elegans.' *Behavioral Neuroscience 111*, 2, 354.

Wilsom, W.J., Ferrara, N.C., Blaker, A.L., and Giddings, C.E. (2014) 'Escape and avoidance in the Eisenia hotensis.' *PeerJ 2*, e250.

Wystrach, A., and Graham, P. (2012) 'What can we learn from studies of insect navigation?' *Animal Behaviour 84*, 1, 13–20.

Chapter 3

DEPRESSION

Depression is a psychological condition impacting millions of people and complicating their lives. Symptoms of depression include feelings of hopelessness, frequent sadness, lack of motivation, and withdrawal. Depression impacts people by itself and also in combination with other conditions. Although depression alone can devastate people's lives, it has greater impact when coupled with chronic diseases such as diabetes and arthritis (Moussavi *et al.* 2007), and even more so when there are other psychological problems involved. Depression is one of the leading causes of disease throughout the world (Richards 2011). Depressive disorders impact people's lives significantly, increase death rates across the entire age spectrum, are often difficult to diagnose and treat in children, complicate the course of patients with chronic illness, and increase overall medical burden in the elderly (Kessler *et al.* 2005).

Depressive disorders make up one of the largest groups of conditions treated by counselors and therapists worldwide. Treating the disease is important because of its toll on people's lives and the economic consequences. A study of depression in Japan conducted in 2005 found that the total cost of depression for that country alone was two trillion yen (Sado *et al.* 2011). This would be the modern equivalent of 16 billion U.S. dollars. Costs for depression include not only direct treatment costs but the indirect costs (including lost financial support for families of individuals who are incapacitated by depression or commit suicide) and costs of lost work production and support services. These costs increase as the severity of the disease increases, which makes treatment important even if only to reduce severity (Kleine-Budde *et al.* 2013).

Depression is a mood disorder that reflects significant emotional distress. It is an emotional disturbance but is also a disorder of behavior. Withdrawal, sleep problems, eating problems, and appearance of hopelessness, helplessness, and distress are all characteristic symptoms of depression that are reflected in behaviors (or lack of behaviors). People can *say* that they feel depressed but also frequently *show* that they feel depressed. Asking a person who may have depression how they feel is an important step in diagnosing depression, but it is rarely ever enough. There are also outward behavioral signs characteristic of depression and which are primary symptoms. You can see this in a standard mental status examination where there is equal emphasis on "affect" (outward expression of emotional state) and "mood" (subjective expression of emotional state).

When you recognize that depression is a behavioral condition as well as an emotional condition you see the ways animal research can help explain depression. Animals cannot say how they feel but they can show how they feel. Animal studies provide useful insights into many of the outward symptoms of depression. While symptoms such as guilt, suicidality, and sad mood are likely purely human features, other aspects of depression exist in laboratory animals. These include helplessness, anhedonia, behavioral despair, sleep disruptions, and appetite problems. These are more behavioral symptoms and do not suggest subjective emotional states. Animal research allows for the study of these outward behavioral symptoms.

Methods used to test depression models

Animal models are used to help understand how depression develops and how depression might be best conceptualized. (*Note:* In this book, we follow Jaccard and Jacoby's lead (2010, p.29) and take "models" and "theories" to mean essentially the same thing.) They focus on overt symptomology as a way of understanding what contributes to those symptoms. Many researchers consider these models to be effective but, as you might expect, there is often difficulty determining just what relevance animal models have for understanding what is primarily considered to be a human disorder. There is debate about whether animals actually get depressed, but it is clear that what is typically referred to as "depression" relates to humans. Animals certainly show defeat, withdrawal, hopelessness (in terms of expecting defeat), and lack of motivation but are not necessarily described as "depressed" when they look that way. And even in the circumstances where "depressed" is used to describe animals (for example, when pet owners say that their pets "look depressed") it is mostly with the understanding that human terms are being used to describe animal behaviors. Animals do show behaviors associated with human depression, show them in situations where "depressed" might describe human behaviors, show them with the same intensity as symptoms of depression, but are not necessarily described as "depressed" when this occurs.

Effectiveness of depression models is usually based on how "valid" that model is for understanding the condition. Validity of depression models is based on the degree to which the model shows effectiveness in understanding depression. This could come from obvious expectations of how depression looks or the degree to which the model is consistent with what is already understood about depression. Models of depression also are judged on how accurately they predict the effectiveness of different interventions. Understanding the degree to which models are consistent with what is already known about depression and depression treatment helps with understanding the degree to which the model predicts effectiveness of other clinical treatments.

Depression models are tested based on four types of validity:

- *Face validity* is the degree to which the model appears to be addressing depressive symptomology.

- *Construct validity* is the degree to which the model is consistent with what is already known about depression.

- *Pharmacological validity* is the degree to which the model can help identify effective antidepressant medications.

- *Pathological validity* is the degree to which the model is validated by pathological or biochemical changes found in human depressed patients. This last type of validity is rather new and difficult to measure, but this is changing with recent advances in biochemical testing and human tissue collection.

Next in this chapter we address the main animal models of depression. These are models that have shown the most validity in terms of understanding depression. There is little evidence to suggest that these models have any less validity, as measured by the types of validity discussed in the previous paragraph, than human models. Our discussion of these models will focus on the main types of validity associated with the model.

Harry Harlow

One of the most eccentric, and sometimes controversial, figures in the history of comparative psychology was Harry Harlow. His work on monkeys in the 1960s and 1970s gave new understanding to depression and the impact of social isolation. He and his associates studied the behaviors of young monkeys confined in chambers for at least 30 days (Harlow and Suomi 1971). These monkeys exhibited significant increases in self-clasping and huddling behaviors and decreases in movement and exploratory activity. These behavioral changes were similar to what happens when human children are separated from individuals with whom they have an emotional attachment. They were also similar to human depressed behaviors.

Harlow's work, and the model of depression it produced, had strong face validity. Those monkeys clearly looked depressed following removal from their chambers. But the impact of social isolation was so significant that the monkeys seemed not only depressed but also sometimes psychotic. He went beyond just studying social isolation for 30 days but studied monkeys who were in total isolation for 3, 6, 12, and even 24 months (Harlow and Zimmerman 1958). And these monkeys showed signs not only of depression but also of several other psychological disturbances. Some of the depressive-like symptoms associated with longer periods of isolation included almost constant self-clutching and rocking. They suffered severe emotional shock and could not recover even when placed with monkeys raised normally.

Face validity of Harlow's model surfaces further when you consider the psychotic-like symptoms it produced. Because psychotic symptoms are often associated with the most severe types of depression, "Major Depressive Disorder with Psychotic Features" is a common diagnostic term for these. Common interpretations of this condition reflect that the neurological impact of severe depression works along the same neurological pathways that trigger psychotic symptoms. Having a model that produces the same type of symptoms associated with severe clinical depression supports this model's face validity.

Harlow's work had face validity but created sufficient controversy that other ways of creating animal models of depression were explored. Research on depressive symptoms in animals over the past twenty years has been of the ethological variety where animals are observed in home cages and not subject to environmental manipulation. For example, different breeds of monkeys (including cynomolgus and rhesus macaques) showed depressive-like behaviors, such as increased levels of immobility and slumped body posture where they appeared to be withdrawn from the environment, when faced with challenges they would face in the wild (Camus *et al.* 2012). These authors found that understanding depressive symptoms does not need experimental manipulation and can be studied using ethological observation methods. This approach to studying depression among different species removes the need for the more controversial methods used by Harlow and his colleagues decades ago.

With the passage of time, critics who examined Harlow's body of work began to see him as insensitive to animal welfare. However, his work actually contributed to animal welfare once zoo biologists began to understand the full impact of social deprivation and changed the way the apes and monkeys were managed in captive settings. For example, zoos once routinely removed infants to protect them from injury or neglect. They stopped doing this when they accepted the criticism that they were damaging infants hand-reared by human caretakers and preventing primiparous (inexperienced) mothers from becoming better mothers with successive births. What zoo professionals learned from Harlow's research led them to adopt better practices and higher standards for primates living in zoos. Biomedical labs and primate research centers also adopted these better practices. There is controversy about Harlow because the scope of his impact is not fully understood. A balanced treatment of Harlow can be found in

Deborah Blum's excellent book *Love at Goon Park: Harry Harlow and the Science of Affection* (2001).

Learned helplessness

Learned helplessness is likely the most familiar theory of depression based on animal research. Seligman and Maier (1967) studied learned helplessness first in dogs; later researchers studied the condition in other animals, including rats, mice, fish, cockroaches, slugs, and flies (Yang *et al.* 2013). In a typical learned helplessness experiment, two groups of animals are subject to some form of mild electric shock. One group can end the shock by their behaviors while the other group receives the same sequence and amount of shock but has no influence on the onset and duration. These two groups are then compared in a different experimental setting where both groups have influence over the shocks. Typically, the second group of animals do not try to escape the shock in the second experimental setting and basically remain inactive. They actually look helpless and look like they are feeling hopeless. In this way, their behaviors reflect the same behaviors associated with clinical depression.

Learned helplessness is a depression model with excellent face, construct, and predictive validity in rats and mice (Vollmayr and Gass 2013). Face validity for this model comes from its similarity to situations that would be expected to produce depression. It is a model that predicts a course for depression that is similar to other models and has produced effective ways of understanding how certain antidepressant medications work. Furthermore, this model is consistent with several physiological concepts of depressive disorders. For example, researchers using this model also predicted several biomarkers of depression, including the habenula as a region centrally important in the pathophysiology of depression and antidepressant therapy. This part of the brain is in the back part of the thalamus and is involved with sending information from the basal ganglia and limbic system to the midbrain. It is an essential part of how the brain processes reward information.

Describing validity as "face validity" for learned helplessness models takes on a new meaning because the faces of animals in these experiments look depressed. If you look at Seligman and

Maier's original experiments, the dogs in the helpless condition look depressed. They look like they are defeated and have no chance of making their lives better. When you consider the facial expression of the animals in those original experiments it is difficult not to say that those animals "look depressed."

One criticism of learned helplessness as a theory of depression is that the impact of learned helplessness situations does not tend to last long. Depression is a condition that endures and any theory of depression needs to account for its lasting impact. Maier (2001) addressed this issue with a summary of research supporting that the behavioral consequences of learned helplessness can be prolonged by exposing the individual again and again to the original stressor environment. Subsequent presentations of cues associated with the original inescapability experience can prolong learned helplessness's impact even if the shock is not delivered during these repeated presentations. This explanation leads to even more questions (e.g. is Maier suggesting that depression is repetitive experiencing of negative events?) but it is one possible way of accounting for this theory's limitations.

Social defeat theory

Another model of depression similar to learned helplessness, and one also based on animal studies, is the "social defeat" theory. This theory addresses more directly the lasting impact of depressive symptoms and involves situations where the animal experiences defeat directly with another animal (Hammack, Cooper, and Lezak 2012). This theory basically posits that social defeat, like learned helplessness, produces behavioral changes similar to those seen in depression. Huhman *et al.* (2003), for example, found that social defeat in hamsters leads to loss of territorial aggression and increased submissive and defensive behaviors in subsequent encounters with smaller, non-aggressive intruders. When these hamsters suffered defeat in social situations, they showed behaviors similar to those exhibited in learned helplessness situations. There were differences, however, in terms of these social defeat experiences having impacts that lasted longer and endured in more types of situations.

Social defeat theory is more consistent than learned helplessness theory with the lasting effects of depression because it addresses both the effects of social conflict and also continued fellowship with the dominant animal (Venzala *et al.* 2012). When animals are made subordinate in social conflicts, those animals remain within the same social environment and around the same animals. This mimics social situations humans find themselves in when their social rank may be significantly impacted but they are still in the same social environment. In this way, social defeat theory addresses directly the lasting impact of negative environmental factors to help with understanding the lasting impact of depression. We can see more why depression tends to last well beyond negative experiences that contribute to that depression. Social defeat has more of an impact than the negative experiences (which were troubling but temporary) because of its lasting impact on the individual's environment.

There is considerable animal research supporting this theory of depression. Several studies have demonstrated that an animal subordinated by dominant individuals of the same species shows signs of stress, social avoidance, anxiety, decreased grooming, hyperactivity, and increased vulnerability to addiction. There also is evidence that these animals show significant changes in brain function, physiology, neurotransmitter level, and hormone levels. Defeat-induced stress in mice persists for weeks or even months and also can be reversed by repeated antidepressant treatment. This supports that the social conflict depression model has pharmacological validity as discussed earlier.

Prior to the social conflict and social defeat theories, Price *et al.* (1994) proposed a very important theory called the "social competition" theory. It is a theory that addresses not only depressed behaviors but also the general issue of what leads animals to face defeat. We often think of evolution as "survival of the fittest" and this is true. But conflicts present the possibility of animals surviving or not surviving. And animals recognize this. So, it is reasonable to conclude that a mechanism is in place to help animals determine whether they have a good chance of winning a conflict. Otherwise, they would just get into every conflict that comes their way and eventually be killed because they chose to participate in conflicts they have no chance of winning. Survival is sustained through submissive behaviors that reduce the likelihood of lethal combat.

"Social competition" theory is similar to the social defeat theory and posits that depression evolved as an unconscious, involuntary losing strategy, enabling the individual to accept defeat in competitions and to accommodate to what would otherwise be unacceptably low social rank. There is frequently conflict between members of species when it comes to things such as territories, sexual opportunities, or making alliances. Some members will win and some will lose. And losing, for animals in the wild, has a much more significant impact and meaning than it does for most humans and even for domesticated animals. Losing often means loss of status, loss of access to resources, and even death. Animals in the wild have many reasons for trying to avoid losing if they can. This often means they have to "fight to win" but also means they are geared towards avoiding conflicts they cannot win.

Animals who lose or are likely to lose need to have some internal mechanisms that will inhibit their challenging behavior. This is an evolutionary necessity leading animals to stay out of conflicts that are likely to end their survival. Struggling on when it is likely they will lose is only likely to intensify conflicts, use valuable energy, and make things more difficult for that individual member. An individual caught in a conflict has the choice of either escalating the situation or de-escalating the situation. Escaping and backing down are two ways animals can de-escalate the situation.

Without having a strategy for determining when it is preferable to de-escalate the situation, animals would engage in conflicts they could not win and would likely be harmed in the process. This theory goes on to propose that primitive de-escalation strategies involved internal biological changes that automatically forced the losing animal to run away, back down, or submit. These de-escalation strategies are associated with behaviors that are similar to the more passive behaviors associated with depression. In this way, de-escalation strategies look very similar to depressed behaviors. These behaviors have the evolutionary benefit of sending signals to deactivate the challenge and attack behaviors of the attacker while also inhibiting the energy that the animal puts into its own attack and challenging behaviors.

These behaviors do not necessarily de-escalate the situation but only send signals that have the potential for de-escalating the situation.

Price's theory proposes that human depression evolved from the strategic importance of having a de-escalation strategy that sends signals to the self and others. It has the survival benefit of inhibiting challenging behaviors that would require the animal to put energy into a fight that it could not (or likely could not) win. It makes the animal appear subordinate, which is not typically preferable from an evolutionary perspective, but does aid in survival, which *is* typically preferable from an evolutionary perspective. Subordinate animals often show the same behaviors associated with depression. They tend to be less explorative, more submissive, withdrawn, and tense. They also have higher levels of stress hormones than more dominant animals and lower levels of neurochemicals such as 5-HT. These are neurological and biochemical differences that are also seen in humans with depression.

When confronted with a social stressor, animals will either seek support, submit, take flight, or attack. If these defensive behaviors are blocked or are ineffective, the animals can remain in a high state of arousal without resolution (Carvalho *et al.* 2013). This is the type of thing that has a downward impact on mood for humans. Submissive behaviors are often associated with these types of situations and are usually aimed at de-escalating or terminating conflicts and attacks. Without these involuntary behaviors signaling submissive status, animals would not be able to resolve conflicts without serious injuries. In humans, submissive behaviors, social anxiety, and poor assertiveness are linked to depression and are known to be vulnerability factors for depression. These are factors that may lead to feelings of inferiority and may act as an internal signal of down-rank that makes an individual feel more inferior and defeated. These feelings occur despite the fact that an individual successfully escaped from a potentially dangerous situation because of feelings of failure. Feelings of failure and inferiority relate in these situations to social competition and social defeat. Humans often feel depressed and feel a sense of failure in those situations without acknowledging that they may have successfully avoided a very damaging type of situation. Successfully avoiding a loss is not the type of thing that humans typically count as a success.

Fournier (2009) conducted an empirical study of social competition theory for adolescents. Social competition was conceptualized in this study as a theory with three main components: (a) social hierarchies form spontaneously when resources are scarce; (b) social rank in the human hierarchy depends partly on attention-holding; and (c) depression constitutes an involuntary response to low social rank, entrapment, and defeat. This study involved 121 male adolescents and the results showed clear empirical support for all three components. First, the adolescents perceived that there was a social hierarchy, agreed on where they stood in the hierarchy, and knew their own place in the hierarchy. Second, the adolescents obtained prominence and influence by being likable. And, third, quantitative measures of the adolescents' places in the hierarchy contributed significantly to the prediction of their levels of self-esteem and depression.

Evolutionary perspectives

Gilbert and Allan (1998) summarized social competition theory from an evolutionary perspective, based on the following points: (1) In pursuing access to any "evolutionary meaningful" resources (e.g. territories, sexual opportunities, or making alliances), there will be others who are pursuing the same resources. (2) This will bring the animals involved into conflict with each other. Before an animal can acquire the resources pursued it must deal with competitors. (3) As a result of conflicts over resources some will win and some will lose. (4) Animals who lose, or are likely to lose, conflicts need to have internal mechanisms that will inhibit their challenging behavior, as struggling on or fighting will only intensify conflicts.

As these authors saw it, these conflict situations provide two basic choices: either the animal escalates the situation (tries harder, threatens, overpowers the competitor) or de-escalates the situation (backs off, retreats, gives up). This view again emphasizes that, without a de-escalation strategy, animals would engage in conflicts they could not win and be harmed in the process. Therefore, a primitive de-escalation strategy involves internal biochemical changes that automatically force the animal most likely to lose the conflict to run away, back down, submit, and generally try to bring the conflict to an end rather than risk injury. It is this de-escalation strategy that is the evolutionary basis of depression.

Slavich and Irwin (2014) summarized the growing body of research supporting that different types of life events often have different effects on depression, depending on their core features and psychological characteristics. Interpersonal loss (i.e. loss of an important person in an individual's life) is the type of event that has received the most attention. This type of loss tends to have the most impact on how people feel and function. Evolutionary theory would predict that this is likely to happen given the adaptive benefits accompanying the maintenance of close social bonds. Human and nonhuman animals alike gain survival benefits from having close social relationships. These benefits include the provision of food, shelter, emotional comfort, and physical security.

Interpersonal losses disrupt these important social bonds and this disruption often evokes intense distress, especially if the losses involve social rejection, which signals a loss of social status, value, and regard. Major life events that involve interpersonal loss and social rejection are hypothesized to be particularly strong in terms of the level of emotional distress that is characteristic of depression. People often respond to losing important others in their life with strong emotional responses and may not necessarily think about the practicalities of what they lose when that important person passes away. And it certainly would not be beneficial for that person's counselor to start talking to them about how they are feeling such intense emotion because losing that person could mean decreased security, assistance in obtaining resources, and possibly even loss of social status. But evolutionary theory does support that at its very base the emotional response people experience when they lose important people in their lives is related to these significant losses.

Nesse (2000) summarized some of the possible evolutionary benefits to depression. This is not to say this author proposed that depression is "good," but that there may be some evolutionary purpose to depressive symptomology that allows it to continue. Some negative and passive aspects of depression may be useful because they inhibit dangerous or wasteful actions in situations characterized by pursuit of an unreachable goal, temptations to challenge authority, insufficient resources to allow action without damage, or lack of a viable life strategy. Low mood and passivity may allow for the conservation of resources in situations where a desired outcome is not likely.

Theories of depression have to address whether depression is an adaptation, an adaption gone wrong, or a pathological state related to any function. There have been dismissals of the possibility that depression could be useful for any evolutionary purpose, whereas others have proposed that there could very well be an evolutionary purpose to depression. This could have practical implications for treatment. Patients who see depression as an expected response to a negative situation might refuse any type of treatment due to fear that they will cover up what really is causing the problem. And then those who believe depression is purely a result of neurological pathology might be reluctant to examine how any aspects of their life might be contributing to their symptoms.

Acute and chronic stressors

One limitation of all evolutionary theories of depression continues to be that they best describe depression as an acute condition. They tend to present a view of how depressive symptoms may develop in a relatively short time and also last a relatively short time. As we discussed earlier, the symptoms discussed in learned helplessness or social defeat strategies are consistent with depressive symptomology. However, they are not consistent with the length of time that depressive symptoms last. Depressive symptoms in humans often last for several weeks or several months and the evolutionary theories do not do as good a job at explaining why this happens. Diagnostically, evolutionary theories do a better job at explaining conditions such as "adjustment disorder," which often lasts for a relatively brief period of time, and not conditions such as "major depression," which carries the possibility of depressive symptomology lasting for months or even years.

Evolutionary theories of depression necessitate some role of genetic predisposition to depression. There is really no other way to explain why the impact of learned helplessness or social defeat lasts so much longer for some individuals than for others. Animal studies on the neurobiology of depression provide a good deal of insight as to possible genetic and biochemical characteristics of individuals with a predisposition to suffer more lasting depressive symptomology.

Incorporating this material into the other theories of depression underscores the possibility that individuals may be more prone genetically and/or biochemically to experiencing depressive symptoms. This would mean that not everybody who experiences stressful events develops clinical depression, but individuals who experience stressful events and also have a genetic predisposition towards depression will develop more lasting depressive symptomology.

Human depression research shows that stressful life events significantly increasing the risk of depressive episodes are typically chronic ones (divorce, financial problems) (Krishnan and Nestler 2008). Animal studies on chronic stress are less common than studies of acute stress, due to the resources needed to maintain chronic stressors. Studying animals in natural environments also does not allow for much study in terms of chronic stressors. But the animal studies on the neurobiology of depression and human studies of chronic stress and depression do support that a combination of chronic stressors and a genetic predisposition is very likely a major factor in the development of depression.

Learned helplessness theory and social defeat theory are best understood as depression theories showing that stressors contributing to depressive symptomology are ones that occur over an extended period of time and involve individuals who have some genetic predisposition to developing lasting depression. These theories are particularly useful for understanding more reactive types of depression (i.e. adjustment disorder), but a combination of genetic factors and chronic stressors most likely contributes to more severe types of depression (i.e. major depressive disorder). These psychological conditions involve a process evolving over time where human and nonhuman animals respond physiologically, cognitively, and emotionally to conflicts they are not likely to win.

Clinical interventions

From a clinical perspective, evolutionary and animal theories of depression offer the most benefit in terms of explanation. Patients often look for an answer about where their depression comes from and these theories can provide some basis for that answer. Remember that these are patients whose level of sadness and despair has become so significant that it impacts on most, if not all, aspects of their daily lives. And even if they are told many times that "depression is more than just sadness" patients will still often interpret their depression as deep, lasting sadness that will not seem to go away. Evolutionary theories of depression in particular offer at least a basic premise for understanding how their depression may very well be based on a process that has been important for human survival. Their particular situation is also likely based on individual factors (e.g. acute and chronic stressors, biochemistry) but the very basis of their depression may be a process that is important and understandable.

Evolutionary theory helps explain depression to patients who are often looking for some understanding of what is happening to them. Helping patients understand depression as a process that may be necessary at its base (even if it has gone astray for an individual) can be very helpful. In this way, patients can be helped to see that there is indeed some meaning, some purpose, to what they are experiencing while also deciding how best to address their difficulties. But helping patients understand depression as anything more than purely a neurochemical disorder can be difficult in places where pharmacology dominates. In fact, an individual reviewing depression treatment literature, including literature involving animal research, could be forgiven for thinking that antidepressant medication makes up the only empirically supported depression treatment. There just seems to be many, many more studies geared towards studying antidepressant medication than counseling and therapy treatments. And this difference becomes even wider if you consider the number of studies involving both medication and counseling, rather than just counseling or therapy alone.

When considering research on depression treatments, it is useful to keep in mind the legitimate criticisms of antidepressant medication research. Antidepressant medication has offered relief to millions of people worldwide but is also big business. And its dominance in the clinical and research communities does not reflect only drug effectiveness but very likely also reflects its financial dominance. Mental health treatment has, in many countries, allowed for medical explanations of depression and other mental health disorders beyond what the scientific evidence suggests (Brezis 2008). Selective choices of what research studies to publish has given reason to call effectiveness of some antidepressant medication into question (Every-Palmer and Howick 2014). Reporting bias has also been shown in antidepressant vs. placebo research (Trinquart, Abbé, and Ravaud 2012). At least one meta-analysis showed antidepressant medications do not consistently show significant advantages over placebo (Moussavi *et al.* 2007). And even editorial boards of prominent medical journals, including the *New England Journal of Medicine*, have strongly questioned the role financial issues play in antidepressant medication research (Angell 2012).

Evolutionary theories provide more comprehensive explanations than the purely biochemical explanation typically associated with treatments emphasizing antidepressant medication. Depression understood from an evolutionary framework does not ignore neurochemical factors but also considers psychological, historical, and environmental factors. Evolutionary theories help explain why medications can work, but also explain how therapeutic interventions and environmental changes can help. In this way, explanations used by pharmaceutical companies are not wrong about depression, but may not be complete. Psychological explanations, like those based on evolutionary theories, allow for equal emphasis on more than just neurochemical and physiological factors. This can benefit patients by helping them understand the complex ways that different parts of their lives contribute to depression rather than seeing their problems just in terms of biochemistry.

Notice how the social competition and evolutionary theories of depression focus on the animal's expectation of whether a battle can be won or lost. There is no basis in the theories about whether the animal actually wins or loses. Because the animal perceives that they might win or lose does not actually determine how likely it is that the outcome will be one way or another. It may very well be that the animal may win a battle even if their perception is that they will lose. From a human perspective, situations that seem insurmountable may not actually be insurmountable. Similarly, learned helplessness experiences show that just because an individual "learns" that a situation is hopeless does not mean the situation is actually hopeless.

Humans' and animals' perceptions of what is the likely outcome of a situation are not always correct. And many times it can be beneficial for individuals to bypass their perception of a situation and only deal with the situation in the "here and now." What this means is that the individual deals with the situation without making any interpretations of whether it is good or bad, winnable or losable, worthwhile or non-worthwhile, and so on. If an individual (and here we are talking about humans) can bypass their initial impressions and reactions to a situation and deal with parts of the situation as they come then they may be able to deal more effectively with that situation.

In this way, evolutionary and animal theories of depression (as those theories are applied to humans) are consistent with other theories of depression in supporting approaches such as mindfulness for treating depression. This is a therapeutic approach used to teach individuals to become more aware of thoughts and feelings and to relate to them in a wider, de-centered perspective as mental events rather than as aspects of the self or as necessarily accurate reflections of reality. This approach to developing a detached and de-centered relationship to depression-related thoughts and feelings is central in helping prevent the escalation of negative thinking patterns at times of potential relapse/recurrence (Teasdale *et al.* 2000). There is little explicit emphasis in mindfulness on changing the content or specific meanings of negative automatic thoughts, as the emphasis is primarily on helping change how the individual reacts to negative thoughts and feelings. Mindfulness has shown moderate effectiveness in a number of studies for the treatment of anxiety and depression (Hofmann *et al.* 2010).

Problem-solving therapy approaches focused on handling interpersonal stressors are used for depression and are consistent with evolutionary theories. If these types of situations indeed trigger imbedded concerns regarding competitiveness then helping individuals determine which approaches maximize success and minimize losses can go a long way towards helping to address these concerns. Working with patients on problem-solving steps for handling conflicts is important, as is working with them on steps for handling losses when they do occur. Cognitive-behavior therapeutic approaches minimizing "catastrophic thinking" help address how an individual deals with losses if they do indeed occur.

Theories addressed in this chapter underscore the significant role that social competition and conflicts can play in depressive symptomology. In humans, this is reflected largely in interpersonal conflicts. These theories support that therapeutic interventions associated with decreasing interpersonal conflicts also hold potential for treating depression. This can include problem-solving and social skills training. There are also certain types of family therapy focused on addressing deviations in hierarchy that might be particularly useful for minimizing the types of interpersonal conflicts that often contribute to depressive symptomology. Therapeutic approaches focusing on cross-generational coalitions may be potentially useful. These are interventions that help strengthen the bonds between family members and help minimize conflict and maximize support between family members.

Cognitive-behavioral therapies that help to address self-esteem issues as a way of helping the individual face competition in more realistic ways can also be helpful. Decreasing "catastrophic thinking" when facing interpersonal competition is one approach that can be particularly beneficial. Helping the individual identify different outcomes and determine realistic ways of handling those outcomes is another potentially helpful approach. Self-esteem in the context of these approaches focuses on helping individuals develop realistic views of how they can handle problem situations and also how they can effectively deal with different outcomes.

Molecular theories in the role of antidepressant medications

Animal research also contributes significantly to the understanding of antidepressant medication. This has been an extensive field of study and continues to be so since animal research is a required part of getting federal approval of psychiatric medication. This chapter will touch only briefly on this topic as psychiatric medication is not this book's focus. But it is worthwhile to look at this subject as a way of understanding another way that animal research helps with understanding depression.

SSRIs (Selective Serotonin Reuptake Inhibitors) make up one of the most commonly-prescribed categories of antidepressant medications over the past decade. Few behavior tests involving animals were available to support the original development of SSRIs (Carr and Lucki 2011) but a number of behavioral tests were developed in recent years that are sensitive to their effects. One of the main reasons there was not a test for these medications initially was because the behavioral effects of SSRIs were not detectable in many of the early animal models of depression or antidepressant tests. After SSRIs were introduced and their clinical efficacy became accepted, their effects were demonstrated to be active in a number of newer behavioral tests and animal models. Because these newer tests have established a broader pharmacological basis for their validity they have replaced the earlier tests for antidepressants for use in drug discovery.

One of the first tests that measure the effects of antidepressant medications in rats was the forced swim test. This test measures the behavioral patterns of the response to stress that are correlated with either an increased vulnerability to stress or treatments for depression. The test involves placing a rat in a container of water from which it is unable to escape. Initially, the rat will try to escape but eventually adopts a pattern of passive behavior characterized by a lack of movement except that which is necessary to keep its nose above the water level. This test usually consists of two swim exposures. The first one is a 15-minute exposure and the second one, conducted 24 hours later, is a 5-minute exposure. In this second exposure, immobility time is the main measure recorded. Effective antidepressants decrease the time that the rat spends immobile by increasing its active coping behaviors. These effects are selective for antidepressant medications and are separate from simple increased locomotor activity that might increase with stimulant medications.

Another test of antidepressant effectiveness is the tail suspension test. This test was developed as a simpler and faster way to test the behavioral response to antidepressants in mice compared with the forced swim test. In this test, mice are attached and suspended from a bar by their tails with adhesive tape. The amount of time that the mouse spends immobile during the six minutes they are suspended is interpreted as a measure of depression-like symptomology. This test has a number of advantages over the forced swim test, including lack of negative effects of cold water, the ability to test mouse strains that might have motor deficits, and increased sensitivity to more types of antidepressant compounds.

Animal research helps identify areas of the brain that should be considered when treating depression. Making an appropriate choice of action requires computing the value for each action based on expected rewards and expected punishments. One way to view this on a neurological level would be to consider that there are neurons that represent both kinds of values. Research over the past decade has shown neurons in the lateral habenula as playing an important role in depression. Neurons in this area of the brain respond to rewards and sensory stimuli predicting rewards. They then send these reward-related signals to dopamine neurons in the substantia nigra (Matsumoto and Hikosaka 2007). They subsequently found that neurons in the same area control signals for both reward-seeking and punishment-avoidant behaviors (Matsumoto and Hikosaka 2009). These authors based their conclusions on research involving monkeys and Li *et al.* (2011) subsequently found the same results on research involving rats.

Mirrione *et al.* (2014) summarized the research about neurological areas associated with sensitivity to learned helplessness. Their research, using Sprague Dawley rats, suggests a group of brain regions involved in sensitivity to uncontrollable stress, and also supported the lateral habenula's important role in depression. Several lines of evidence suggest that behavioral helplessness resulting from uncontrollable stress is caused by habenula-activated brainstem structures. The habenula drives serotonin release in the dorsal raphe during uncontrollable stress, which is necessary for expression of behavioral helplessness. Habenula hyperactivity is involved in severe depression and decreases following antidepressant treatment. These data, coupled with rodent studies demonstrating habenula-stimulation induced impairments in hedonic activity and elevations in habenula activity in congenital learned-helplessness rat strains, support exploration of habenula circuitry as a potential target in treating depression.

Different medications show potential effectiveness for treating depression based on the results of animal research. Yamada *et al.* (2014) investigated the effects of Istradefylline, a medication used for the treatment of Parkinson's Disease, on the learned helplessness of rats. They found that the medication increased the frequency with which rats tried to escape from situations where they experienced shocks. They proposed that this supported the use of this medication for depression in Parkinson's Disease. Arakawa et al. (2012) studied the possible effects of Minocycline for treating depression. They studied this medication, which is known to suppress certain types of cells, using learned helplessness (LH) rats. These rats showed significantly higher serotonin activity (a chemical action related to depressive symptomology) in the orbitofrontal cortex and lower levels of brain-derived neurotrophic factor (BDNF, another type of chemical action related to depression) in the hippocampus than control rats. However, these alterations in serotonin turnover and BDNF activity remained unchanged after treatment with Minocycline. Use of this medication in the LH rats not only showed no change in these activities but also showed significant increases in the levels of dopamine and its metabolites in the amygdala when compared with untreated LH rats. Taken together, all of these results supported that Minocycline may be a therapeutic drug for the treatment of depression.

CASE STUDY

Leonard was a 54-year-old engineer who presented for psychotherapy to address significant problems with depression. He reported that his main symptoms were lack of motivation and frequent periods of increased sadness. He described himself as feeling hopeless much of the day and as having no interest in doing things that might help to improve his mood. He described depression as having been a significant problem for the past decade but reported that the symptoms increased significantly following his wife passing away about two years ago. He was retired after having worked as an engineer for about 30 years. He said that he retired following increased difficulties that he had with his boss. He reported that his boss at the time he retired was putting him down often and was giving him more menial responsibilities. He described himself as having had significant problems with bosses over the years but said that his last boss treated him the worst of all his bosses.

Leonard reported daily symptoms of depression. He reported that one of his main difficulties is that he cannot quite understand what is happening to him. He is sad every day and cannot seem to bring himself out of his sadness. He is looking for an explanation of what is happening to him. He can identify that the losses in his life have contributed significantly to his depression but cannot understand why they have impacted him for so long and to such an extent. He was someone who put a great deal of emphasis on his work and saw it as a significant loss in his life when he had to leave. He described himself as feeling less important to the company as time went on and he was treated worse and worse by bosses. His marriage provided a great deal of support to him and his wife was very encouraging. She passed away after at least a year of battling cancer. He was very involved with her care during that time.

Leonard also reported that he and his wife shared a history of family difficulties. They both had negative relationships with their families and had a history of both sides making unreasonable demands of both of them. During their years together, Leonard and his wife would support each other in addressing these problems and would actually be involved together in dealing with both sides of the family. In this way, they worked together to address the problems on each side and lessen the emotional load of dealing with each side of the family. Leonard went on further to say that since his wife passed away both sides of the family have continued to make unreasonable demands of him. This had increased his level of emotional distress over the past year or so.

Leonard was a patient who benefited considerably from the explanation of depression from an evolutionary perspective. As a scientifically minded individual, he appreciated the role that evolution could play in helping him understand what was happening. But he benefited even more from having an explanation for his depression that took into account more than just his biochemistry. His physician had prescribed him an antidepressant and it had helped somewhat. But he knew that there had to be more than just his biochemistry playing a role and talked about this during sessions. His previous therapist had emphasized cognitive-behavioral therapy and had talked about learning and thinking as playing major roles in his depression. This made sense to him but did not seem to give a clear overall picture of what was happening. These seemed to be pieces of what was happening but did not reveal a clear general explanation. He appreciated an evolutionary explanation (with its emphasis on how depression may relate to the process used to conserve energy and resources when a desired outcome is not likely) as a way of understanding of why this depression was having such a significant impact on him.

During his treatment, Leonard came to see that much of his withdrawal and low energy related to his not wanting to participate in the high-stress conflicts associated with family relationships. He had faced a number of "battles" in the past year (conflicts with bosses, "battling" his wife's cancer) and had essentially lost them. He was facing more of these "battles" with families on both sides and did not see any of them as winnable. He could see that he hadn't actually lost energy but just had not been willing to exert any energy into situations where he felt helpless. He could particularly address how he had "learned helplessness" following his wife's death as he had no one around to help him deal with family difficulties. He also was able to see how the conflicts with his bosses, and particularly those with his most recent boss, had led him to lose rank and status at work and see himself in general as having moved lower in social rank. He had put such an emphasis on his role at work that, when he had been treated as less important by his boss, he related this to significant changes in his social status.

As Leonard was helped to understand his depression more, he was receptive to finding more effective ways of handling the issues that had contributed to his depressive symptoms. Cognitive-behavioral therapy focused on his negative view of himself and on helping him develop a more realistic yet positive view. This helped his self-esteem as the focus was on him developing a view of himself that took into account more than just what he had done for a living. Assertiveness training also helped him develop the skills to help him feel less defeated when he dealt with family conflicts. He also benefited from some work on his social skills and comfort level in social situations to help him develop more positive social relationships. This certainly did not replace the support he felt from his wife but did provide a small degree of increased social support compared with what he had after his wife passed away. Work on family dynamics also helped him identify family members who might be more receptive to help him navigate the family conflicts effectively and decrease his view of being all alone when dealing with those conflicts. All of these interventions helped to significantly decrease the level of depression Leonard experienced and within four months he reported that his depression interfered significantly with his functioning an average of only two days per week.

Summary

Understanding depression is essential for counselors and therapists due to the number of people impacted by depression and the degree to which depression impacts on individuals' functioning. Animal research has been beneficial in developing theories to help understand depression. Learned helplessness, social conflict, and social competition are three of the main animal theories of depression. These theories share in common a focus on how perceived losses (i.e. loss of control, loss of social rank, loss of social support) impact mood. Notice here that the emphasis is on losses that the individual perceives rather than on actual losses (although these losses may be actualized if the individual's perception is correct). Depression may be an outgrowth of the process, developed throughout an organism's evolution, whereby an individual organism tries to limit the impact of losses. Patients may benefit from understanding depression as an extension, although likely a pathological one, of the natural process of deciding when a battle is worth fighting rather than seeing depression as just the result of neurobiology. This view can help set the stage for counselors to use cognitive-behavioral, problem-solving, assertiveness training, and family therapy interventions to help address these clinical issues.

References

Angell, M. (2012) 'Is academic medicine for sale?' *The New England Journal of Medicine 24*, 59–62.

Arakawa, S., Shirayama, Y., Fujita, Y., Ishima, T., *et al.* (2012) 'Minocycline produced antidepressant-like effects on the learned helplessness rats with alterations in levels of monoamine in the amygdala and no changes in BDNF levels in the hippocampus at baseline.' *Pharmacology Biochemistry and Behavior 100*, 3, 601–606.

Blum, D. (2011) *Love at Goon Park: Harry Harlow and the Science of Affection.* New York: Basic Books.

Brezis, M. (2008) 'Big pharma and health care: unsolvable conflict of interests between private enterprise and public health.' *Israel Journal of Psychiatry and Related Sciences 45*, 2, 83.

Camus, S.M., Rochais, C., Blois-Heulin, C., Li, Q., Hausberger, M., and Bezard, E. (2014) 'Depressive-like behavioral profiles in captive-bred single- and socially-housed rhesus and cynomolgus macaques: a species comparison.' *Frontiers in Behavioral Neuroscience 8*, 47.

Carr, G.V. and Lucki, I. (2011) 'The role of serotonin receptor subtypes in treating depression: a review of animal studies.' *Psychopharmacology 213*, 2–3, 265–287.

Carvalho, S. Pinto-Gouveia, J., Pimentel, P., Maia, D., Gilbert, P., and Mota-Pereira, J. (2013) 'Entrapment and defeat perceptions in depressive symptomatology: through an evolutionary approach.' *Psychiatry 76*, 1, 53–67.

Every-Palmer, S. and Howick, J. (2014) 'How evidence-based medicine is failing due to biased trials and selective publication.' *Journal of Evaluation in Clinical Practice 20*, 6, 908–914.

Fournier, M.A. (2009) 'Adolescent hierarchy formation and the social competition theory of depression.' *Journal of Social and Clinical Psychology 28*, 9, 1144–1172.

Gilbert, P. and Allan, S. (1998) 'The role of defeat and entrapment (arrested flight) in depression: an exploration of an evolutionary view.' *Psychological Medicine 28*, 3, 585–598.

Hammack, S.E., Cooper, M.A., and Lezak, K.R. (2012) 'Overlapping neurobiology of learned helplessness and conditioned defeat: implications for PTSD and mood disorders.' *Neuropharmacology 62*, 2, 565–575.

Harlow, H.F. and Suomi, S.J. (1971) 'Production of depressive behaviors in young monkeys.' *Journal of Autism and Childhood Schizophrenia 1*, 3, 246–255.

Harlow, H.F. and Zimmermann, R.R. (1958) 'The development of affectional responses in infant monkeys.' *Proceedings of the American Philosophical Society 102*, 501–509.

Hofmann, S.G., Sawyer, A.T., Witt, A.A., and Oh, D. (2010) 'The effect of mindfulness-based therapy on anxiety and depression: a meta-analytic review.' *Journal of Consulting and Clinical Psychology 78*, 2, 169–183.

Huhman, K.L., Solomon, M.B., Janicki, M., Harmon, A.C., *et al.* (2003) 'Conditioned defeat in male and female Syrian hamsters.' *Hormones and Behavior 44*, 3, 293–299.

Jaccard, J. and Jacoby, J. (2010) *Theory Construction and Model-Building Skills: A Practical Guide for Social Scientists.* New York: Guilford Press.

Kessler, R.C., Berglund, P., Demler, O., Jin, R., Merikangas, K.R., and Walters, E.E. (2005) 'Lifetime prevalence and age-of-onset distributions of DSM-IV disorders in the National Comorbidity Survey Replication.' *Archives of General Psychiatry 62*, 6, 593–602.

Kleine-Budde, K., Müller, R., Kawohl, W., Bramesfeld, A., Moock, J., and Rössler, W. (2013) 'The cost of depression – a cost analysis from a large database.' *Journal of Affective Disorders 147*, 1, 137–143.

Krishnan, V. and Nestler, E.J. (2008) 'The molecular neurobiology of depression.' *Nature 455*, 7215, 894–902.

Krishnan, V. and Nestler, E.J. (2011) 'Animal Models of Depression: Molecular Perspectives.' In J.J. Hagan (ed.) *Molecular and Functional Models in Neuropsychiatry.* Berlin and Heidelberg: Springer.

Li, B., Piriz, J., Mirrione, M., Chung, C., *et al.* (2011) 'Synaptic potentiation onto habenula neurons in the learned helplessness model of depression. *Nature 470*, 7335, 535–539.

Maier, S.F. (2001) 'Exposure to the stressor environment prevents the temporal dissipation of behavioral depression/learned helplessness.' *Biological Psychiatry 49*, 9, 763–773.

Matsumoto, M. and Hikosaka, O. (2007) 'Lateral habenula as a source of negative reward signals in dopamine neurons.' *Nature 447*, 7148, 1111–1115.

Matsumoto, M. and Hikosaka, O. (2009) 'Representation of negative motivational value in the primate lateral habenula.' *Nature Neuroscience 12*, 1, 77–84.

Mirrione, M.M., Schulz, D., Lapidus, K.A., Zhang, S., Goodman, W., and Henn, F.A. (2014) 'Increased metabolic activity in the septum and habenula during stress is linked to subsequent expression of learned helplessness behavior.' *Frontiers in Human Neuroscience 8*, 29.

Moussavi, S., Chatterji, S., Verdes, E., Tandon, A., Patel, V., and Ustun, B. (2007) 'Depression, chronic diseases, and decrements in health: results from the World Health Surveys.' *Lancet 370*, 9590, 851–858.

Nesse, R.M. (2000) 'Is depression an adaptation?' *Archives of General Psychiatry 57*, 1, 14–20.

Price, J., Sloman, L., Gardner, R., Gilbert, P., and Rohde, P. (1994) 'The social competition hypothesis of depression.' *British Journal of Psychiatry 164*, 3, 309–315.

Richards, D. (2011) 'Prevalence and clinical course of depression: a review.' *Clinical Psychology Review 31*, 7, 1117–1125.

Sado, M., Yamauchi, K., Kawakami, N., Ono, Y., *et al.* (2011) 'Cost of depression among adults in Japan in 2005.' *Psychiatry and Clinical Neurosciences 65*, 5, 442–450.

Seligman, M.E. and Maier, S.F. (1967) 'Failure to escape traumatic shock.' *Journal of Experimental Psychology 74*, 1, 1–9.

Slavich, G.M. and Irwin, M.R. (2014) 'From stress to inflammation and major depressive disorder: a social signal transduction theory of depression.' *Psychological Bulletin 140*, 3, 774–815.

Teasdale, J.D., Segal, Z.V., Williams, J.M.G., Ridgeway, V.A., Soulsby, J.M., and Lau, M.A. (2000) 'Prevention of relapse/recurrence in major depression by mindfulness-based cognitive therapy.' *Journal of Consulting and Clinical Psychology 68*, 4, 615–623.

Trinquart, L., Abbé, A., and Ravaud, P. (2012) 'Impact of reporting bias in network meta-analysis of antidepressant placebo-controlled trials.' *PLOS One 7*, 4, e35219.

Venzala, E., Garcia-Garcia, A.L., Elizalde, N., Delagrange, P., and Tordera, R.M. (2012) 'Chronic social defeat stress model: behavioral features, antidepressant action, and interaction with biological risk factors.' *Psychopharmacology 224*, 2, 313–325.

Vollmayr, B. and Gass, P. (2013) 'Learned helplessness: unique features and translational value of a cognitive depression model.' *Cell and Tissue Research 354*, 1, 171–178.

Yamada, K., Kobayashi, M., Shiozaki, S., Ohta, T., *et al.* (2014) 'Antidepressant activity of the adenosine A2A receptor antagonist, Istradefylline (KW-6002) on learned helplessness in rats.' *Psychopharmacology 231*, 14, 2839–2849.

Yang, Z., Bertolucci, F., Wolf, R., and Heisenberg, M. (2013) 'Flies cope with uncontrollable stress by learned helplessness.' *Current Biology 23*, 9, 799–803.

Chapter 4

AGGRESSION

Introduction

Aggression is violent behavior directed towards another individual. It is the physical manifestation of anger directed in a manner to physically harm another. As such, aggression constitutes a significant problem for human society. Murder, physical abuse, stabbings, shootings, and battery are all aggressive acts impacting society. Aggressive acts make up the majority of criminal acts throughout every country in the world. Every culture has some form of aggression causing harm to its people. There really is no place immune from the impact of human aggression.

Aggression is the physical expression of anger. It is fitting, therefore, that a discussion of aggression should follow a discussion of depression. Depression and anger have been linked throughout the history of psychology. This is illustrated clearly in the popular saying "Depression is anger turned inward," used as a basic summary of psychodynamic theory. This relationship between anger and depression has been supported through research throughout the history of psychology (e.g. Riley, Treiber, and Woods 1989).

Aggression constitutes one of the most straightforward topics in comparative psychology. Aggression serves a direct purpose of getting something that the individual wants (e.g. food, territory, sex). Aggression is also used by animals to prevent other animals from harming them. Animals use aggression to get what they need. It has a direct function in that way. How the animal goes about using aggression and when they use aggression differs depending on the species. Some species are more aggressive than others and, therefore, individuals of that species will need to rely more on physical aggression. Some are more domesticated and individuals will rely less on aggression. What does not change is that when aggression is used it serves a definite purpose.

Animal research and aggression

Aggression from a comparative psychology standpoint means physical aggression (not, for example, verbal aggression). When discussing animals, the goal of aggression is primarily to harm the other individual and very often to kill the other individual. Removing the other individual from competition is what the aggressor is looking to do as a way of removing an obstacle from the goal. When species rely less often on aggression this is typically because aggression has been less effective for getting the animal what they need. It could also be because the animals find more effective ways of reaching goals.

Domesticated animals rely less often on aggression than wild animals. They simply need aggression less often because they have other ways of getting want they want. In fact, domesticated animals are often hindered if they rely too much on aggression. A domesticated dog who seeks out food through aggression will not tend to be a dog that humans want. Such a dog would likely be without an owner and would find itself without a source of food and protection. What we see when we look at domesticated animals is that a decreased reliance on aggression, from an evolutionary standpoint, is primarily one based on need. There is no physiological need for animals to be less aggressive over time. If aggression is less likely to get an individual species what they need then it is less likely they will rely on it.

There are specific reasons and contexts in which aggression occurs. Primates, for example, use aggression as a strategic response to appropriate environmental conditions (Wilson and Wrangham 2003). Aggression is not inevitable, from this perspective, but occurs in specific situations for specific reasons. Natural selection throughout evolution shapes basic psychological mechanisms for solving wide ranges of problems, including obtaining access to mates and managing conflicts between groups (McDonald, Navarrete, and Van Vugt 2012). There is a purpose to aggression and seeking to find ways of explaining aggression requires that you find the contexts and goals of aggressive acts. Taking this approach allows for a more directive and focused way of trying to find out why aggression occurs.

When looking for reasons aggression occurs, you want to ask, "Why would this individual exert so much energy and other physical resources to commit such an act?" Because aggression is indeed costly to the individual. Aggressive behaviors require energy, physical strength, and physical exertion (as evidenced by, for example, rapid heartbeat, heavy breathing, and muscle tension). As a result, males in good physical condition tend to win more contests than males in poor physical condition. Larger males outcompete smaller males due to their being stronger and better able to defend themselves. Studies of primates, spiders, birds, lizards, and even field crickets have all shown the aggressive dominance of larger, physically fit males over smaller, less fit ones (Bertram *et al.* 2011). While this is not surprising, it is important for understanding just how costly aggression can be. Because requiring physical exertion and strength for aggression is really the only reason why larger males would be so dominant over smaller ones.

Aggression's demand for physical resources requires that animals must have developed strategies for determining when aggression is worthwhile. We touched on this concept in the previous chapter when we looked at how animals determine when it is not worthwhile to put up a fight. Deciding when aggression is warranted by an attacker depends on things such as perceived benefit for survival (i.e. can it get the individual food?) and reproductive potential (i.e. can it get the individual sex?). Deciding when aggression is warranted by a defender depends on things such as the perceived strategy of the potential attacker and the associated threat to the defender's reproductive fitness (Horton, Hauber, and Maney 2012). There are a number of behavioral theories positing how animals develop these strategies and most of them posit that animals have developed, through natural selection, ways of interpreting signals exhibited by other members of their species. Animals develop ways of observing and processing information about potential opponents and situations to gather signals for determining if aggression is warranted and potentially beneficial. These signals depend on taking into account such things as physical disparities (size, strength, weaponry), resources, outcomes of previous fights, and social upbringing (Stevenson and Schildberger 2013).

Animals develop skills for determining whether aggressive behaviors are worthwhile and likely to be beneficial. Basically, animals develop ways of determining if the "cost–benefit" ratio for aggression is better than for non-aggression. This may be how we think of humans making decisions about aggression (i.e. asking the question, "Will aggression get me what I want without demanding too much of me?") but it is interesting to note that this is true of all animals. There are patterns that have developed throughout evolution where animals make decisions about whether their aggressive behaviors will get them what they want without requiring too many resources (including exertion of physical strength and too much energy).

Aggressiveness evolved among humans because humans could compete with relatively low cost of lethal injury or extreme energy depletion. For much of human history, competition for resources involving humans only involved physical aggression. This occurred because each human faced competitions with a relatively low level of expectation that they would be harmed severely or killed. Humans are not particularly large compared with other animals, nor do they have claws or horns that can cause severe physical harm. As such, human competitions preserved a low level of potential for lethal altercations or significant physical damage. Notice here that we see again how just because humans make decisions about the potential for being harmed or killed does not mean their decisions are correct. Clearly, humans making decisions about the likelihood they will be harmed or killed make the wrong decision. You could say that in each physical altercation there are two individuals making the decision that they could come out victorious but there is always one individual who comes out wrong. Just because the human makes the decision that they are unlikely to be harmed does not mean they make the correct one. But the tendency for humans to not perceive a strong likelihood they will be harmed or killed is one reason why humans showed a preference for physical aggression throughout evolution.

Development of projectile weapons is relatively new in the history of human evolution but has quickly impacted humans' reliance on aggression. Humans have relied less on physical aggression for determining every conflict as there has been more of a likelihood of injury or death. Humans have also relied less on physical aggression as it has been more difficult to develop cues about who is likely to be the victor. It is difficult to determine from physical cues or even past events who will be the victor in a conflict if both individuals are using machine guns. It is even more difficult to use these cues to determine the victor if two individuals or groups of individuals are using artillery shells or missiles to exert physical damage. Even though it may not seem this way from the news, there actually is a historical trend throughout human history towards a general reduction in relying on aggression (Pinker 2011).

One theory of how anger and aggression work is called the "recalibrational theory" (Sell 2011). This is a cognitive-evolutionary model of aggression emphasizing how individuals calculate cost–benefit ratios for aggression (called "welfare-tradeoff ratios" or WTRs). WTRs are described in this theory as the likelihood that aggressive behaviors will increase survival or that the other individual does not hold the individual's welfare highly when making decisions that impact them both. They are the mental representations of the calculations individuals make when they decide how much weight to give to the welfare of another compared with themselves when making decisions that affect them both (Tooby *et al.* 2008). Aggression kicks in either when the individual calculates that aggression can benefit them or that the other individual is more likely than not going to harm them. Aggression serves here as a tool, designed throughout evolution, used to gain dominance in situations that will lead to more reproductive success (either by improving that success or keeping it from being lessened by the individual being harmed or killed) and WTRs are the mental processes by which animals determine the likelihood of success. Animals are looking for the opportunity to modify and create situations that increase the likelihood they will be able to reproduce. This assures survival of the individual and survival of the species.

Aggression in recalibrational theory does not necessarily mean anger, although in humans anger is often inferred from aggressive behaviors (Averill 1983). According to this model, aggression is basically a computational system that kicks in when an animal detects cues of a low WTR in others (i.e. cues that the other individual does not weight the angry individual's welfare highly when making decisions that impact them both). Four factors, according to this theory, determine if aggressive behaviors are employed: (1) the target of aggression gives an indication that they hold a low WTR towards the individual; (2) signals given off by the target provide supporting evidence that the target's WTR is too low; (3) the target resists early, low-cost attempts to resolve the situation without aggression; and (4) using aggression is determined by the individual to be more efficient than not using aggression.

Neurological research studies yield a good deal of information related to the neurological circuits involved in aggressive behaviors. There are three primary areas involved in impulsive/reactive aggression: (1) subcortical neural systems where aggressive impulses are produced; (2) decision-making circuits and social-emotional information processing circuits where decisions are made regarding the potential consequences of aggression; and (3) frontoparietal regions that are involved in regulating emotions (Coccaro *et al.* 2011). We will not go here into the specific neural areas where each of these systems exist but there are specific areas of the brain associated with these systems. Addressing that these systems exist is a way of showing the process by which aggressive impulses occur and how those impulses end up with aggressive behaviors. Looking at aggression here from a neurological perspective emphasizes once again that aggression occurs because something triggers aggressive impulses (either because the individual feels threatened or sees a potential benefit to aggression); the individual computes on a neurological level the cost–benefit ration of aggression and then acts out on the decision through areas controlling emotion regulation.

Competition and aggression

Aggressive behaviors occur for reaching certain goals. These behaviors evolved over time as a way of accomplishing things that animals needed accomplished. In their article on the evolution of human aggression, Buss and Shackelford (1997) proposed seven adaptive problems which aggression might have evolved to solve: (1) co-opting the resources of others; (2) defending against attack; (3) inflicting costs on same-sex rivals; (4) negotiating status and power; (5) deterring rivals from future aggression; (6) deterring mates from sexual infidelity; and (7) reducing resources expended on genetically unrelated children. These are the primary types of contexts in which aggressive behaviors occurred throughout evolution and are similar to the contexts in which aggression evolved for nonhuman animals. Notice how competition is a significant issue for each of these contexts as they relate to one individual or one group of individuals vying for resources against another individual or group of individuals.

Natural selection is driven primarily by differences among individuals in reproductive success and this serves as the main function of evolution. Any risky behavior has evolutionary significance depending on its cost–benefit with respect to the organism's reproductive potential (i.e. the likelihood that the individual can contribute offspring to future generations). Competition results in aggression only when there is some reason for the individual to see potential benefit of that competition. Individuals strive for tangible goals (primary goals being food, safety, status, sex, and parental investments) that reliably led to reproductive success over evolutionary history. Evolution adds another layer of complexity in humans, causing people to strive for culturally defined goals that do not necessarily contribute to genetic fitness. Humans look to maximize cultural and social resources that help increase the likelihood that they will have offspring and that their offspring will survive successfully. As a result, natural selection shaped human neurobiological mechanisms to detect and respond to costs and benefits associated with different environments. Humans respond to environments in ways that are not arbitrary but function to help create developmental and behavioral strategies that match those environments and maximize the likelihood of reproductive success (Ellis *et al.* 2012).

There are two primary types of aggression: reactive aggression and proactive aggression. Reactive aggression is the defensive response related to perceived or actual provocation (Carré, McCormick, and Hariri 2011). This is what occurs when an animal perceives (rightly or wrongly) that another animal is about to attack them or otherwise try to cause them harm. Reactive aggression is characterized by anger and impulsivity and is often accompanied by disinhibition, affective instability, and high levels of bodily arousal. Proactive aggression, also referred to as "instrumental aggression," is goal-oriented and occurs in the absence of direct provocation. This is the type of aggression that occurs when the individual is trying to gain some resource or advance their reproductive potential. This is the type of aggression occurring when the animal wants to "get something" rather than wanting to "protect something." In contrast to reactive aggression, proactive aggression is characterized by low physiological arousal. Proactive aggression in humans is the type that tends to receive widespread media attention (e.g. serial killings). The reactive form likely accounts for most societal problems associated with aggression and is the type of aggression most seen in individuals who seek counseling.

What you notice when you compare reactive and proactive aggression is the role of perception. They are both types of aggression that occur when the individual "perceives" that something is happening or could happen (i.e. physical threat for reactive, potential gaining of resources for proactive). Perception is an important factor when considering aggression. Perception accounts for the main reasons for aggression and those perceptions are not always accurate. Perception also plays a role in determining what the animal will fight for. Animals often make the error of fighting for mates of a different species because they perceive that the potential mates are of the same species. Individuals of different species often fight over space, and those conflicts may arise spontaneously when populations of closely related territorial species first come into contact. Ordinarily, males of the two different species (e.g. species of insects who live close to each other) do not compete for mates, but when males of the different species cannot distinguish females of their own species, those females may effectively become a shared resource (Drury *et al.* 2015). Aggression here occurs because the insects *perceive* they are fighting for females of their own species but they are *actually* fighting for females of a different species. As is often the case with aggression, perception plays a key role in determining aggression, and that perception is not always consistent with reality.

We will look later in detail at implications of aggression research for clinicians. But it is worth pointing out here that this issue of "perception" in aggression should be familiar for counselors and therapists. Patients who present with aggression problems often talk about their perception that others were trying to harm them or were threatening their social status. Issues of "respect" are common when humans talk about aggression being used as a way of preventing social downgrading and this is often an issue of perception (Morris 2012). Criminal gang members, for example, are notorious for justifying the use of aggression to confront "disrespect" from others who threaten to attack their standing in the gang hierarchy. Also, many parents seeking help for children will describe their children as getting aggressive "for no reason." Their inability to determine the reason is often the result of the child's perception of what is happening not being consistent with what the parent perceives is happening. In his book on collaborative problem-solving (used for treating anger problems in children), Ross Greene (2005, p.8) summarized the importance of understanding this: "Dealing more effectively with explosive children requires, first and foremost, an understanding of why these children behave as they do." Understanding that individuals, including children, act from perceptions that may not be clear to others is an essential part of helping to treat aggression.

Animal species and aggression

Aggression always serves a function. This is the lesson gained from comparative psychology studies across many different animal species. Studies of different animal species yield a great deal of understanding with regard to aggression. Aggression often serves different functions for different species but always serves a function. There is always a purpose to aggressive behaviors, whether it be for sex, territory, food, or dominance. It might not always seem to the outside observer that aggression is the most effective way of obtaining the desired resources but that is irrelevant. What matters here is that a study of aggression across species reveals that it serves the function of obtaining some desired result. Studying aggression across species also provides insight into how animals move away from aggression and come to rely on more cooperative goal-reaching approaches. We can learn about the nature of aggression when we look at how it occurs across different species.

Lions and chimpanzees are two species who show that aggression is one reason why they form groups. Individual physical threats and fights are still the most common types of competition throughout the animal world for gaining access to potential sexual partners (Geary *et al.* 2003). More dominant males as individuals have preferential access to potential mates or to the resources that potential mates need to raise offspring (e.g. nesting territories). But many species will form groups or coalitions so as to increase the access to potential mates and territories. This tendency to form competitive coalitions appears to evolve only for species in which coalitions are more likely to gain access to mates than are lone individuals. Smaller members of the species may join these coalitions, with the primary benefit being that they will have more access to females. The primary cost of this type of coalitional behavior is that sexual access to females must be shared among coalitional males. This leads to a decline in the number of offspring sired by each male. In lions, coalitions frequently outcompete lone males for access to prides. Although lions will occasionally form alliances with non-kin, the largest and most competitive coalitions are among brothers and other male kin. Chimpanzees also engage in coalitional competition and this is primarily defined by coalitions of related males that defend a territory. Small coalitions of males cooperate within these communities to achieve social dominance over other male coalitions. Aggressive behaviors serve as the impetus for more social cooperation between members of these species.

Processes such as cooperative problem-solving occur across animal species as an alternative to aggression. In this way, the control of aggression serves a purpose in the same way that aggression serves a purpose. Research on foxes, chimpanzees, and bonobos shows that animals develop cooperative problem-solving when it offers the most effective route to gaining desired resources (Hare *et al.* 2007). This process likely develops through animals' neural processes that control emotional systems, such as fear and anger. Evolution comes into play because these cooperative systems can only develop over time and through natural selection. Cooperation fails when animals show no tolerance for working with others and increases only as the animals develop an understanding that they need other individuals' help to solve problems. Only animals who develop a greater tolerance for working with others, mainly through the neural areas controlling social emotions reacting less strongly to others, develop the behavioral flexibility to work cooperatively.

Aggression and sex are strongly correlated in many animal species. There have been many studies that have addressed specifically how sexual behaviors, and the potential for sex, contribute to aggression. For example, wild male bonobos frequently compete for access to estrous females and aggression tends to be much higher on days when mating is most likely. This tends to be successful for bonobos, as aggressors tend to have higher rates of mating than non-aggressors. Sex is one of the main reasons for male–male aggression in bonobos. Female aggression against males occurs frequently but appears to be independent of mating behavior. Being in close association leads to male and female bonobos being aggressive towards each other less often and mating much more often than at other times (Hohmann and Fruth 2003). Reasons for sexual aggression are similar across species, with some differences. For example, bonobos and chimpanzees have three functions of sexual activity in common: paternity confusion, practice sex, and exchange for favors (Wrangham 1993); but only bonobos use sex purely for communication about social relationships.

Research on bonobos also shows how social behaviors lead to reduced aggression. This is a relationship common throughout different animal species, but is particularly prominent in bonobos. These apes tend to form more stable relationships and tend to rely less on aggressive behaviors than chimpanzees (Engh *et al.* 2006). They show a preference, compared with chimpanzees, against aggression and towards more domesticated behaviors (Hare, Wobber, and Wrangham 2012). Bonobos also form relatively stable coalitions where females are more gregarious than males and that contain a larger proportion of the community than those of chimpanzees. These coalitions allow for the formation of female alliances, which are much more frequent and effective against male aggression in bonobos than in chimpanzees. This is an approach, developed through natural selection, where female bonobos use social coalitions to defend against male aggression. Female bonobos have evolved to where they have longer periods for potential reproduction and this is due to their reliance on social coalitions. They have defended against male aggression and this has allowed them to develop longer periods of time where they can mate and reproduce. This allows them to attract males over longer periods of time than the brief periovulatory period associated with chimpanzees. As a result, males compete less intensely for each mating opportunity and this lowers the benefits of high male rank among bonobos. Less aggressive males then avoid both the risks and the costs of physical aggression and alternative means to access females are favored over more aggressive males. Natural selection would no longer favor attempts to attack and injure other bonobos since there would not be a benefit of this type of behavior (Wrangham 1999).

Domesticated animals often move away from relying on aggression through natural selection. There are also wild animals who, through the evolutionary process, show a preference in development that favors less aggressive behaviors. This part of the evolutionary process is known as the "self-domestication" process and has been studied in a number of domesticated species, including the domesticated fox (Trut, Oskina, and Kharlamova 2009). This term was first used by Morey (1994) as a way of explaining how domestication occurred in dogs over time. The process involved natural selection where less aggressive and fearful animals gained a selective advantage because they were able to approach human settlements relatively easily and therefore better exploit opportunities such as human garbage and feces. These opportunities provided nourishment without animals relying on aggression. Non-aggression was favored for survival for animals who wanted to survive around humans. This theory also shows how humans came to rely on more domesticated behaviors over time as they needed more cooperation from other humans (e.g.Leach 2003).

This "self-domestication" theory does not explain changes in aggressive behaviors for all species. There are some animals who do not develop more domesticated (e.g. less aggressive) behaviors no matter for how many generations they are around humans. Being raised in captivity does not explain the difference in aggressiveness between some wild ancestors and domesticated animals. For example, Künzl et al. (2003) kept wild cavies (Cavia aperea) in captivity for 30 generations without any prior selection for domestication. Despite multiple generations being reared in captivity, there was no evidence of these animals changing their aggressive behavior. They had to be kept in single male groups to prevent adult males from attacking and potentially killing their fully grown sons. Their behavior contrasted considerably with that of domesticated guinea pigs where the decrease in aggression over time allowed multiple males to be housed in single groups without risk.

When animals develop decreased reliance on aggression they often also have changes in other behavioral characteristics. Research involving macaque species shows a number of traits with regard to conflict resolution that tend to change together as species evolve (Thierry *et al.* 2008). These traits are known as "conciliatory tendencies," "explicit reconciliatory contacts," "kin bias," and "levels of counter-aggression." "Concilatory tendencies" refers to the frequency with which the individual exhibits friendly gestures after an antagonistic episode. "Explicit reconciliatory contacts" refers to the degree to which the individual is otherwise obvious in their attempts to be friendly following antagonistic episodes. "Kin bias" refers to how much more often and more quickly the members try to reconcile with relatives than nonrelatives. "Levels of counter-aggression" refers to how often the individual engages in alternative nonaggressive behaviors. Notice that all of these related traits are associated with the tendency of species to show very clearly that they are trying to reconcile after potentially aggressive episodes. These are behaviors that develop as a way of increasing the likelihood that a less aggressive animal will be met with aggression. Having a tendency to rely less on aggression is necessarily associated with an increased tendency to make very clear that the individual is not trying to be aggressive and is trying to reconcile.

Social behaviors evolve over time and evolution's direction tends to be towards increased socialization. But different animal species develop different types of social behaviors as they evolve. Modern humans differ from other primate species (and likely their hominid ancestors) in terms of increased stable breeding bonds, more male parental investment, extended bilateral kin networks, and concealed ovulation. All of these evolved along the same lines as the ability for humans to develop intensive social coalitions. Humans and chimpanzees share some general cooperative behaviors but for the most part have very different social behaviors. Chimpanzees will, for example, rarely fight group against group. Chimpanzee border patrols usually will attack solitary individuals or small groups but not large congregations. "Great apes" (gorillas, orangutans, chimpanzees, and bonobos) do not have alliances between communities to attack/defend themselves from other groups. They also do not control mating or marriage relationships in terms of there being consequences for relationships between relatives (Flinn, Ponzi, and Muehlenbein 2012).

Animal research also shows that aggressive behaviors often move beyond the point where the animal is trying to gain something. Many different species utilize aggressive behaviors in their play.

Aggressive behaviors may be used purely for play or may also be used in a type of play where the individual is supposed to learn something. For example, in a study by Himmler *et al.* (2013), the play of juvenile rats from a colony of wild rats maintained in captivity was compared with that of a strain of domesticated rats (e.g. Long Evans Hooded). Data showed that the play of laboratory rats involved the same target (i.e. the nape of the neck) and tactics of defense as those used by wild rats. However, the laboratory rats initiated playful attacks more frequently, and were more likely to use tactics that promoted bodily contact. Aggressive behaviors were utilized in what was considered to be purely playful activities. Humans also use aggressive behaviors in playful ways, and children in particular may often have problems with their playful behaviors being described as "too aggressive."

One common characteristic across different animal species is the way teenagers rely on aggression. In many different species, teenagers show a tendency towards using aggression as a way of maintaining social rank. This is true of both human and nonhuman animals. It is during the adolescent years when members of many species start to develop a pattern of relying on aggressive behaviors. Adolescents, even more than adults, of many species also have a tendency to be more significantly impacted by the potential loss of social standing. Certainly this is common among human teenagers where any type of embarrassment or reflection of decreased social standing can have a significant behavioral and emotional impact. Adolescent nonhuman animals also often show evidence of being significantly impacted by any type of social defeat. For example, Coppens *et al.* (2012) found a tendency towards increased attack latencies after social defeat in adolescent rats even though the total time spent on offensive aggression was unaffected by social defeat.

In terms of aggression's neurochemistry, a wide range of research shows that testosterone is critical for male aggression. This is the most common neurochemical when it comes to aggression used to gain reproductive advantage. In fact, one of the most consistent findings for neurochemical research and aggression is the primary role of this neurochemical. For example, Marshall and Hohmann (2005) found in their review of the research that testosterone plays similar roles in aggression for both chimpanzees and bonobos. Even though these two species of great apes have many differences when it comes to aggression and social organization, the primary role of testosterone is one area of similarity. This type of research finding is one of the reasons why testosterone has been and will continue to be the main focus when it comes to researching possible pharmaceutical treatments for aggression.

Clinical applications

As we have seen throughout this chapter, comparative psychology research emphasizes the goals (or "functions") of aggression. Aggressive behaviors always have a purpose, even if it is not clear to others what that purpose might be. Aggressive behaviors occur when animals calculate that they would be the most effective means of accomplishing that goal. But, again, it is important to keep in mind that just because they determine that aggression will help accomplish goals does not mean they are correct. Animals calculate the likelihood that aggressive behaviors will help them reach goals that will maximize their reproductive potential. These are calculations based on processes developed over generations of evolution. Animals are looking for aggression to aid not only their survival but also the survival of their species.

Aggression serves purposes across all animal species, including humans. If aggression in humans is both purposeful and effective for achieving certain goals, this decreases the expectation that interventions such as social skills or sensitivity training are likely to be globally effective (Hawley 2007). Aggressive humans may indeed be socially astute and sensitive to the needs of others but still utilize aggression to obtain certain goals. Their reliance on aggression, if viewed through the lens of comparative psychology research, likely obtains certain goals and can be reduced if the individual is helped to find alternative ways of obtaining the same goals. Counselors and therapists working with aggressive individuals need to start with an understanding of what goals are relevant for the aggressive individual and how their behaviors are helping them to reach those goals.

Functional behavioral assessment is a key component of identifying the purposes and goals associated with behaviors. This is an assessment where the goal is to identify the purpose or "function" of particular behaviors. It is a key component of any type of behavioral therapeutic intervention as it addresses what contributes to the behavior problems and what purpose it serves. In this way it is consistent with what we have covered throughout this chapter as it is an assessment procedure that does not focus on identifying whether a behavior is a problem or not, but addresses in a nonjudgmental way what are contributing factors to the behavior in question. There are four primary steps to effective functional behavioral assessment. First, the behavior of concern must be identified in very specific terms. Second, the behavior must be defined as specifically as possible using terminology that helps make it clear when the behavior occurs. Third, data is collected about the behavior from a variety of different sources. Data collected at this step includes how frequently the behavior occurs, what happens before the behavior, and what happens after the behavior. It is important at this step to make clear that you are not looking for "causes" of the behavior but looking simply for what occurs before and what occurs after. Finally, data is reviewed with a focus on determining what conclusions can be drawn about what functions the behaviors serve and what antecedents and consequences contribute to the current behavior in question.

Comparative psychology research also shows that reliance on aggression decreases as animals learn more effective ways of reaching goals. Aggression continues for as long as it is calculated to be the most effective means of gaining desired outcomes. Whether it is access to mates, social standing, or resources for survival, there are specific things animals are looking to gain with aggression. There are instincts, evolved over generations, that lead animals to use aggression as a way of gaining desired outcomes. But once other skills become more effective for gaining those outcomes then reliance on aggression lessens. This is the case with social behaviors, as evolution leads most animals to rely more on social behaviors than on aggression for gaining desired outcomes. Social cooperation and group formations are used more to get these outcomes as they become more effective and aggression becomes less effective.

If we extend what we learn from comparative psychology research, we see that an effective aggression treatment would incorporate a detailed and objective assessment of the goals (or "functions") of the target behaviors and a focus on developing skills for more effectively gaining those desired outcomes. Since we are talking about humans here, it is important to note that one way of defining "effective" is that these skills will help decrease the person's use of aggression. Humans face legal outcomes for aggression that are not the case for animals. There is no equivalent to human legal consequences for murder or aggravated assault in the animal world. Keeping away from the legal ramifications for aggressive behaviors would be one part of defining "effective" goal-reaching that would apply only to humans and not to nonhuman animals.

Cognitive-behavioral therapy has emerged as the most common approach and most effective therapy approach to anger management. This fits right in with the comparative psychology research as cognitive-behavioral therapy emphasizes skills-building for reaching goals without the use of aggression. A meta-analysis of the clinical literature, based on 50 studies incorporating 1640 subjects, found that patients who received cognitive-behavioral therapy were better off than 76 per cent of untreated subjects in terms of aggression and anger reduction (Beck and Fernandez 1998). This effect was statistically significant, robust, and homogeneous across all the different studies. These findings strongly supported the efficacy of cognitive-behavioral therapy for anger management treatment.

Beck and Fernandez's meta-analysis focused primarily on cognitive-behavioral therapy such as Stress Inoculation Therapy. This is a cognitive-behavioral approach to treating aggression where clients identify situational "triggers" that precipitate the onset of their anger response. They then rehearse self-statements intended to reframe the situation and facilitate healthy responses. This then leads to the second phase of treatment, which requires the acquisition of relaxation skills. Cognitive self-statements, taught during the first treatment phase, are then coupled with relaxation as clients use these approaches, after exposure to triggers, to mentally and physically soothe themselves. In the subsequent rehearsal phase, clients are exposed to anger-provoking situations during the session utilizing imagery or role-plays. They practice the cognitive and relaxation techniques until the mental and physical responses can be achieved automatically. This basic outline of stress inoculation therapy can also be supplemented with alternative techniques such as problem-solving, conflict resolution, and social skills training. Each of these approaches emphasizes developing and using skills to more effectively accomplish goals without relying on aggressive behaviors.

There are two other research reviews showing the benefits of cognitive-behavioral therapy for aggression management. Hofmann *et al.* (2012) examined the effects of cognitive-behavioral therapy, cognitive therapy alone, relaxation, and other types of therapy (including social skills training and communication training) on various anger problems leading to aggression. These problems included driving anger, anger suppression, and anger expression difficulties. They found that cognitive-behavioral therapy for reducing these anger problems produced medium effect sizes compared with the other treatments and control conditions. Del Vecchio and O'Leary (2004) conducted a meta-analytic review where they analyzed the effects of different therapies on various aspects of anger. This meta-analysis included 65 per cent of studies that were not previously reviewed. Studies used in this review were compiled from a computer search of published and unpublished anger treatment studies conducted between January 1980 and August 2002. The search resulted in 23 studies containing one or more treatment groups and a control group, with effect sizes derived for each anger problem within each treatment category. This meta-analysis resulted in medium to large effect sizes across each of the different therapies. Cognitive-behavioral therapy was shown to be most effective for addressing driving anger, anger suppression, and trait anger. These results also supported the use of relaxation training as a main treatment for situational anger.

One limitation of the cognitive-behavioral therapy approach is that it is limited to more objective material. Focusing on behaviors and ways of thinking is straightforward but many would argue does not address all aspects of aggression. Aggression relates to anger and anger is an emotion. There is considerable argument within the therapy and counseling community that cognitive-behavioral therapy does not address the deeper emotional processes associated with anger and aggression. Psychodynamic theory, in particular, posits that aggression serves the purpose of accomplishing goals but that those goals are more on the subconscious and unconscious levels. Aggression serves the function of helping to resolve emotional conflicts that sit at the root of each individual's personality. Some psychodynamic therapies emphasize not only the deeper emotional needs of individuals but also the importance of social connections. Object relations therapy is one approach to psychodynamic therapy that has the potential for treating aggression (e.g. Lennings 1996) as it incorporates an emphasis on social behaviors, shown in comparative psychology research to correlate with animals reducing their reliance on aggression, and also on deeper emotional processes contributing to behaviors.

There is an approach to behavioral therapy that incorporates aspects of psychodynamic therapy and behavioral analysis. This therapy approach is called Functional Analytic Therapy and is a useful step forward following the use of functional behavioral assessment. This is a useful therapeutic approach to keep in mind for professionals who want to incorporate cognitive-behavioral therapy and empirical support for treating aggressiveness into an approach that gives consideration to important aspects of psychodynamic therapy. In this approach, practitioners focus on the functional benefits of aggressive behaviors and address them with a therapeutic approach that is in line with psychodynamic approaches. This approach to therapy includes the following methods: being aware of clients' clinically relevant behaviors; evoking clinically relevant behaviors during the sessions; reinforcing improvements with therapeutic approaches; and using behavioral interpretations to help clients generalize changes to daily life.

Sleep is an additional key element to help keep aggression under control. Various experimental studies in rats suggest that sleep deprivation may increase aggression (Kamphuis *et al.* 2012). When an individual gets an adequate amount of sleep there is more likelihood of that individual finding ways of handling situations other than aggressive behaviors. Therapists and counselors can help their patients manage their aggressive behaviors better by helping them get more sleep. Behavioral therapy and pharmaceutical therapy have been found to be equally effective for treating sleep problems (Smith *et al.* 2002).

CASE STUDY

Gerald was a middle-aged male who was court-ordered to counseling following his third arrest for aggravated assault. He had gotten into a fight with a co-worker who had accused him of not doing a job that he was assigned. Gerald insisted that the co-worker had been mistaken and, when confronted on what the co-worker accused him of, Gerald had become physically aggressive and had sent the co-worker to the emergency room with a broken finger. Gerald was not only facing possible jail time because of his multiple arrests for aggravated assault but also was facing the possibility of being fired from his job unless he could show that his tendency towards aggression had been successfully treated.

Gerald presented to psychological therapy as a very resistant patient. He stated outright that he thought his aggression was justified given that he did not like what the co-worker said. He also stated that he thought the previous episodes of aggravated assault had been justified because he had also been angry at what other people said. He stated that he had gotten so angry in each of those episodes that he had not fully recalled what he had done. But he also stated that he was not regretful for how he handled the situation and that he was glad that his behavior had resulted in the co-worker stopping his accusations that Gerald had not done the work he was assigned.

There was a long history of Gerald getting into trouble in work and school environments for his anger management problems. He had received disciplinary actions such as detentions and suspensions multiple times when he was in school. He was not in any sort of special classes, nor did he receive behavioral support when he was in school. But he had received disciplinary actions a number of times throughout the time that he was in school due to his handling of anger in an aggressive manner. He had also been fired previously from jobs because of his being verbally aggressive towards bosses, but said that this was not a problem for him because he did not like those jobs anyway. He recently spent a brief period of time in jail because of the incident with the co-worker but had been let out on bail. He recognized that he was facing longer jail time because of what he had done, and did exhibit and report some increased emotional distress as he faced the possibility of going to jail. He also stated that he liked his job and was concerned that he might lose it due to his aggressive behaviors.

Following a clinical interview where his social history and medical history were reviewed, Gerald was given the opportunity to discuss his perspective on what had happened. He talked at some length about how he recognized that he does get very angry at people when they seem to be causing difficulties for him. He talked with some degree of anger about how he had significant difficulties handling situations where he believed people were treating him in a disrespectful manner. He talked about how he thought his behaviors were acceptable because it "gets people to shut up." He described situations where other people were acting towards him in a way that he perceived as trying to "knock him down a peg or two" and he felt the need to address the situation first before these other individuals had the opportunity to cause problems for him.

As Gerald was given the opportunity to talk about his anger in a nonjudgmental environment, his resistance to talking about his anger seemed to lessen. When the counselor assured him that the only goal of having him talk about his anger was to figure out what purpose it served, his resistance went down even further. He did not pay much attention to what the counselor said at the beginning of the session, but seemed to pay a bit more attention when the counselor went into an explanation of how aggressiveness often serves a purpose and one of the goals of counseling is to help individuals find alternative ways of addressing that purpose. And he stated outright agreement for the first time when the counselor talked with him about how his aggressiveness would be discussed in session not as something that was "wrong" but more as something that was "ineffective." He initially was not comfortable with the presentation of comparative psychology research supporting that aggression has a purpose and he did not like having himself compared to animals. But he did agree with the general premise that psychological research and theories support that aggressive behaviors serve a function and that there may often be alternative ways of serving the function. He did express some increased comfort level in later sessions with discussing all of this in the context of comparative psychology research.

Gerald's functional behavioral assessment showed that his aggressive behaviors occurred in situations where he saw others acting towards him in ways that he deemed to be disrespectful. He described these as situations where he perceived other people as doing things that could decrease his standing in certain situations or cause him to have a worse reputation in work or school settings. He presented a number of different perspectives on why people might do this type of thing, including people wanting his job, people not liking how he addressed certain situations, or people just feeling better about themselves when they could make someone else feel worse. His behaviors when trying to deal with those situations mostly included verbal and physical aggression and served the function of altering or terminating situations that he found problematic and/or emotionally upsetting. These were behavior problems that he acknowledged as being problematic and that he reported did not occur on a regular basis but did cause significant difficulties for him when they occurred.

After discussing his aggressive behaviors in a nonjudgmental way and in a manner that reflected the potential purposes of those behaviors, Gerald was more open about discussing his recognition that his behaviors had caused significant difficulties for him. He could identify the reasons why he used those behaviors but was more willing to admit that the outcomes of the approaches he chose were not particularly good ones. Even though he had come into the session being very adamant that losing his job or facing jail time was worthwhile given that it got his co-worker to "shut up," he admitted following the functional behavioral assessment that he was quite concerned about the difficulties he faced because of his behaviors. This was when he took up more of a willingness to describe his behaviors as "ineffective" and acknowledged that it would be beneficial for him to find other ways of dealing with anger, and particularly ways of handling situations where he was angry about how others acted towards him.

Therapeutic discussions of the types of issues that concerned him were in line with the concept of Gerald feeling that his social rank was jeopardized by behaviors of others. He described himself as somebody who is very concerned about his standing in social environments and after several sessions was able to relate this to his having been treated very badly as a child and young teenager. He had been bullied quite often and had been made fun of given that he grew up in a rather poor household. As he got older he was able to prove himself physically through sports and work activities and developed quite a positive reputation in those environments.

He saw that his physical abilities were what helped him gain progress in social settings but also acknowledged that this led to him developing a tendency to rely on his physical abilities for handling difficult situations. So whenever he saw his self-esteem threatened by the behaviors of others, or his standing in social settings being threatened by others, he would rely on the physical abilities that had gained him higher social standing. He was able to acknowledge that he could find alternative ways of dealing with situations where he felt threatened by other people while also not having to listen to criticism of what he had been able to accomplish through his use of physical abilities.

Cognitive-behavioral therapy with Gerald progressed with a focus on helping him identify specific types of situations where he was starting to feel threatened by the behaviors of others. He was able to identify the types of situations in which those feelings occurred and could define more specifically how those behaviors impacted. He came to recognize these antecedents as they occurred, in part because functional analytic therapy approaches were used to help him identify during sessions when he was starting to have those feelings as he described potentially difficult situations. There were several times during sessions where he clearly was becoming angry, and this was often the opportunity to use functional analytic therapy approaches to help him recognize that this was occurring. He then was able to use this information to generalize his recognition of when problem situations were occurring outside of session. Once he was able to consistently identify those triggers he was then able to use cognitive approaches to talk himself through the situations in a more realistic way and find assertive approaches that could help him deal more effectively with those situations. He particularly benefited from a focus on assertiveness training that he could use as a way of standing up for himself without becoming verbally or physically aggressive. Gerald particularly benefited from the discussion of assertiveness that focused on helping him recognize that being assertive was a strong middle ground between backing down all the time and becoming physically aggressive as a way of addressing a problem situation.

Gerald made progress in terms of decreasing the frequency with which he had significant problems dealing with anger. His therapy lasted a total of ten sessions and by the end of those sessions he was able to report several incidents where he had felt threatened by the behaviors of others but had not responded in any sort of aggressive manner. By the end of those sessions he had gone more than a month with no significant problems related to anger management at work or at home. He was able to keep his job and could identify several situations at work where he had been able to defuse difficulties with the use of assertive behaviors. He recognized these as being situations where his social rank was being threatened and could identify more effective ways that he could use for maintaining his social rank without engaging in behaviors that threatened his position. He was also able to avoid jail time as the judge accepted the counselor's recommendation that he be given the opportunity to prove that he could avoid the use of aggressive behaviors for dealing with problem situations. He was given a probationary period of one year where he needed to stay away from aggressive behaviors and was able to complete that probationary period with no significant difficulties.

Summary

Comparative psychology research shows that aggression is used for different reasons across different species. There also is a considerable amount of variability across different species in terms of the degree to which they rely on aggression for reaching goals. There are some species that rely on aggression more than others and there are also species that show a preference for alternatives to aggression. This chapter covers a wide variety of research addressing how different species utilize aggression and what factors contribute to whether species show a preference for aggressive behaviors. But what remains constant across species is that aggression serves a purpose. There is little benefit in therapy and counseling to focus on aggression being "wrong" rather than addressing aggressive behaviors as often being "ineffective." Aggression always serves a purpose, but it is often the case for humans that there are more effective ways than aggression for accomplishing that purpose. What clinicians need to do is help their patients recognize the ineffectiveness of aggression and find more effective approaches that can serve the same function as aggressive behaviors. Functional behavioral assessments, cognitive-behavioral therapy, and functional behavioral therapy are three of the clinical interventions that can help accomplish this task.

References

Averill, J.R. (1983) 'Studies on anger and aggression: implications for theories of emotion.' *American Psychologist 38*, 11, 1145–1160.

Beck, R. and Fernandez, E. (1998) 'Cognitive-behavioral therapy in the treatment of anger: a meta-analysis.' *Cognitive Therapy and Research 22*, 1, 63–74.

Bertram, S.M., Rook, V.L., Fitzsimmons, J.M., and Fitzsimmons, L.P. (2011) 'Fine- and broad-scale approaches to understanding the evolution of aggression in crickets.' *Ethology 117*, 12, 1067–1080.

Buss, D.M. and Shackelford, T.K. (1997) 'Human aggression in evolutionary psychological perspective.' *Clinical Psychology Review 17*, 6, 605–619.

Carré, J.M., McCormick, C.M., and Hariri, A.R. (2011) 'The social neuroendocrinology of human aggression.' *Psychoneuroendocrinology 36*, 7, 935–944.

Coccaro, E.F., Sripada, C.S., Yanowitch, R.N., and Phan, K.L. (2011) 'Corticolimbic function in impulsive aggressive behavior.' *Biological Psychiatry 69*, 12, 1153–1159.

Coppens, C.M., de Boer, S.F., Steimer, T., and Koolhaas, J.M. (2012) 'Impulsivity and aggressive behavior in Roman high and low avoidance rats: baseline differences and adolescent social stress induced changes.' *Physiology and Behavior 105*, 5, 1156–1160.

Del Vecchio, T. and O'Leary, K.D. (2004) 'Effectiveness of anger treatments for specific anger problems: a meta-analytic review.' *Clinical Psychology Review 24*, 1, 15–34.

Drury, J.P., Okamoto, K.W., Anderson, C.N., and Grether, G.F. (2015) 'Reproductive interference explains persistence of aggression between species.' *Proceedings of the Royal Society of London B: Biological Sciences 282*, 1804, 20142256.

Ellis, B.J., Del Giudice, M., Dishion, T.J., Figueredo, A.J., *et al.* (2012) 'The evolutionary basis of risky adolescent behavior: implications for science, policy, and practice.' *Developmental Psychology 48*, 3, 598.

Engh, A.L., Beehner, J.C., Bergman, T.J., Whitten, P.L., *et al.* (2006) 'Female hierarchy instability, male immigration and infanticide increase glucocorticoid levels in female chacma baboons.' *Animal Behaviour 71*, 5, 1227–1237.

Flinn, M.V., Ponzi, D., and Muehlenbein, M.P. (2012) 'Hormonal mechanisms for regulation of aggression in human coalitions.' *Human Nature 23*, 1, 68–88.

Geary, D.C., Byrd-Craven, J., Hoard, M.K., Vigil, J., and Numtee, C. (2003) 'Evolution and development of boys' social behavior.' *Developmental Review 23*, 4, 444–470.

Greene, R. (2005) *The Explosive Child.* Harper: New York.

Hare, B., Melis, A.P., Woods, V., Hastings, S., and Wrangham, R. (2007) 'Tolerance allows bonobos to outperform chimpanzees on a cooperative task.' *Current Biology 17*, 7, 619–623.

Hare, B., Wobber, V., and Wrangham, R. (2012) 'The self-domestication hypothesis: evolution of bonobo psychology is due to selection against aggression.' *Animal Behaviour 83*, 3, 573–585.

Hawley, P.H. (2007) 'Social Dominance in Childhood and Adolescence: Why Social Competence and Aggression May Go Hand in Hand.' In P.H. Hawley, T.D. Little, and P.C. Rodkin (eds) *Aggression and Adaptation: The Bright Side to Bad Behavior.* Mahwah, NJ: Lawrence Erlbaum.

Himmler, B. T., Stryjek, R., Modlinska, K., Derksen, S.M., Pisula, W., and Pellis, S. M. (2013) 'How domestication modulates play behavior: a comparative analysis between wild rats and a laboratory strain of Rattus norvegicus.' *Journal of Comparative Psychology 127*, 4, 453–464.

Hofmann, S.G., Asnaani, A., Vonk, I.J., Sawyer, A.T., and Fang, A. (2012) 'The efficacy of cognitive behavioral therapy: a review of meta-analyses.' *Cognitive Therapy and Research 36*, 5, 427–440.

Hohmann, G. and Fruth, B. (2003) 'Intra- and inter-sexual aggression by bonobos in the context of mating.' *Behaviour 140*, 11, 1389–1413.

Horton, B.M., Hauber, M.E., and Maney, D.L. (2012) 'Morph matters: aggression bias in a polymorphic sparrow.' *PLOS One 7*, 10, e48705.

Kamphuis, J., Meerlo, P., Koolhaas, J.M., and Lancel, M. (2012) 'Poor sleep as a potential causal factor in aggression and violence.' *Sleep Medicine 13*, 4, 327–334.

Künzl, C., Kaiser, S., Meier, E., and Sachser, N. (2003) 'Is a wild mammal kept and reared in captivity still a wild animal?' *Hormones and Behavior 43*, 1, 187–196.

Leach, H. (2003) 'Human domestication reconsidered.' *Current Anthropology 44*, 3, 349–368.

Lennings, C.J. (1996) 'Adolescent aggression and imagery: contributions from object relations and social cognitive theory.' *Adolescence 31*, 124, 831.

Marshall, A.J., and Hohmann, G. (2005) 'Urinary testosterone levels of wild male bonobos (Pan paniscus) in the Lomako Forest, Democratic Republic of Congo.' *American Journal of Primatology 65*, 1, 87–92.

McDonald, M.M., Navarrete, C.D., and Van Vugt, M. (2012) 'Evolution and the psychology of intergroup conflict: the male warrior hypothesis.' *Philosophical Transactions of the Royal Society B: Biological Sciences 367*, 1589, 670–679.

Morey, D.F. (1994) 'The early evolution of the domestic dog.' *American Scientist 82*, 336–347.

Morris, E.J. (2012) 'Respect, protection, faith and love major care construsts identified within the subculture of selected urban African American adolescent gang members.' *Journal of Transcultural Nursing 23*, 3, 262–269.

Pinker, S. (2011) *The Better Angels of Our Nature: The Decline of Violence in History and its Causes.* London: Penguin.

Riley, W.T., Treiber, F.A., and Woods, M.G. (1989) 'Anger and hostility in depression.' *Journal of Nervous and Mental Disease 177*, 11, 668–674.

Sell, A.N. (2011) 'The recalibrational theory and violent anger.' *Aggression and Violent Behavior 16*, 5, 381–389.

Smith, M.T., Perlis, M.L., Paik, A., Smith, M.S., *et al.* (2002) 'Comparative meta-analysis of pharmacotherapy and behavior therapy for persistent insomnia.' *American Journal of Psychiatry 159*, 1, 5–11.

Stevenson, P.A. and Schildberger, K. (2013) 'Mechanisms of experience dependent control of aggression in crickets.' *Current Opinion in Neurobiology 23*, 3, 318–323.

Thierry, B., Aureli, F., Nunn, C.L., Petit, O., Abegg, C., and De Waal, F.B. (2008) 'A comparative study of conflict resolution in macaques: insights into the nature of trait covariation.' *Animal Behaviour 75*, 3, 847–860.

Tooby, J., Cosmides, L., Sell, A., Lieberman, D., and Sznycer, D. (2008) 'Internal Regulatory Variables and the Design of Human Motivation: A Computational and Evolutionary Approach.' In A. J. Elliot (ed.) *Handbook of Approach and Avoidance Motivation, 251.* Mahwah, NJ: Lawrence Erlbaum.

Trut, L., Oskina, I., and Kharlamova, A. (2009) 'Animal evolution during domestication: the domesticated fox as a model.' *Bioessays 31*, 3, 349–360.

Wilson, M.L., and Wrangham, R.W. (2003) 'Intergroup relations in chimpanzees.' *Annual Review of Anthropology 32*, 363–392.

Wrangham, R.W. (1993) 'The evolution of sexuality in chimpanzees and bonobos.' *Human Nature 4*, 1, 47–79.

Wrangham, R.W. (1999) 'Evolution of coalitionary killing.' *American Journal of Physical Anthropology 110*, s29, 1–30.

Chapter **5**

SUBSTANCE ABUSE

Introduction

Drug and alcohol abuse are two of the most significant health problems across the world. Questions about the nature of substance abuse include how people become addicted to substances in the first place and what serves to maintain their use of substances. People will continue to use drugs and alcohol for years following the point where they start to develop a tolerance and require much heavier amounts of drugs and alcohol to obtain the same physiological effect. This gets to the heart of the matter with regard to why substance abuse is such a significant problem. People will give up so much of their lives to maintain their use of drugs and alcohol, and it is not clear why. Comparative psychology research provides important results that help advance the professional community's understanding of drug and alcohol abuse.

To understand drug and alcohol abuse it is important to note that there is a significant difference between the use of substances and the abuse of substances. There also is a significant difference between drug use, even heavy drug use, and drug addiction. A person can use drugs and/or alcohol recreationally without reaching the point where they are abusing those substances. Similarly, an individual can abuse drugs and alcohol for even long periods of time without being said to have been addicted to those substances. An individual can be using substances over a long period of time without developing an addiction. Understanding substance abuse requires an understanding of what separates recreational use from abuse and what distinguishes abuse from addiction. Animal research covered in this chapter provides important findings to help clarify this distinction.

Drug studies involving animals typically involve rats who are not familiar with drugs and who are given adequate food. Other animals have been used in drug abuse research but rats are primary. Rats tend to respond to drugs the same way as humans and also are relatively easy to study in terms of how they respond when given ready access to substances. They are given access to low dosage of the drugs and are tested for drug self-administration. This is measured in terms of the number of sessions needed to reach a specified level of drug intake. There are several factors that have consistently been shown to predict vulnerability to higher levels of drug self-administration and these include dopamine release in brain regions associated with drug reward, genetic strain, impulsivity, age, and gender (Lynch *et al.* 2010).

Alcohol use has been more difficult to study in rats. This is because rats tend not to consume alcohol, even when it is easily available (Bell *et al.* 2012). They have a natural aversion to drinking alcohol and it is therefore more difficult to get them to drink alcohol readily than it is to get them to use a drug, like cocaine, readily. Researchers have had to use genetic manipulation to develop their own strain of rats who are more susceptible to alcohol consumption and alcohol effects (McBride and Li 1998). These alcohol-preferring rats will self-administer alcohol readily and will usually require less alcohol to feel the effect than would other rats.

Several symptoms of drug-addicted behaviors have been shown to occur in laboratory animals. These symptoms include escalation of drug use, neurocognitive deficits, resistance to extinction, increased motivation for drugs, preference for drugs over nondrug rewards, and resilience to punishment. These symptoms of drug addiction are the same as those found in humans. These findings support that addictive behaviors can occur and be studied in animals (Vanderschuren and Ahmed 2012) and that the outcomes of drug abuse and addiction are similar for animals and humans.

Drug use vs. drug addiction

Studying drug use in animals is relatively easy since animals have positive responses to the same types of drugs that humans find pleasurable. They become motivated to take opportunities made available for obtaining drugs they find pleasurable. In animals, as in humans, there is a significant difference between drug use and drug addiction. Most animals can use drugs over a long period of time and even on regular basis and still not develop addiction. Actually, it turns out that developing drug addiction in animals is relatively complicated. Resilience to drug addiction is basically the norm in rats and very few rats are actually vulnerable to addiction when using drugs (Ahmed 2012). This is the same as arises with human research as only a small percentage of humans who use drugs actually develop addictions. There clearly are factors contributing to drug addiction other than just the frequency and amount of drug use.

Research involving rats helps explain the differences between drug use and drug addiction. The nucleus accumbens and ventral striatum both have dopamine-enhancing effects and play a major role in the reinforcing effects of stimulant drugs. This is what leads to the reinforcing effects underlying drug use. Animals and humans use drugs because they have a pleasurable effect. Dopamine is the neurochemical most often associated with rewards so any drug that can enhance its impact will be one that has a pleasurable effect. Impacting the dopamine system is one of the reasons drug use is often pleasurable and something human and nonhuman animals want to do.

Dopamine is clearly involved in the pleasurable and reinforcing effects of drug use. But its role in the development of drug addiction is less clear. This is because it is often difficult to distinguish the behavioral conditioning associated with addictive behaviors from the rewarding and motor impact of the drugs themselves (Everitt and Robbins 2013). Individuals addicted to drugs seek them out and take them compulsively. This happens at the expense of other sources of reinforcement and despite negative consequences. As individuals become more addicted to drugs it is difficult to determine whether it is still the pleasurable effects of the drugs themselves contributing to their use or whether is compulsive behaviors caused by the drugs.

As addiction progresses, drug-seeking and drug-taking become habitual and often continue even when the drugs' value has decreased. Counselors frequently see the impact of this as addicts present with difficulties related not only to their taking drugs but also to increasing their use of drugs even as they develop a tolerance. Viewing this as habitual, which is supported both through behavioral and neurological research, helps address the question of why addicted individuals do not just stop using drugs when their initial rewarding impact wears off. What is less clear is whether the habit develops more because of the continued pleasurable impact of the drug, which tends to wear off quickly over time unless more drugs are used, or whether it is habitual behaviors caused by the neurological impact of drugs over time.

There actually is very little evidence in the literature to clearly indicate what separates animals who develop drug dependence from those who do not. Extended drug exposure and increased drug motivation over time do not lead animals to lose control over the self-administration of drugs. Studies involving cocaine use show that about 90 per cent of rats who have long-term exposure to cocaine do not lose their ability to abstain from cocaine for another nondrug pursuit when it is available. Regular and continued use of cocaine does not lead to addiction in rats. This is consistent with human research showing that only a minority of cocaine users become addicted (Degenhardt, Bohnert, and Anthony 2008).

Reward processing and substance abuse

Animal studies show that the rewarding effects of drugs are critically involved in addiction but that the strength of involvement varies depending on the stage of the addiction process. Rats find the use of drugs rewarding, but how much the rewarding properties of the drug impact on the drug use changes as addiction progresses. These rewarding effects involve several brain regions, primarily the ventral tengmedial area, nucleus accumbens, and prefrontal cortex. Animal studies involving deep brain stimulation have shown that the nucleus accumbens (NAc) is the most effective primary area for targeting with patients who have treatment-resistant drug addiction (Luigjes et al. 2012). This is one key area of the brain involved in the impact of reward and the feeling of pleasure. There are other brain areas involved, and all of these areas together are critical in processing rewarding behaviors (Koob 2003).

Compulsive drug-seeking is often associated with addiction. Individuals who get addicted to drugs spend a great deal of energy and resources trying to get that drug. One proposed interpretation of this type of behavior is that it represents the behavioral manifestation of an extreme motivational state. Individuals addicted to drugs may be neurologically geared towards more intensely seeking out the pleasurable effects of drugs. Neurologically, this change often involves an increased sensitivity to dopamine in the midbrain. When this type of neurological change takes place, it increases how quickly the individual responds to pleasurable and rewarding stimuli (such as those associated with drug-taking) and this leads to increased drug self-administration (Vezina 2004). Chronic use of drugs has a tendency to produce the sensitivity that further supports the ongoing use of that drug. Additional research suggests that the neurological aspects associated with negative reinforcement, which would be experienced in humans through the alleviation or avoidance of a negative emotional state, also help reinforce the compulsive use of drugs (Koob 2008). This is consistent with the view of drug addiction being used by individuals to self-medicate emotional difficulties.

When we discuss the issue of motivational state related to substance abuse it is important to recognize the rewarding effects of the drugs and alcohol used by people who are addicted. There is a warped type of reward system associated with abuse where the individual is getting a positive outcome by utilizing a behavior that is harmful to themselves and/or other people. It is not just that the substances provide some sort of positive outcome, but more that a positive outcome is so overwhelming for the individual that they tend to ignore other consequences. People become so focused on the rewarding effects of the drug that they tend to ignore anything else, including other things that could provide rewarding effects. Animal research supports that drug abuse in particular tends to make the individual more sensitive to the positive outcome they experience from using drugs. This can go a long way in explaining how substance abuse and substance addiction develops.

Context also plays an important role in substance abuse (Maren, Phan, and Liberzon 2013). When drugs are administered, human and nonhuman animals show a strong sensitivity to the context in which they experience the pleasurable impact of those substances. Context also plays an important role in determining the quantity and the type of drugs that are consumed. Animals tend to self-administer drugs in the same sort of environments and situations where they originally started using the drugs. This is in large part because those are also the same sorts of environments where they first experienced the rewarding effects of the substances. There is a strong connection, supported by human and nonhuman animal research, between frequent drug use and the contexts in which the drug use occurs and where it first occurred. Drug abuse is most likely to continue when there is continued access to the types of contexts and/or situations where the drug use started.

Addiction and impulsivity

Impulsivity is another key factor in addiction to many drugs. Dalley *et al.* (2007) found that about seven per cent of a Lister hooded rat sample showed high levels of impulsivity. These highly impulsive rats then also showed an escalated response to self-administering cocaine on a schedule consistent with binge usage. This pattern was more consistent for some drugs (e.g. cocaine) than others (e.g. heroin). Subsequent research found that the use of an ADHD drug (Atomoxetine) helped reduce heroin-seeking behaviors among rats but not compulsive cocaine-seeking behaviors (Fernando *et al.* 2012).

Impulsivity can be defined as goal-directed behavior that is characterized by poor judgment in obtaining rewards. Using this definition, impulsivity is often associated with behaviors characterized by increased novelty and/or poor decision-making. These are behaviors that typically have disadvantages and problematic consequences (Vitacco and Rogers 2001). Psychiatric disorders commonly identified with substance abuse comorbidity are typically ones associated with impulsivity (Moeller *et al.* 2001; Evenden 1999). A subsequent definition of impulsivity (Dalley, Everitt, and Robbins 2011) described it as a premature responding to an attentional task. They found that animal research supported that impulsivity is consistent with a tendency towards escalation in cocaine self-administration. Their findings also supported that impulsivity is related to a tendency towards cocaine-seeking in rats and a relapse into cocaine use following abstinence.

Understanding the role that impulsivity plays in drug abuse helps in understanding why drug abuse tends to occur with higher frequencies in adolescents. There is a heightened propensity for teenagers to act impulsively and ignore the negative consequences of their behaviors. This may be due in large part to the relatively late development of brain circuits involved with judgment, emotion, and inhibitory control. This could be what increases the risk for substance abuse during adolescence. Adolescents tend to act more impulsively and as a result tend to engage more with experimentation and chronic use of drugs and alcohol. What we see here is one of the clearer reasons to suspect that impulsivity plays a major role in the development of substance abuse and substance addiction problems.

Impulsivity and contextual processing deficits often interact when it comes to substance abuse problems. These are two factors commonly associated with substance abuse in animals which are also starting to show importance in human substance abuse research. Papachristou *et al.* (2012) found that individuals who indulge in heavy alcohol drinking and also show higher impulsivity tend to react more strongly to alcohol-related contextual cues. They concluded that deficit response inhibition related to impulsivity presents as a risk factor for heavier alcohol use because it is associated with increased cravings for alcohol use. Their conclusions supported that individuals who tend to be more impulsive also tend to develop stronger sensitivities to the contextual cues associated with craving alcohol. In this way individuals who abuse alcohol and drugs tend to have stronger cravings for alcohol and drugs in more situations similar to the ones where they previously experienced the positive impact of using those substances.

Drug abuse also tends to occur when there is a meshing of problems often associated with the teenage years along with increased impulsivity and novelty-seeking of those developmental years. Isolation is one major factor that tends to increase the likelihood that an adolescent or young adult will develop substance abuse problems. Isolation and separation from important attachment figures are shown in animal research to correlate with higher levels of problematic drug use. Rats in their adolescent years who were raised in isolation were found to self-administer cocaine at a much higher rate than rats raised in groups (Ding *et al.* 2005). Longer maternal separation impacted significantly on ethanol use in adolescent rats regardless of the environment in which they were raised (Daoura, Haaker, and Nylander 2011). Research in rodents shows a U-shaped resilience function with regard to the maternal separation and drug abuse-related behaviors. Brief maternal separation (<15 minutes) generally protects animals against drug self-administration compared with controls. Prolonged maternal separation (>60 minutes) can reverse that protection and increase the animals' self-administration of drugs compared with controls. Isolation for 15 minutes or more can lead to increased alcohol self-administration in rodents. This may be because isolation is a more severe stressor than maternal separation (Neisewander, Peartree, and Pentkowski 2012). This research on maternal separation and isolation is consistent with human research supporting that parental neglect is a significant risk factor for substance abuse (Altman *et al.* 1996).

Animal studies have been particularly beneficial in understanding how adolescent development impacts on novelty-seeking behaviors. Periadolescent rats show higher levels of exploratory behaviors in a novel open field and engage in more social play than younger and older rats (Spear and Brake 1983). Environmental novelty provokes dopamine release in the ventral striatal area of the brain. This produces locomotor behavior in rats that is similar to that produced by addictive drugs (Lipska *et al.* 1992). Chambers, Taylor, and Potenza (2014) produced a summary of the relevant research showing that novelty and the drive to have unknown and/or unfamiliar experiences is a motivation that is particularly strong in adolescence, which could account for why substance abuse occurs most often in adolescence and young adulthood. There are dopamine systems that are associated with the neurological impact associated with motivation. Direct pharmacological stimulation of these dopamine systems through the use of addictive drugs may mimic the natural motivational propensity associated with novel experiences.

Periadolescent mice show a greater baseline preference for novel experiences than adult mice (Adriani, Chiarotti, and Laviola 1998). Periadolescent rats also showed greater behavioral sensitization and striatal dopamine release after repeated injections of psychostimulants than adult rats (Laviola *et al.* 1995; Laviola,

Pascucci, and Pieretti 2001). Adolescent novelty-seeking behaviors and impulsivity may be associated with maturation of the brain's dopamine system. Research on monkeys shows that the development of dopamine-bearing endings in pre-synapses of the brain mature to the full adult level during adolescence while the areas that produce neurochemicals that block dopamine reach their full levels by two weeks after birth (Lambe, Krimer, and Goldman-Rakic 2000). These findings support that greater dopamine activity may be characteristic of adolescent development.

Animal research supporting impulsivity as a major factor in substance abuse is consistent with recent human substance abuse research. Human research in recent years has shown a strong role for impulsivity in drug abuse (Perry and Carroll 2008). Impulsivity contributes not only to the development of drug abuse but also to its maintenance and escalation. This has also been the case with alcohol abuse research (Courtney *et al.* 2012). Genetic research shows that genetic factors often make individuals more impulsive and, as a result, make them more susceptible to drug abuse and addiction (Kreek *et al.* 2005).

Evolutionary factors and substance abuse

Understanding the evolutionary perspective on substance abuse requires an understanding of the evolutionary perspective on emotions. This theory was initially explained well in a review article by Randolph Nesse in the mid-1990s (Nesse 1994). Emotions are complicated from an evolutionary perspective because they can serve multiple functions. Fear, for example, can communicate danger but also inhibit socially unacceptable behaviors. Emotions are different from other traits because they relate not to specific functions but more to specific types of situations. All emotions can be positive or negative to some degree, depending on the situations. Understanding the adaptive importance of the positive and negative aspects of drugs can similarly help understand why people abuse drugs and why stopping drug use can be so difficult.

Experiences that increase the positive aspects of emotions tend to arouse pleasure and tend to be repeated. These positive experiences can include sex, friendship, having children, and being accepted by others.

These tend to produce benefits for survival. They are experiences that lead to reproductive advantages and, from a Darwinian perspective, tend to have survival advantages. Psychoactive drugs tend to stimulate the same grade circuitry as these pleasurable activities but do so in a way that bypasses perception and cognition.

This evolutionary perspective on drug use helps with understanding this type of behavior when certain aspects are taken into account. First, like the emotions they trigger, drug use has both positive and negative attributes. Any clinician, family member, or support person who tries to help someone using drugs from the perspective that the person can gain nothing positive from drug use is denying reality and can likely provide no help for that person. Helping the drug abuser requires acknowledging that the person is gaining some benefit from drug use. Treating drug use will often require reaching an agreement that the negative aspects of the drug use outweigh the very real positive aspects. Certainly the history of psychiatry shows that drug use has positive aspects since it played an essential role in Sigmund Freud's work and his development of psychoanalysis (vom Scheidt 1973).

A second aspect important for understanding the evolutionary perspective on drug use is recognizing that there is not really a clear distinction between the potential appeal of legal drugs and illegal ones. Many recognize this by acknowledging that alcohol is not necessarily a "better" drug than cocaine just because it is legal. In this same vein, prescribed psychiatric drugs cannot be seen as necessarily "better" simply because they are legal. All psychoactive drugs have some type of impact on the pleasure centers of the brain and tend to stimulate positive experiences without involving perception or cognition. Viewing drug use as a continuum, with the potential cost–benefit ratio for each drug marking different points on the continuum, allows for a clear understanding of how some drugs are more problematic even if they have similar physiological effects to other drugs.

Clinicians can best help individuals suffering from drug abuse by acknowledging that their use of any type of drug likely has some type of benefit for them. Using the drugs clearly has significant motivations associated with them, as evidenced by drug abusers' tendency to increase the use of drugs and to find different ways of taking the drugs. Drug abusers tend to increase their use of their drugs of choice rather than fully acknowledge that the impact of the drug and the benefits it provides have started to wear off. Chronic drug abusers also tend to find different ways of getting drugs into their system as evidenced by, for example, heroin users shooting heroin in between their toes when they no longer can find veins in their arms. This behavior makes absolutely no sense if a clinician does not recognize that there is a strong degree of motivation associated with taking the drug. From an evolutionary perspective, the individual is motivated to find alternative ways of getting the drugs into the system because of the physiological impact that the drug has on their brain circuitry associated with pleasurable activities and, as a result, this tends to be the type of behavior that the person tries to repeat. It may be difficult to view drug use as actually having some degree of evolutionary benefit but this really would be the only way that clinicians can implement drug abuse treatment in a way that is likely to be beneficial. Denying this reality can only serve to make it more difficult for the clinician to make any sort of connection with the drug abuser and have any way of helping the drug abuser make progress.

Clinical applications

Carroll and Onken (2005) summarized the cognitive-behavioral approach to drug abuse treatment that is most in line with evolutionary theory. This approach emphasizes that the clinician do a functional analysis of the substance abuse behaviors. This requires that you identify what sort of function the substance abuse is serving for the individual. What you do here is very difficult in terms of it going against the grain for how many people view substance abuse. Acknowledging that the substance that the individual is abusing might actually have some benefit for them is not something that comes easily to drug abuse clinicians. But it is essential since research shows that there clearly is some positive benefit that is being served for the individual using the drugs. Taking a functional analysis helps to identify what gain the person is obtaining from the use of drugs and then this information can be used to develop a treatment plan to help the individual find alternative ways of obtaining the same gains.

We looked earlier at some of the physiological gains that could be obtained from using drugs. Many psychoactive drugs (including alcohol) stimulate parts of the brain that are associated with pleasurable effects. What the use of these drugs provides is a way of stimulating certain parts of the brain associated with pleasurable activities without the complexities associated with cognition and experience. One potential gain that can be obtained from the use of drugs is being able to gain pleasurable experiences without actually having to do much personal work in order to obtain them. This can be very motivating, and that motivation can increase if the person is having difficulties in other aspects of their lives. Being able to have positive experiences without adding additional complexities beyond just obtaining a drug or buying a bottle of alcohol can have a strong appeal. What the person may be gaining from the use of drugs is the ability to have pleasurable parts of their brains stimulated in a way that is consistent with the types of behaviors that would tend to be repeated. This would be consistent with the evolutionary research discussed earlier in this chapter related to how pleasurable behaviors are often associated with increased reproductive potential and are therefore likely to be repeated.

Cognitive-behavioral treatments often focus on helping the individual learn more effective skills for obtaining the same results that are obtained from the drugs. This can be difficult since it is unlikely that initially the individual would be able to gain anywhere near the same level of physiological benefits that they obtained from the use of drugs. But skills training can help to at least obtain some of the positive experiences that might be associated with drugs and as a result help decrease the desire for using them. In this case it would be particularly important for helping to clarify for the person their motivation for decreasing their use of drugs. Remember that taking out the cognitive processes that are associated with obtaining pleasurable results is one of the reasons why drugs may be attractive to an individual. If you put those cognitive processes back into the skills that the person uses when making decisions this can help to decrease their tendency to go quickly for drugs or alcohol.

Motivational interviewing is an approach to starting substance abuse treatment that has shown a great deal of promise in terms of effectiveness. What happens in this process is that a collaborative effort between the clinician and patient is emphasized as a way of helping to clarify for the person why they are trying to stay away from drugs. This decision is not forced on the individual by the clinician but is rather obtained through a collaborative process where the patient is helped to clarify what motivates them to stay away from their drug of choice. What is happening here is that the person is helped to start making more informed decisions about how to obtain the positive results they desire. This process helps to bring back the cognitive processing into the decision-making that occurs when the person tries to obtain positive results. Where this fits from an evolutionary perspective is that the individual is still trying to reach the same desired goals that would be associated with the drug use but is implementing cognitive processes that would help them stay away from behaviors that actually have more negative consequences associated with them. In this way the individual is approaching a way of obtaining the desired results in a way that is less harmful to them. Motivational interviewing helps to set the individual on a path where they can reach the desired outcomes but in a way that is less likely to cause them significant harm.

Impulsivity is one clinical area not often included in substance abuse treatment. Animal research supports that this is an area that should be given more attention in treatment approaches. As shown in the material summarized in this chapter, impulsivity is clearly a major factor associated with substance abuse problems. You could picture that an individual who has a high level of impulsivity could be similar to the rats discussed in drug abuse studies that tend to self-administer drugs at a higher rate. Individuals who recognize that they have significant difficulties associated with their drug use but also have a high level of impulsivity would be more likely to self-administer drugs without being impacted by their knowledge about what their drug use could mean. This would be similar to the rats in the study who showed higher levels of impulsivity and tended to self-administer drugs at a much higher rate than other rats. Helping individuals decrease the impact of impulsivity could help decrease the likelihood that these individuals will use drugs; or at least increase the likelihood that they will think through more completely how the drugs could impact their lives.

Psychotherapeutic treatments of impulsivity have usually been associated with treatment of ADHD. This would be expected, given that ADHD is often presented as having impulsivity as a major component. In many cases the focus is on helping to increase the attention the individual gives to their behaviors as a way of decreasing the likelihood that they will act in an impulsive manner. Using skills to stop impulsive behaviors soon after they start is another type of approach that can be helpful for decreasing the impact of impulsivity. Behavior therapy is the most common type of therapeutic approach used for treating impulsivity. Interpersonal therapy and family therapy are also effective approaches to help address the interpersonal factors that tend to contribute to the person making impulsive decisions. Family therapy and interpersonal therapy can also be used as a way of helping to bring family members and other supportive individuals into the process where the person is trying to make better decisions about handling situations that present the potential for drug and/or alcohol use.

Distraction-based strategies are cognitive-behavioral approaches that are used to decrease alcohol and drug cravings. Theories about why these types of strategies can be effective are often associated with the impaired contextual deficits that were discussed earlier. These strategies involve the therapist or counselor teaching the individual to use cognitive restructuring so as to change craving-related thinking and also teaching the individual strategies for distancing themselves from alcohol and drug stimuli. Murphy and MacKillop (2014) conducted a study comparing mindfulness and distraction-based strategies for heavy alcohol cravings. They predicted that mindfulness would be more effective but actually found that the distraction-based strategies were more effective.

Animal research discussed earlier supported that substance abuse is often associated with impulsivity and also a higher sensitivity to the cues associated with drug and/or alcohol cravings. Distraction-based strategies focus on helping the person distance themselves from those cravings and contextual responses through the use of cognitive strategies. Behavioral strategies that might also help in this situation would be working with the individual on problem-solving skills and decision-making skills to help them make better decisions about how to handle situations where they are likely to crave alcohol or drugs.

Skills training and problem-solving are two of the most effective behavior therapy approaches used to decrease difficulties related to impulsivity. In terms of skills training the individual is taught to implement skills that help them focus more consistently. As a therapist or counselor you will work with the patient on helping them put effort into focusing whenever they are making decisions. Problem-solving skills involve you working with the person in terms of them taking more effective steps to address problem situations. In the therapy session you can work with the individual in terms of role-playing where they will practice focusing more and using more effective steps for deciding how to address problem situations. You can use these therapy sessions as a way of helping them practice what steps they will take whenever they encounter any sort of situation where they are faced with the potential for using drugs. You can also work with the person in terms of helping them use effective problem-solving and decision-making skills for addressing ways that they can avoid the types of situations that often lead them to use drugs.

Animal studies vs. human studies

It could be easily argued that animal studies have revealed all they can about substance abuse. Animal research on substance abuse involves giving drugs and alcohol to animals and then testing their impact on behaviors. Since the goal is not to treat substance abuse in animals but, rather, substance abuse in humans, there is considerable room to argue that humans should be the focus of research. There is, the argument goes, no real benefit any longer to getting animals hopped on drugs when that area of research has already contributed what it is going to contribute.

Animals react positively to the effect of the same types of drugs to which humans react. Animal research has shown that pleasure centers of the brain are heavily involved in the initial use of drugs but that other areas become involved as addiction develops. These are aspects of drug use that are similar between animals and humans. They are also conclusions that have been reached over decades of research involving animals and drug use. Clearly this research has been beneficial in terms of understanding drug abuse and the impact of drug use on human and animal functioning. It would be difficult to argue that the research done so far has not been beneficial in terms of understanding the impact of drug use. However, it could be argued that there is very little else to be gained by continuing to subject animals to drug use and that the time may have come for focusing drug abuse research exclusively on humans. Making the case one way or another in detail is beyond the scope of this book but it is important to at least address the possibility that the time may have come to stop animal research involving drugs since such research may have resulted in as much information as is likely to benefit humans.

A review of drug research articles over the past five years or so involving animals shows that the focus has been almost exclusively on finding neurological centers of the brain that impact on drug abuse. Certainly the main purpose of that research is to identify drugs that could help with substance abuse problems. Whether or not such research is actually beneficial and worth the impact that it has on animals involved in the studies is worth considering given that the benefit would be almost exclusively for pharmaceutical treatments. This particular type of treatment has a certain problematic circular logic associated with it in that the focus is on helping individuals decrease their use of illegal psychoactive drugs by increasing their use of legal psychoactive drugs. Whether helping to advance this type of treatment approach is worthwhile in terms of the resources necessary for animal studies is certainly an argument worth having.

CASE STUDY

Samantha was an adult female who presents with a history of alcohol abuse spanning the past 20 years. She started drinking alcohol heavily in college and has continued to drink hard liquor several times per week most months of the year. She had been able to go several months at a time without drinking but always returned after those periods of sobriety. She did not identify any specific triggering factor that might have led her back to alcohol after these periods. She did talk about how there may have been a tendency for her to start using alcohol again when there did not seem to be anything particularly interesting going on in her life and she did not have periods of looking forward to anything in particular. But she was quite tentative about this explanation and stated that she was not certain whether there actually was a connection.

Samantha presented to her counselor for substance abuse counseling after she received her second DUI. She had been drinking bourbon and vodka at a bar with several friends. There was no particular reason for this outing and she reported that she had similar outings several times throughout most weeks.

She missed work a few times over the past decade because of hangovers but did not have a history of facing formal disciplinary actions at work because of her drinking. She last received a DUI about five years earlier and received the present DUI after she swerved driving home from a bar. She knew that she was in danger of having significant consequences related to her license if she had another DUI and said that this was the reason that she had chosen to seek alcohol abuse counseling.

Samantha's counseling started with motivational interviewing. This type of interviewing involves pursuing in detail with the person their motivations for improving. In this case Samantha was encouraged to talk about her own reasons why she is trying to stay away from alcohol. She could identify her recent DUI and potential problems with her license as one major reason why she was trying to stay away from alcohol. She also talked about how alcohol use led her to get into arguments with people and had significantly impacted some of her relationships over the years. She also talked about how she is getting older and knows that heavy drinking several times per week is likely to impact significantly on her health. Samantha went on to talk about how she just wanted to stop engaging in behaviors that she knows are potentially dangerous for her.

Samantha did talk about finding the motivational interviewing helpful. And she was able to finish the motivational interview with a stated commitment that she wanted to find a way to stay away from alcohol. But it was only after several sessions that she started to really seem engaged in the therapy. This followed some discussion several sessions after her initial evaluation where the focus turned more to talking about the positive consequences that she associated with drinking. This went beyond the discussion of just talking about why she drinks and focused more on what her motivation was for continuing to drink. Initially Samantha was hesitant about this part of the discussion as she did not really want to acknowledge that there had been any time where she actually saw alcohol in a positive way. But as therapy progressed and the therapeutic relationship grew she seemed to be more comfortable in terms of discussing honestly what it was about alcohol that had such a strong appeal. She talked openly about how she felt she was able to be more honest with people when she drank alcohol and how her inhibitions lessened. She talked about social events being much more interesting when she had the chance to be inebriated. Samantha related how many of the difficulties in her life seemed to either disappear or become less significant whenever she was inebriated. These were all issues that she discussed over the course of two sessions when the discussion turned more to discussing what the positive impact of alcohol use might be.

Once the point had been reached where Samantha was more open about how alcohol had actually been a positive factor for her she then seemed more receptive to discussing ways that she might lessen her use of it. Earlier in the sessions she seemed to tense up and not really put much effort into discussions about ways she might be able to stay away from alcohol. She kept insisting that she knew the things that she was supposed to do but just did not think she could do them. But after there was more opportunity for discussion about alcohol being a positive force for her she seemed more receptive to discussing ways that she could decrease her use of it. Her responses indicated that this was because she felt that she was being more honest now about the impact that alcohol had on her and could then also be more honest about what she needed to do in order to stop drinking. She was able to admit that she was not happy about having to give up alcohol but recognized that this was best for her.

A subsequent functional analysis revealed the positive consequences that she experienced from alcohol use and also the antecedents to her alcohol use. This led to a discussion of what triggers might increase her use of alcohol. There clearly was a pattern where she had started using alcohol in certain situations and then broadened that to different contexts over the years. Much of the positive impact that alcohol had on her was then carried over to the different contexts. She had learned that positive consequences can result from alcohol use and had extended that learning to a number of different environments. Part of the reason that her alcohol abuse had become such a problem was that she had continued to use alcohol regardless of changes in her environment. It did not matter where she was living or where she was spending her time, she would seek alcohol out and described herself as having the same types of positive experiences from alcohol use regardless of the environments.

Triggers for alcohol use that Samantha identified included work stressors and also boredom. When her work became more stressful she would resort to using alcohol more often as a way of helping her deal with the stress. And when her life became increasingly boring she would then seek out alcohol as a way of bringing some excitement back. She could identify specific situations over the past ten years where increased work stress or increased boredom would precede the termination of her abstinence or increase in alcohol use. When she talked about boredom she often described it as feeling that her life did not really have a purpose and that she did not really have anything to which she could look forward.

Samantha's functional analysis revealed triggers that were often associated with her use of alcohol. This then led to a discussion of specific steps that she could use to avoid those triggers. A discussion of the contexts in which her alcohol use tended to occur naturally led to a discussion of ways to avoid those contexts that could trigger cravings. This was not presented as any sort of panacea in terms of stopping her alcohol use but was discussed as a good first step. Samantha was assigned to self-monitor how often she had to deal with those triggers and then what steps she took to avoid them in the weeks between sessions. Her self-monitoring of the behaviors that preceded her alcohol use improved and she was able to talk about steps that she took to specifically stay away from alcohol use.

Cognitive strategies were used to help decrease the level of stress that Samantha experienced when she faced difficulties at work. She was helped to develop some specific ways of talking herself through problems that she faced at work. Stress inoculation was used to help identify the types of negative thinking that increased her stress and find ways to help decrease the thinking associated with that stress. She also developed a type of self-talk that specifically addressed ways to encourage her to stay away from alcohol and to recognize that she did not need alcohol to deal with stressors. She used the strategies to help encourage herself to stay away from alcohol whenever she acknowledged that she was having increased stress in her life.

Behavioral strategies focused on helping her find ways to bring more meaningful activities into her life. She objectively defined boredom as not feeling that she had anything meaningful in her life or anything to which she could look forward, and these were specific issues that were addressed with problem-solving steps to help her find ways of improving how she viewed her life. By finding ways to make her life more meaningful she could be helped to decrease the level of boredom that she experienced. She was also encouraged to develop self-talk that she could use to focus herself on not relying on drinking alcohol as a way to deal with boredom and problem situations.

Impulsivity was also identified as a significant problem for Samantha. She was able to talk about how she would often react very quickly when it came to using alcohol. She also could identify ways that she had been impulsive throughout her life. She worked with her counselor on developing cognitive strategies she could use to keep herself focused on what she was doing and take specific steps to deal with problem situations. This helped her focus more on what she was doing and allowed her to incorporate decisions about drinking as part of the steps she used. Samantha walked herself through a series of steps whenever she was facing situations where she was even thinking about drinking. She would incorporate a decision about whether she should drink as one of those steps and was able to increase the number of alternative steps she could take other than drinking for handling situations where her alcohol cravings increased.

Over a period of six months Samantha decreased significantly her use of alcohol. During that time she did not stop using alcohol altogether but decreased the amount of times that she used alcohol each week. She then had a close call where she almost obtained another DUI and knew that she could lose her license altogether. So at that point she continued with therapy but also then started attending Alcoholics Anonymous meetings with a focus on staying away from alcohol altogether. With the help of both counseling and AA meetings she was able to stay clean of alcohol for a period of six months when the decision was made to terminate counseling.

Summary

Comparative psychology research reveals the rewards associated with substance abuse and some of the factors that distinguish substance abuse from the more typical substance use. Animal research has supported much of the same conclusions about drug and alcohol abuse that have been revealed through human research. Impulsivity and impaired contextual processing are two factors associated with substance abuse that were strongly implicated in animal research. Counselors and therapists working with individuals who have substance abuse problems need to consider the functional aspects of alcohol and drug use and particularly focus on the positive benefits that individuals are getting from using those substances. They also need to consider the degree to which impulsivity and contextual processing difficulties play significant roles in alcohol and substance abuse. Cognitive-behavior therapy focused on problem-solving, distraction strategies, focusing, and contextual processing are therapeutic approaches that are supported from animal research findings discussed through this chapter.

References

Adriani, W., Chiarotti, F., and Laviola, G. (1998) 'Elevated novelty seeking and peculiar d-amphetamine sensitization in periadolescent mice compared with adult mice.' *Behavioral Neuroscience 112*, 5, 1152–1166.

Ahmed, S.H. (2012) 'The science of making drug-addicted animals.' *Neuroscience 211*, 107–125.

Altman, J., Everitt, B.J., Robbins, T.W., Glautier, S., *et al.* (1996) 'The biological, social and clinical bases of drug addiction: commentary and debate.' *Psychopharmacology 125*, 4, 285–345.

Bell, R.L., Sable, H.J., Colombo, G., Hyytia, P., Rodd, Z.A., and Lumeng, L. (2012) 'Animal models for medications development targeting alcohol abuse using selectively bred rat lines: neurobiological and pharmacological validity.' *Pharmacology Biochemistry and Behavior 103*, 1, 119–155.

Carroll, K.M., and Onken, L.S. (2005) 'Behavioral therapies for drug abuse.' *American Journal of Psychiatry 162*, 8, 1452–1460.

Chambers, R.A., Taylor, J.R., and Potenza, M.N. (2014) 'Developmental neurocircuitry of motivation in adolescence: a critical period of addiction vulnerability.' *American Journal of Psychiatry 160*, 6, 1041–1052.

Courtney, K.E., Arellano, R., Barkley-Levenson, E., Gálvan, A., *et al.* (2012) 'The relationship between measures of impulsivity and alcohol misuse: an integrative structural equation modeling approach.' *Alcoholism: Clinical and Experimental Research 36*, 6, 923–931.

Dalley, J.W., Everitt, B.J., and Robbins, T.W. (2011) 'Impulsivity, compulsivity, and top-down cognitive control.' *Neuron 69*, 4, 680–694.

Dalley, J.W., Fryer, T.D., Brichard, L., Robinson, E.S., *et al.* (2007) 'Nucleus accumbens D2/3 receptors predict trait impulsivity and cocaine reinforcement.' *Science 315*, 5816, 1267–1270.

Daoura, L., Haaker, J., and Nylander, I. (2011) 'Early environmental factors differentially affect voluntary ethanol consumption in adolescent and adult male rats.' *Alcoholism: Clinical and Experimental Research 35*, 3, 506–515.

Degenhardt, L., Bohnert, K.M., and Anthony, J.C. (2008) 'Assessment of cocaine and other drug dependence in the general population: "gated" versus "ungated" approaches.' *Drug and Alcohol Dependence 93*, 3, 227–232.

Ding, Y., Kang, L., Li, B., and Ma, L. (2005) 'Enhanced cocaine self-administration in adult rats with adolescent isolation experience.' *Pharmacology Biochemistry and Behavior 82*, 4, 673–677.

Evenden, J.L. (1999) 'Varieties of impulsivity.' *Psychopharmacology 146*, 4, 348–361.

Everitt, B.J. and Robbins, T.W. (2013) 'From the ventral to the dorsal striatum: devolving views of their roles in drug addiction.' *Neuroscience and Biobehavioral Reviews 37*, 9, 1946–1954.

Fernando, A.B., Economidou, D., Theobald, D.E., Zou, M.F., *et al.* (2012) 'Modulation of high impulsivity and attentional performance in rats by selective direct and indirect dopaminergic and noradrenergic receptor agonists.' *Psychopharmacology 219*, 2, 341-0352.

Koob, G.F. (2003) 'Neuroadaptive mechanisms of addiction: studies on the extended amygdala.' *European Neuropsychopharmacology 13*, 6, 442–452.

Koob, G.F. (2008) 'A role for brain stress systems in addiction.' *Neuron 59*, 1, 11–34.

Kreek, M.J., Nielsen, D.A., Butelman, E.R., and LaForge, K.S. (2005) 'Genetic influences on impulsivity, risk taking, stress responsivity and vulnerability to drug abuse and addiction.' *Nature Neuroscience 8*, 11, 1450–1457.

Lambe, E.K., Krimer, L.S., and Goldman-Rakic, P.S. (2000) 'Differential postnatal development of catecholamine and serotonin inputs to identified neurons in prefrontal cortex of rhesus monkey.' *Journal of Neuroscience 20*, 23, 8780–8787.

Laviola, G., Pascucci, T., and Pieretti, S. (2001) 'Striatal dopamine sensitization to D-amphetamine in periadolescent but not in adult rats.' *Pharmacology Biochemistry and Behavior 68*, 1, 115–124.

Laviola, G., Wood, R.D., Kuhn, C., Francis, R., and Spear, L.P. (1995) 'Cocaine sensitization in periadolescent and adult rats.' *Journal of Pharmacology and Experimental Therapeutics 275*, 1, 345–357.

Lipska, B.K., Jaskiw, G.E., Chrapusta, S., Karoum, F., and Weinberger, D.R. (1992) 'Ibotenic acid lesion of the ventral hippocampus differentially affects dopamine and its metabolites in the nucleus accumbens and prefrontal cortex in the rat.' *Brain Research 585*, 1, 1–6.

Luigjes, J., Van Den Brink, W., Feenstra, M., van den Munckhof, P., *et al.* (2012) 'Deep brain stimulation in addiction: a review of potential brain targets.' *Molecular Psychiatry 17*, 6, 572–583.

Lynch, W.J., Nicholson, K.L., Dance, M.E., Morgan, R.W., and Foley, P.L. (2010) 'Animal models of substance abuse and addiction: implications for science, animal welfare, and society.' *Comparative Medicine 60*, 3, 177.

Maren, S., Phan, K.L., and Liberzon, I. (2013) 'The contextual brain: implications for fear conditioning, extinction and psychopathology.' *Nature Reviews Neuroscience* *14*, 6, 417–428.

McBride, W.J. and Li, T.K. (1998) 'Animal models of alcoholism: neurobiology of high alcohol-drinking behavior in rodents.' *Critical Reviews in Neurobiology 12*, 4, 339–369.

Murphy, C.M. and MacKillop, J. (2014) 'Mindfulness as a strategy for coping with cue-elicited cravings for alcohol: an experimental examination.' *Alcoholism: Clinical and Experimental Research 38*, 4, 1134–1142.

Neisewander, J.L., Peartree, N.A., and Pentkowski, N.S. (2012) 'Emotional valence and context of social influences on drug abuse-related behavior in animal models of social stress and prosocial interaction.' *Psychopharmacology 224*, 1, 33–56.

Nesse, R.M. (1994) 'An evolutionary perspective on substance abuse.' *Ethology and Sociobiology 15*, 5, 339–348.

Papachristou, H., Nederkoorn, C., Havermans, R., van der Horst, M., and Jansen, A. (2012) 'Can't stop the craving: the effect of impulsivity on cue-elicited craving for alcohol in heavy and light social drinkers.' *Psychopharmacology 219*, 2, 511–518.

Perry, J.L. and Carroll, M.E. (2008) 'The role of impulsive behavior in drug abuse.' *Psychopharmacology 200*, 1, 1–26.

Spear, L.P. and Brake, S.C. (1983) 'Periadolescence: age-dependent behavior and psychopharmacological responsivity in rats.' *Developmental Psychobiology 16*, 2, 83–109.

Vanderschuren, L.J. and Ahmed, S.H. (2012) 'Animal studies of addictive behavior.' *Cold Spring Harbor Perspectives in Medicine*, 1–14.

Vezina, P. (2004) 'Sensitization of midbrain dopamine neuron reactivity and the self-administration of psychomotor stimulant drugs.' *Neuroscience and Biobehavioral Reviews 27*, 8, 827–839.

Vitacco, M.J. and Rogers, R. (2001) 'Predictors of adolescent psychopathy: the role of impulsivity, hyperactivity, and sensation seeking.' *Journal of the American Academy of Psychiatry and the Law 29*, 4, 374–382.

vom Scheidt, J. (1973) 'Sigmund Freud and cocaine (English translation).' *Psyche: Zeitschrift für Psychoanalyse und ihre Anwendungen 27*, 5, 385–430.

Chapter 6

GAMBLING
PROBLEMS

Introduction

Gambling is prevalent throughout the world. It is an activity that often involves a great deal of money changing hands. There are many, many people who lose a great deal with gambling and many people who gain a great deal. Gambling itself is not necessarily a problem and is legal in many countries. However, gambling becomes a problem and becomes the arena of mental health professionals when it becomes pathological. There are many different definitions of what makes up pathological gambling. Most of the main definitions emphasize that pathological gambling is distinguished by gambling behaviors that result in an individual having significant damage to the personal, financial, family, professional, and/or legal aspects of their lives (Blaszczynski and Nower 2002). There are millions of people throughout the world who find their lives in a great deal of turmoil because they have developed gambling addiction.

For humans, gambling addiction is a problem because of what people lose. Like drugs and alcohol, there is a difference between typical gambling and gambling addiction. Most people who gamble are able to control it. They bet on some horse races, play casino games, try the slot machines, or place wagers on sporting events, but walk away when they are in danger of losing too much. Problem gamblers, those with addictions, will keep playing until they have nothing left to lose. And those losses have a much more direct effect on their lives and their family's lives than alcohol and drug addictions. When someone has drug or alcohol problems they may still be able to cover up the effects, at least for a while, so losses do not become prevalent. But gambling involves money and only money. So, once a person starts losing, their cars, homes, and college funds will start disappearing almost immediately. Preventing this sort of thing from happening is where counselors and therapists come in.

Counselors and therapists need an understanding of gambling behaviors in order to understand how to help pathological gamblers. There are aspects of gambling appealing to many more people than those who develop gambling addiction. Something about games of chance and the ability to bet sums of money, with the chance to win much more money, pulls people in. But for the vast majority of people it pulls them in only temporarily. Gambling addicts get pulled in but then have a much more difficult time pulling away than other people. It is not that the attraction is different but that the attraction's strength is much greater. Understanding not only that attraction but also what makes it stronger for certain individuals is the key to finding ways of helping to treat gambling addiction.

Animal research and "gambling" behaviors

Animals take chances in much the same ways humans do. They perceive potential benefit in taking risks and are often attracted by situations involving risks. Animals, much like humans, will engage in riskier behaviors if there is a chance of a large payoff at the end. They will also approach situations that are riskier but allow for higher payoffs even if it means ignoring a situation with less risk but also less of a payoff. These are the aspects of gambling behaviors that are similar between human and nonhuman animals.

Studying gambling behaviors among animals can be helpful in terms of understanding the types of behavioral factors impacting on gambling. But there are significant differences between human and nonhuman animals with regard to gambling behaviors. Animal studies of gambling actually involve behaviors that are similar to gambling but are not exactly the same (at least not the same as what humans call "gambling"). One difference is that the loss of reinforcers used in animal studies is not consistently parallel to the human experience of "loss" when it comes to gambling (Zeeb, Robbins, and Winstanley 2009).

Animals suffer the removal of reinforcers in gambling studies but those reinforcers do not typically have the same potential meaning to animals as do the money losses associated with human gambling.

In order to understand the differences between animal and human gambling studies, particularly understanding the outcomes related to gambling, it is useful here to veer into a discussion of "primary" and "secondary" reinforcers. This is because the difference in losses for humans and animals when it comes to gambling behaviors is that gambling usually involves loss of secondary reinforcers rather than primary reinforcers. Primary reinforcers are biological reinforcers such as food and sex. Secondary reinforcers are reinforcers that gain their strength by being associated with primary reinforcers. Most human reinforcers are secondary reinforcers while most animal reinforcers are primary reinforcers. Money is a good example of a secondary reinforcer. It does not, by itself, meet any sort of biological need (e.g. you cannot eat it) but it is associated with obtaining biological reinforcers.

Behavioral associations with primary reinforcers are usually straightforward. Gaining access to food is important for animals because it gets them the specific food they want. There is a direct relationship. But a secondary reinforcer, such as money, has more multi-faceted associations. Money can gain a lot of different things. It is more flexible in that it allows for the person to gain what they need or want at any particular moment. There is not as much of an immediacy to its value. You do not need to take advantage immediately of what money can get you but can "sit on" your money for a while and build up more opportunity for getting things you need or want. For this reason, money has more opportunity for gaining humans social status over time. It has immediate value and also long-term value in what it can gain. Humans can even distance themselves from other people if they have money. As Vohs and Baumeister (2011) put it in their article on money, "You don't need others if you have money." All of these factors give money a stronger connection for humans than any particular primary reinforcer has for animals.

Even though "gambling" behaviors for nonhuman animals are different than gambling for humans, there is still a lot that animal research can teach related to gambling. There are enough similarities between the two to make comparisons useful. Both animal and human gambling research addresses risk-taking behaviors. Both involve behaviors related to giving up a certain amount of resources to get more (or possibly get more) resources later. We are not looking to see how any specific animal species are similar to humans in terms of their behaviors. We are looking for general patterns that help explain different types of behaviors across different species. Capuchin monkeys do not act like humans. Capuchin monkeys act like capuchin monkeys. It is not important how much they look like humans. But it is important to what degree factors impacting their behaviors, including gambling behaviors, are similar to those impacting human behaviors. Through this comparison, we see general patterns that are important for understanding behaviors across species.

Animal studies allow for study of gambling-like behaviors free from the cultural, language, and social biases that may influence human gambling. Researchers do not have to be as concerned about the real losses animals would suffer in gambling tasks or the difficulties associated with humans getting into gambling patterns. Basically, studying animals allows researchers to see the patterns of reinforcement that strengthen gambling without concerns that the animals will become addicted to gambling or suffer the real losses humans suffer when they gamble. This is one of the trade-offs that makes animal research on gambling useful even if it is not the equivalent of human gambling.

Reinforcers and pathological gambling behaviors

Decisions humans make when they gamble are often based on emotions, irrational thought, and misunderstanding of probabilities. This is different from the types of decisions humans make most of the time, although not different from decisions humans make a large percentage of the time. Animals also often make decisions about risks based on misunderstanding possible outcomes. Humans and animals face decisions where they have to weigh risks and cost–benefit trade-offs across a variety of contexts. These situations include finding food and finding mates. These are tasks involving a structured assessment of different risks involved. They are tasks that usually require rational and objective approaches. But humans and animals often respond irrationally and emotionally to these tasks. They often respond to situations where they have to gauge risks in irrational ways that lead them to make ineffective, and sometimes harmful, decisions. What we have here is confusion about why there are situations where human and nonhuman animals tend to make irrational decisions about risk and potential outcome. Identifying why individuals would make these types of decisions is important for understanding the appeal and potentially addictive nature of gambling.

There is considerable evidence that the potential for larger payoffs reinforces more irrational gambling behaviors. Studies involving rhesus monkeys (Macaca mulatta) in a visual gambling task showed that riskier options tended to be preferred when there was an expectation of a larger payoff. Having the potential for a larger payoff played a critical role in determining willingness for risk of the individual macaques (Hayden and Platt 2007). Rhesus macaques tended to prefer risky rewards to safe ones. Why would these animals prefer more risk while other animals might prefer safer outcomes?

When reviewing the results, these authors proposed that the issue may have been the types of tasks associated with the gambling situation. What may have looked like a preference for risk may have actually been a preference for situations where there were more gambling opportunities over shorter periods of time. These animals may have been motivated by the opportunities to take risks rather than the specific risks themselves. Situations like these may look like high-risk but may actually be preferred by some animals because they involve very small stakes at any one time and also provide short delays between trials and task parameters that are more easily learned (Heilbronner and Hayden 2013).

This study shows some limitations of gambling research involving animals. For one, it shows the difficulty of determining what are "high risk" stakes for animals. Researchers aren't going to let animals starve so if food is what is being gambled, the animals will just get food from another source. Humans who lose money lose direct access to things they want or need but it is not clear how often this is actually the case for animals who take risks. Also, it takes some time to address whether there are issues common across species. The study addressed in the previous paragraph is one specifically involving rhesus monkeys and there has not been enough additional research to determine if the same type of results are consistent across other animal species.

Laboratory animals will work particularly hard for reinforcers where the number of wins per reinforcer is unpredictable (Madden, Ewan, and Lagorio 2007). These authors concluded that the strength of unpredictable rewards (consistent with what is called the "delayed discounting model" of gambling) affects problem gamblers who find unpredictable rewards to be of greater value than predictable ones. These are results that have been obtained across a variety of different species and is consistent with much of learning theory based on empirical research showing unpredictable schedules of reinforcement to be stronger than predictable schedules. These types of reinforcement schedules are the ones that reinforce the types of behaviors that the individuals perceive are going to result in desired outcomes. Gambling behaviors are reinforced in this way as the individuals perceive that the behaviors can get them what they want. In fact, one of the difficulties with gambling behaviors is that people do actually win things, but when they win something is unpredictable. Having the rewards associated with gambling occur on an unpredictable basis actually helps reinforce the gambling behaviors more than if they were provided on a predictable basis.

In a study by Zentall (2011), pigeons showed a preference for alternatives that are associated with a low level of reinforcement over alternatives with higher levels of reinforcement. These pigeons initially showed a preference for variable reinforcement schedules over fixed reinforcement schedules, which is consistent with basic behavioral analysis principles. But, as the authors further studied their behaviors, pigeons also chose the opportunity to obtain ten food pellets 20 per cent of the time over the opportunity to obtain three food pellets 100 per cent of the time. That is, they showed a preference for obtaining more reward less often than lower rewards more often. Notice, also, that they showed a preference for the higher rewards option even though they were *guaranteed* to obtain food pellets with the lower-quantity option. This is consistent with gamblers who choose activities with low probability of higher payoffs over alternatives where they have higher probability of lower payoffs.

Zentall's article also addressed another issue relevant to understanding pathological gambling. Pigeon research summarized in the article showed a preference for reinforcement clearly signaled to situations where the signals were more ambiguous. This is consistent with research showing that animals and humans prefer situations where the possibility for reinforcement is clearly signaled, or at least perceived to be clearly signaled, over situations where this is not the case. One example of this type of "signalled reinforcement" occurs in experiments where animals receive a verbal tone five seconds before food arrives as a signal that it is about to arrive. Gambling behaviors also show increased frequency when gamblers perceive there is a signal for possibly winning. This is evident in research on "near-misses" in gambling. Clark *et al.* (2009) described neural activity, involving striatal and insula brain circuits and the anterior cortex area of the brain, occurring when gamblers had unsuccessful attempts that were close to what they needed to win (otherwise known as "near-misses"). This neural activity acted as a "signal" that then increased the likelihood that the individual would gamble again. This is consistent with other research showing that gambling behaviors increased after "near-misses" (Chase and Clark 2010; Kassinove and Schare 2001). It is quite possible that this neural activity is the signal that pathological gamblers experience, increasing their perception that a win is close at hand. If this is the case, and more research is needed, then these results would help explain not only gambling behaviors but also the neurological differences distinguishing problem gamblers from typical gamblers.

In a study of six female Norway hooded rats, Peters, Hunt, and Harper (2010) also found that "response latencies" changed as a function of reinforcer magnitude and near-miss trials (they used the term "near-wins"). They defined response latencies as the time period between the outcome of one gamble and the initiation of the next. These authors determined that outcomes close to the desired outcomes served as discriminative stimuli signaling that reinforcement is likely in the future. This may be one explanation for the effect of near-wins in this study. Another possibility is that the near-wins became conditional reinforcers because they have a temporal association with the gambling reinforcers. Either way, their results also showed an association between near-wins and the likelihood of gambling again.

Research on pathological gambling in humans shows a significant impact of impulsivity. This is consistent with the research on other addictions. Pathological gambling is particularly interesting to study when it comes to impulsivity because there is very little neurological impact of the addiction (Verdejo-García, Lawrence, and Clark 2008). People who gamble heavily do not suffer any sort of neurological impairment because of their habits. Drug addiction involves impulsivity but there is also indication that the drugs themselves can impact on the further development of impulsivity. Heavy drug, and alcohol, habits are not only possibly caused by neurological factors but also impact neurological functioning. That is not the case with gambling behaviors. So, it is often difficult to know how much of the drug and alcohol addiction is due to the individual's impulsivity and how much of the addiction is due to the neurological impact of substances that the person uses. Studying gambling addiction does not involve these same difficulties.

There are some similarities between drug addiction and gambling addiction. Animal studies show that highly impulsive individuals are more prone to problematic gambling behaviors than other less impulsive individuals (Winstanley et al. 2010). Impulsivity is also consistent with individuals who show a preference for novel types of situations. Molander et al. (2011) found that rats who were impulsive exhibited a preference for novel types of situations. Gambling addiction, like drug and alcohol addiction, tends to develop most often during adolescence, which is when impulsivity is at its height (van den Bos et al. 2013). As we saw in Chapter 5, impulsivity and preference for novel situations is often associated with drug abuse. What we see here is that these same tendencies are also consistent with gambling addiction. Animal studies also show that the same neurochemical changes that can help lessen drug-addictive behaviors also can have an impact on gambling-addictive behaviors. Drugs that target D2 receptors, which are drugs that help to address substance addiction, tend to have the most impact on addictive gambling behaviors in animals (Winstanley 2011).

Neurochemical factors and gambling

Gambling addiction research reveals the same neurochemical patterns associated with other types of addictions, particularly drug addiction. This is consistent across different animal studies and shows that dopamine in particular is a significant factor in gambling addiction. Dopamine sensitivity, usually involving what are called "D3-related mechanisms," has been shown to be heavily involved in behavioral addictions such as gambling. This level of dopamine sensitization is consistent with the neurological impact of dopamine associated with drug addiction (Boileau *et al.* 2014). There were also similar findings of the involvement of D2- and D3-related mechanisms in persistent gambling behaviors involving rats (Clark *et al.* 2013). And, once again, when looking at gambling addiction you do not have the same impact of the source of addiction as you do with drug addiction. Many of the drugs associated with addictions also impact on dopamine production so it can be difficult to establish what role the addiction itself plays in the dopamine pattern and what role the specific drugs have in the dopamine patterns. But, as we saw earlier, this is not a complicating factor when it comes to gambling addiction as gambling itself does not directly impact on neurochemical production.

Lobo *et al.* (2014) also found support for the involvement of D3 mechanisms in the development of gambling addiction. They conducted this research specifically in the context of understanding how gambling behaviors develop in animals. Animal research plays a major role in the initial stages of developing psychoactive drugs, so this information is important for when researchers try to develop drugs for pathological gambling. These authors found the involvement of the DRD3 receptors, a specific type of D3-mechanism receptor for dopamine, in rats who developed gambling-like addictions. This was also consistent with neurochemical findings of humans who developed gambling addictions. Once again, we see here that the dopamine mechanisms consistent with drug addiction are also consistent with gambling addiction.

Decision-making research and pathological gambling

All animal species work to avoid losses and may take steps to avoid losses that are not necessarily effective. Loss aversion may be innate for all animal species rather than learned (Chen, Lakshminarayanan, and Santos 2006). For gambling, this means that individuals will take steps that they expect will help them avoid losses and that this relates to an innate motivation to keep from losing resources that are important. But what gambling behaviors indicate is that the way individuals go about making the decisions with regard to what will help them avoid losses is not necessarily the most effective way. Just because an individual perceives that certain behaviors will help them avoid losses does not necessarily mean that they will actually avoid losses. What you see when you look at gambling and gambling-like behaviors, among most animal species, is that the individuals are trying to avoid losses and maximize gains but are often not making decisions that are going to be the most effective for those outcomes.

People do not want to lose things that are important to them. Animals do not want to lose things that are important to them. Those species will work hard to do what they can to avoid those losses. At the same time, humans and animals want to maximize gains and do what they can to bring in resources that are important to them. Avoiding losses also means avoiding the loss of opportunities. When we look at gambling behavior we often see an attempt to avoid the loss of opportunity for material gains and for reinforcement gains. There is a clear motivation among humans and other animals to do what they can to avoid losing what they need and avoid the loss of opportunity to gain more of what they need. What we see when we look at the empirical research on gambling among humans and animals is that individuals perceive they are gaining something from the process and fall into an addictive behavior as a way of trying not to lose what they gain from the gambling-like behaviors.

There is a pattern of learned behavior associated with gambling. Gambling behaviors among humans and animals involve the individual learning what options are likely to result in desired outcomes. When this type of behavior becomes addictive it is often due to a hypersensitivity to the types of rewards associated with that behavior. The majority of rats can evaluate and deduce favorable options more or less rapidly despite the level of complexity. They can gather and use accurate and relevant information to help them make appropriate decisions. Rivalan, Ahmed, and Dellu-Hagedorn (2009) found, however, that the tendency to take on risk was not related to poor decision-making or a failure to acquire relevant information but more to a hypersensitivity to rewards and higher risk-taking in novel situations.

This tendency to be impulsive and have a hypersensitivity to risk and novel situations is one that develops early. Anselme, Robinson, and Berridge (2013) found in a study of adult rats that early exposure to conditioned cues predicting highly uncertain rewards tends to sensitize those rats to responding in the long term. The rats, exposed to uncertain environments early on, showed a hypersensitivity to unpredictable rewards later on. This sensitization continued despite a gradual reduction in the level of uncertainty throughout the study. There was no behavioral sensitization apparent to highly uncertain rewards after those rewards were provided with certainty early on. So, rats exposed to uncertainty early on showed a hypersensitivity to uncertain rewards later on but rats not exposed to uncertainty early on did not show the same hypersensitivity. This finding is consistent with human gambling behavior, showing that persistent gambling is more likely to occur in people who have experienced unpredictable environments and gambling situations early in their lives.

Gambling and evolutionary theory

Anselme (2013) proposed an evolutionary hypothesis of gambling behaviors. They proposed that when a significant object or event has a low predictability, motivational processes compensate for the inability to make correct predictions. Animals, from this perspective, are motivated by the lack of predictability and uncertainty rather than the reward itself. Anselme presented this hypothesis to help explain why animals, if given a choice between certain and uncertain rewards, tend to prefer uncertain rewards. They show this preference even if they do not gain as much from the uncertain reward schedule as the certain one. Animals tend to be more responsive to reward-related cues and uncertain situations. This is in opposition to the general theory of reinforcement, positing that animals will prefer an option associated with the highest reward rather than an option with a lower reward. Risk-taking, particularly the type associated with gambling, goes against the basic tenets of reinforcement. It may be that unpredictability enhances the individual's motivation to seek stimuli that will allow them to predict events in their environments. Animals are looking for predictable environments and being in unpredictable environments might increase their motivation to find predictability.

Gambling behavior could have an evolutionary benefit when individual members of the species have a better chance of survival in complex and dynamic environments. Pathological gambling might be an exaggeration of a natural tendency to show preference for uncertainty. Motivation may continue to be increased in uncertain situations despite, or even because of, repeated losses. Uncertainty provides excitement, which is equivalent to physiological arousal, and that tends to be highly reinforcing (Glickman 1960). Uncertainty also increases the motivation to find some degree of predictability. Evolution would give preference to those individuals who are able to keep stimulated and keep motivated and would also give preference to those individuals who are able to gain big payoffs in terms of resources. Trying to find predictability, even in unpredictable environments, would be a benefit for survival. Impulsive individuals who have a preference for novel situations would seek out those types of stimulation and would have a hypersensitivity to unpredictable rewards.

Clinical interventions

When we look at gambling-type behaviors as covered in this chapter we see that there are a number of factors that contribute to the more irrational nature of gambling. There is a tendency among human and nonhuman animals to prefer choices that involve the potential for higher outcome and have more unpredictable results. This means that individuals will make decisions about what routes to take for obtaining certain results that are not necessarily the best results on a very practical level. They are influenced by what would be considered more irrational choices. When you look at it through the lens of empirical comparative psychology research you see the need for helping individuals take steps to increase their use of rational decision-making skills when approaching gambling tasks.

Impulsivity is a key aspect of gambling behaviors. This is what we have seen through the research summarized in this chapter. What animal research shows is the key role that impulsivity plays in gambling behaviors. Gambling addicts show the same type of impulsivity shown to be a major factor in gambling-like behavior exhibited by animals. This is consistent across research involving different animal species. Helping to decrease this level this level of impulsivity will be key for helping to decrease problems related to gambling behaviors.

Highly impulsive individuals have significant problems with self-monitoring (Takács *et al.* 2015), so therapeutic approaches to address self-monitoring can be helpful for decreasing impulsiveness and therefore are likely to be helpful for addressing gambling behaviors. Self-monitoring techniques are an important part of cognitive-behavioral therapy. In this part of the chapter we need to look at how self-monitoring techniques can be used as part of therapeutic approaches for treating gambling.

Therapeutic approaches to self-monitoring involve a series of steps. Self-monitoring tends to be the initial part of therapeutic interventions. When it comes to gambling, clinicians will want to focus self-monitoring on gambling behaviors, starting with trying to identify the specific types of gambling behaviors that tend to be problematic and then putting steps in motion for helping to increase self-monitoring of that behavior and of the types of situations that lead to that behavior.

Dissatisfaction at the start of self-monitoring is essential for effective self-monitoring of addictive behaviors (Maas *et al.* 2013). Using some of the motivational interviewing techniques that are helpful for drug and alcohol abuse can be beneficial for helping to clarify the dissatisfaction at the beginning of therapy. This involves the therapist providing a number of open-ended questions for the individual, helping them to identify the specific reasons why they are looking to stay away from gambling. It is important here to stay away from any sort of lecture or attempt at education identifying why gambling is a problem. You can remind the individual of what may have led them to go into therapy and what sorts of problems they faced, but it is important at this stage to stay away from being seen as some sort of lecturer. You are helping the person to identify on their own what problems gambling has caused, and this can help to increase the person's recognition and acceptance of their own dissatisfaction with their behaviors. Providing your own opinions about whether they need to stay away from gambling is only likely to lessen the individual's recognizing on their own why they need to stay away from this type of behavior.

If we look at gambling through the lens of evolutionary theory, as was discussed earlier this chapter, you can see why lecturing an individual about why they should stop their gambling behaviors is not likely to be effective. If the individual clearly does not recognize the reason why they need to stop, you might want to provide a basic explanation. However, it is very likely that the person recognizes what sorts of difficulties their behaviors have caused. But evolutionary theory posits that there are reasons the person is gambling. There may also be benefits that the person experiences related to their gambling behaviors. Choosing to stay away from gambling is more of a cost–benefit type of analysis rather than a definitive choice that one behavior is necessarily better than another. This can be difficult for clinicians to recognize, as they tend to see problems that addictive behaviors cause and may see those problems as something that everyone else should see as well. This is not likely to be the case and, in the case of addictions, there is a real experience for the individual that their gambling behaviors have benefit. This is not something they are likely to admit, but if you do not leave open the possibility (that they may be experiencing some real positive outcomes associated with their addictive behaviors) then it is not likely that they are going to be motivated on their own to make changes.

Self-monitoring techniques start with having the person objectively define what sorts of behaviors they are looking to address. When it comes to gambling it is important to help clarify with the individual what sorts of behaviors might be defined as gambling. Lottery tickets and smaller games of chance might be overlooked here but it is important to clarify that they would also be the same types of behaviors falling under the category of gambling. You would then work with the individual to develop a system by which they would pay attention to when these sorts of behaviors occur and under what circumstances they occur. There is a twofold reason for this type of approach. One is to get the individual to start thinking more specifically about what sorts of behaviors they are addressing and increasing their attention to those specific behaviors. Attention is one step in the rational thinking process and if you can get the person to pay more attention to their behaviors you can increase the frequency with which they use at least some steps in rational thought to address those behaviors. Keep in mind that in this step you are not necessarily trying to get the person to reduce their behaviors, and you do want to encourage them not to put pressure on themselves to have to change the behaviors immediately because they are paying attention to them.

You certainly do not want to discourage the person from taking steps to avoid the behaviors once they pay attention to them and it is very likely that the behaviors themselves will reduce once they are paying more attention to them.

Another benefit to the self-monitoring techniques in the early stages of gambling treatment is helping the person identify specific types of antecedents and consequences that are associated with their gambling behaviors. This will be important for helping the individual to recognize the type of environments where the gambling occurs. Remember, from the animal studies reviewed earlier in this chapter, that there is a strong association between the types of situations involving the potential for high risk and high reward and the likelihood of problematic gambling behaviors. Again, what you are doing at this stage is helping the individual to recognize the situations with the expectation that just by increasing their focus on the situations they can take steps on their own to start reducing how frequently they put themselves in those types of situations.

Following the initial stages of self-monitoring, the goal is to further increase the attention and amount of rational thought that the individual gives to the situations where gambling is likely to occur. You are looking here to decrease the frequency of more impulsive behaviors by increasing the frequency with which the person monitors their own behavior. As you move on in therapy, you are looking to provide the individual with frequent opportunities during the session and outside of the session through the use of homework assignments to increase the attention they give to their behaviors and to the frequency with which they put themselves into potentially problematic situations. This type of approach helps to increase the frequency with which the individual addresses potentially problematic environments in more rational ways. You also want to work with the individual on identifying antecedents and consequences of gambling situations with the goal of helping them take different approaches for avoiding those situations and handling those types of situations differently.

When you utilize self-monitoring you can also obtain information that can be helpful for addressing the emotional issues that are likely contributing to the individual's gambling behaviors. Animal research and human research supports that experiences of abandonment and lack of social environments can help contribute to more addictive behaviors. As you move past the initial stages of the self-monitoring process you can help the individual identify what sorts of thinking they are associating with the potentially problematic situations. This then provides the potential for connecting the thoughts with emotional material that may be contributing to the gambling behaviors. Remember that the empirical research we summarize throughout this chapter indicates that gambling behaviors often involve decision-making that would be considered irrational. There is considerable reason to believe, based on this research, that if you could increase the consistency with which the person uses more rational thinking and decreases the level of emotional material impacting on their rational decision-making you would increase the likelihood of decreasing their gambling behavior.

Functional analytic therapy is one type of therapeutic approach that offers the possibility of helping the person increase their self-monitoring and also increase their recognition of the type of thinking and emotional material contributing to their addictive behaviors. In this sort of therapeutic scenario you can work with the individual during the session on pointing out when they clearly are not paying attention to their behavior. You can also focus during the sessions on specifically identifying the types of behaviors that occur and often serve as a precursor to their gambling behaviors. When pointing out these behaviors it is often useful to then ask the person what sort of thinking or what sort of emotions they are experiencing at that precise moment. You then have the opportunity to work with them on finding more effective ways of overcoming that emotional material in decreasing the impact that the emotional aspects of their gambling has on their behaviors.

Extinction techniques also have the potential for decreasing the frequency of gambling behaviors. When you look at animal studies, you see that aversion to losses lessens the more losses the individual experiences. This continues to be consistent with the premise that individuals will avoid losses but will not necessarily learn effective patterns for avoiding those losses. If the individual is not willing or able to stop their gambling right away then working with them to at least decrease the frequency with which they gamble might be one effective step. If you can work with the person to make a commitment to gamble at a casino only two times when they are in the place, you could help to decrease the frequency with which they have losses and decrease the aversion to those losses. Remember also that the risk of high reward is one of the major reinforcing aspects of pathological gambling. So getting the person to participate only in low wagering types of betting might be another way of decreasing the reinforcing aspect of gambling. One example might be to get the person to commit to staying away from casinos while allowing themselves to buy lottery tickets that have relatively small monetary outcomes. If you are running the risk that the person may win with a lottery ticket but actually only end up winning a few dollars, as opposed to having the potential to win a few hundred or a few thousand dollars, then you might have a good chance of decreasing the reinforcing aspect of the behavior. Keep in mind that the only way this process can be effective is by making the extinction process ongoing and gradually taking additional steps to decrease the reinforcing aspect of gambling behaviors.

CASE STUDY

Janet was a young adult female who presented to therapy with significant problems related to slot machines. She lived in an area where gambling was not actually legal but where there were several local bars that had slot machines. What would happen is that patrons would use the slot machines and then would get paid for certain outcomes. This was not technically legal in the area where Janet lived but it was not considered to be a crime that received a lot of attention. Janet spent much of each week's paycheck on the slot machines and would tend to continue playing the machines until she lost a large portion of it. Even if she won, she would then tend to spend more on the slot machines and end up losing the same amount of money as she would during weeks when she did not win.

Janet reported that she was in considerable financial distress because of her addiction to slot machines. She could identify the few times where she won a large amount of money but also reported that it was those events that reinforced her going back to the slot machines. She had been so excited about the times when she did win big that this kept her coming back to try to obtain that same level of excitement. She also talked about finding the social aspect of being in bars around familiar people to be another aspect of the gambling that she found reinforcing. She had been to casinos in areas where gambling was legal but continued to return to the slot machines at her local establishments.

A clinical history revealed that Janet did have a history of impulsive behaviors. She did adequately in school but tended to do poorly on longer tests because she would impulsively give answers without clearly thinking through what was being asked. She did not have disciplinary problems in school but did have some difficulties in social relationships because she would say things without thinking through potential outcomes. She described her relationships with her parents as being emotionally distant. She also reported that she had initially learned about the slot machines in local bars because she had accompanied her father on a number of occasions to bars where she played similar types of slot machines. She did not report that her father had significant financial difficulties related to playing slot machines and said that her father seemed better able than her to control his gambling behaviors.

Self-monitoring techniques made up the initial part of Janet's therapy. Her therapist worked with her on objectively defining the behaviors that made up gambling and worked out a schedule by which Janet kept detailed notes about incidents where she engaged in gambling or where she felt like she wanted to gamble. She kept a therapeutic notebook that detailed these incidents and the antecedents and consequences associated with the situations where she felt tempted to gamble. Her therapist also worked with her during the sessions on increasing the amount of time that she spent focusing on situations where she was about to gamble as a way of increasing the attention that she paid to his gambling behaviors.

Janet reported that she decreased the frequency with which she used slot machines by an average of one time per week by the time of her second session. She related this directly to the increase in her self-monitoring and the increased amount of attention that she was paying to her gambling behaviors. This was a result of the homework assignment that she was given, which was to pay attention to when she engaged in any type of gambling behavior, and also to the amount of time that she spent discussing her gambling behaviors during sessions. Janet also acknowledged during sessions that her impulsivity seemed to play a major role in her gambling behaviors. She would give considerable thought to many decisions that she made during the week but seemed to make decisions about gambling behaviors rather impulsively. Her therapist was able to isolate with Janet the type of thinking associated with her gambling behaviors based on her recognition that this was the type of behavior to which she gave the least amount of thought when compared with other decisions that she made during each week.

Therapeutic interventions also helped Janet open up about the emotional aspects to her gambling behaviors. As she discussed her childhood, Janet recognized that she tended to feel much closer to her father when she accompanied her father to the bar. As therapy went on, Janet acknowledged that the few visits to the bar with her father that she reported at the beginning of therapy actually constituted a large number of visits during her childhood. She talked about actually having gone to the bar where her father gambled several times per month as a child. She also talked about this being the one time that she felt emotionally close to her father. Recognizing this helped Janet develop some statements that she could make to herself when she felt like gambling, where she would acknowledge that one of the reasons she was doing this was probably because it made her feel better emotionally. She would then remind herself that there were other ways she could feel better emotionally that did not run the risk of damaging her finances. Using these statements to herself helped increase the attention that she gave to her behaviors whenever she was faced with gambling situations.

Janet also agreed to take steps towards extinguishing her gambling behaviors. After a detailed discussion of the environments where she gambled, she noted that scratch-off lottery tickets were also available in the bars. She estimated that she would spend an average of four hours in front of the slot machines during the times that she was in the bar. She also acknowledged that she had never won more than two dollars on a scratch-off lottery ticket. Janet agreed for a trial period of one week to take the four hours that she spent in the bar and not change anything except that instead of putting money into the slot machine she would buy a lottery ticket each of the four hours. She was allowed to gamble on the lottery ticket but agreed that she would see what happened if she just played the lottery ticket and then waited another hour before buying another lottery ticket. This would allow her to gamble but would decrease the amount of reward that she could gain from gambling. This would also lessen the frequency of losses that might help to decrease her aversion to losses as she would be engaging in only one gambling activity during the hour rather than a multitude of gambling activities. During the first week she was able to stick to lottery tickets but ended up buying one every half hour. Even with this pattern she still spent less than half of the money that she would have spent on the slot machines. After some time she was then able to further decrease the frequency with which she played the lottery tickets.

Janet's therapy over a four-month period focused on her self-monitoring of gambling behaviors and also extinguishing techniques used to lessen the reinforcement strength of her gambling behaviors. She also was able to explore the emotional material that contributed to her impulsivity and stood as obstacles to her making more rational decisions about her behaviors. In addition, she used the time that she saved by playing scratch-off lottery tickets rather than slot machines as a way to find other things that she could enjoy doing while visiting the establishments. She made progress in terms of what she did in the establishments, although she was not willing to stop visiting the establishments altogether as they provided a large percentage of her social relationships. But over the course of her therapy she was able to decrease significantly the amount of gambling in which she engaged when she visited those establishments. She accomplished this primarily through a process of increasing her self-monitoring and decreasing the reinforcement strength of gambling behaviors.

Summary

Gambling decisions are often irrational and based on a misunderstanding of probabilities. Humans and animals take gambles as ways of trying to minimize loss and maximize beneficial outcomes. But the choices they make are not necessarily ones that *actually* result in these positive outcomes but are often only ones that the individuals *perceive* as having the potential for positive outcomes. Individuals often misinterpret what outcomes are likely based on the strength of reinforcers and reinforcement schedules.

Reinforcers obtained on an unpredictable schedule are consistently more valuable than those obtained on a predictable schedule. Human and nonhuman animals will often show preference for gambling behaviors that they associate with the potential for larger payoffs.

Pathological gambling is different from typical gambling as it involves the individual damaging important parts of their lives to maintain their gambling behaviors. This type of gambling behavior is often associated with impulsivity. Neurochemical research across different species shows that the physiological processes associated with impulsivity are strongly associated with pathological gambling. This is one of the reasons why pathological gambling so often starts during adolescence as this is the time when individuals have the highest degree of impulsivity.

Gambling addiction may be a malformation of the evolutionary preference for unpredictable results. Animals recognize that nature is often unpredictable and show a preference for outcomes that gain them some degree of predictability in mostly unpredictable environments. Animals also show a preference for larger payoffs as the unpredictability of nature leads them to try and gain the highest amount of desired resources with the lowest amount of effort. Looking to benefit from these two aspects of the natural environment leads to a preference for unpredictable results and larger payoffs. This is at the heart of gambling behaviors although there likely are neurochemical impairments contributing to the development of pathological gambling.

Therapeutic interventions for pathological gambling focus on decreasing the frequency of gambling. Increasing self-monitoring and modifying the reinforcement strength of gambling behaviors are important aspects of therapy that can help to reduce gambling behaviors. Decreasing impulsivity starts with an increase in self-monitoring. Animal research also shows that isolation often increases more addictive behaviors. Addressing emotional and social isolation associated with pathological gambling is also an important step in gambling treatment. Extinction approaches in therapy are also important for decreasing the reinforcement strength of gambling behaviors.

References

Anselme, P. (2013) 'Dopamine, motivation, and the evolutionary significance of gambling-like behaviour.' *Behavioural Brain Research 256*, 1–4.

Anselme, P., Robinson, M.J., and Berridge, K.C. (2013) 'Reward uncertainty enhances incentive salience attribution as sign-tracking.' *Behavioural Brain Research 238*, 53–61.

Blaszczynski, A. and Nower, L. (2002) 'A pathways model of problem and pathological gambling.' *Addiction 97*, 5, 487–499.

Boileau, I., Payer, D., Chugani, B., Lobo, D.S.S., *et al.* (2014) 'In vivo evidence for greater amphetamine-induced dopamine release in pathological gambling: a positron emission tomography study with [11C]-(+)-PHNO.' *Molecular Psychiatry 19*, 12, 1305–1313.

Chase, H.W. and Clark, L. (2010) 'Gambling severity predicts midbrain response to near-miss outcomes.' *Journal of Neuroscience 30*, 18, 6180–6187.

Chen, M.K., Lakshminarayanan, V., and Santos, L.R. (2006) 'How basic are behavioral biases? Evidence from capuchin monkey trading behavior.' *Journal of Political Economy 114*, 3, 517–537.

Clark, L., Averbeck, B., Payer, D., Sescousse, G., Winstanley, C.A., and Xue, G. (2013) 'Pathological choice: the neuroscience of gambling and gambling addiction.' *Journal of Neuroscience 33*, 45, 17617–17623.

Clark, L., Lawrence, A.J., Astley-Jones, F., and Gray, N. (2009) 'Gambling near-misses enhance motivation to gamble and recruit win-related brain circuitry.' *Neuron 61*, 3, 481–490.

Glickman, S.E. (1960) 'Reinforcing properties of arousal.' *Journal of Comparative and Physiological Psychology 53*, 1, 68.

Hayden, B.Y. and Platt, M.L. (2007) 'Temporal discounting predicts risk sensitivity in rhesus macaques.' *Current Biology 17*, 1, 49–53.

Heilbronner, S.R. and Hayden, B.Y. (2013) 'Contextual factors explain risk-seeking preferences in rhesus monkeys.' *Frontiers in Neuroscience 7*, 404–410.

Kassinove, J.I. and Schare, M.L. (2001) 'Effects of the "near miss" and the "big win" on persistence at slot machine gambling.' *Psychology of Addictive Behaviors 15*, 2, 155.

Lobo, D.S.S., Aleksandrova, L., Knight, J., Casey, D.M., *et al.* (2014) 'Addiction-related genes in gambling disorders: new insights from parallel human and pre-clinical models.' *Molecular Psychiatry 20*, 1002–1010.

Maas, J., Hietbrink, L., Rinck, M., and Keijsers, G. P. (2013) 'Changing automatic behavior through self-monitoring: does overt change also imply implicit change?' *Journal of Behavior Therapy and Experimental Psychiatry 44*, 3, 279–284.

Madden, G.J., Ewan, E.E., and Lagorio, C.H. (2007) 'Toward an animal model of gambling: delay discounting and the allure of unpredictable outcomes.' *Journal of Gambling Studies 23*, 1, 63–83.

Molander, A.C., Mar, A., Norbury, A., Steventon, S., Moreno, M., Caprioli, D., Theobald, D.E., Belin, D., Everitt, B.J., Robbins, T.W., and Dalley, J.W. (2011) 'High impulsivity predicting vulnerability to cocaine addiction in rats: some relationship with novelty preference but not novelty reactivity, anxiety or stress.' *Psychopharmacology 215*, 4, 721–731.

Peters, H., Hunt, M., and Harper, D. (2010) 'An animal model of slot machine gambling: the effect of structural characteristics on response latency and persistence.' *Journal of Gambling Studies 26*, 4, 521–531.

Rivalan, M., Ahmed, S.H., and Dellu-Hagedorn, F. (2009) 'Risk-prone individuals prefer the wrong options on a rat version of the Iowa Gambling Task.' *Biological Psychiatry 66*, 8, 743–749.

Takács, Á., Kóbor, A., Honbolygó, F., and Csépe, V. (2015) 'Does rare error count in impulsivity?' *Journal of Psychophysiology 29*, 2, 64–72.

van den Bos, R., Davies, W., Dellu-Hagedorn, F., Goudriaan, A.E., *et al.* (2013) 'Cross-species approaches to pathological gambling: a review targeting sex differences, adolescent vulnerability and ecological validity of research tools.' *Neuroscience and Biobehavioral Reviews 37*, 10, 2454–2471.

Verdejo-García, A., Lawrence, A.J., and Clark, L. (2008) 'Impulsivity as a vulnerability marker for substance-use disorders: review of findings from high-risk research, problem gamblers and genetic association studies.' *Neuroscience and Biobehavioral Reviews 32*, 4, 777–810.

Vohs, K.D., and Baumeister, R.F. (2011) 'What's the use of happiness? It can't buy you money.' *Journal of Consumer Psychology 21*, 2, 139–141.

Winstanley, C.A. (2011) 'Gambling rats: insight into impulsive and addictive behavior.' *Neuropsychopharmacology 36*, 1, 359.

Winstanley, C.A., Olausson, P., Taylor, J.R., and Jentsch, J.D. (2010) 'Insight into the relationship between impulsivity and substance abuse from studies using animal models.' *Alcoholism: Clinical and Experimental Research 34*, 8, 1306–1318.

Zeeb, F.D., Robbins, T.W., and Winstanley, C.A. (2009) 'Serotonergic and dopaminergic modulation of gambling behavior as assessed using a novel rat gambling task.' *Neuropsychopharmacology 34*, 10, 2329–2343.

Zentall, T.R. (2011) 'Maladaptive "gambling" by pigeons.' *Behavioural Processes 87*, 1, 50–56.

Chapter 7

AUTISM SPECTRUM DISORDERS

Autism is a "heterogeneous neurodevelopmental disorder defined by behavioral characteristics" (Gadad *et al.* 2013). These characteristics include social deficits, language abnormalities, and repetitive behavioral patterns. Autism symptoms vary considerably and this is one reason why the more general term Autism Spectrum Disorder is used for individuals presenting with these symptoms. Calling this condition a "spectrum disorder" reflects the variety of different behavioral presentations associated with autism. Autism disorders present difficulties in a number of different areas, primary of which are social difficulties, even though the three primary symptom areas (communication difficulties, poor social comprehension, and repetitive patterns of behaviors) are typically required for a diagnosis.

When a counselor or therapist works with someone with autism spectrum disorder, chances are they are being asked to help them in the social arena. This might be helping them develop more positive social relationships or get along better with people at work or at school. It could also include more severe problems such as frequently running out of the classroom at school or being physically aggressive towards peers or teachers (Brookman-Frazee *et al.* 2012). Referral problems also often reflect the degree to which other autism symptoms (e.g. repetitive behaviors) impact on social interactions. People with autism often have very limited social relationships, if any at all, and helping address this issue is frequently the reason individuals with autism spectrum disorders start therapy or counseling. It is not always the case that the individual themselves will start the therapy or counseling; rather, it may be someone else (e.g. a parent) who has determined that the lack of social relationships is a problem that needs to be addressed. Individuals with autism spectrum disorders may often be less bothered by their limited social relationships and more bothered by how concerned important people in their lives seem to be about these.

Repetitive behaviors associated with autism spectrum disorders can be of two main types. Both of these behavioral types can cause significant difficulties in terms of interfering with the person's ability to focus and difficulties in how other people respond to them. "Stereotypical movements" are repetitive movements such as rocking or arm-flapping that occur for no apparent reason. They may at times seem like a self-calming technique but this is not consistently the reason for those behaviors. Stereotypical movements occur frequently and usually last for at least several minutes (although the duration can vary considerably). "Perseverative behaviors" are typically verbal behaviors where the individual focuses on the same subject for extended periods of time. These can also be nonverbal behaviors where the person focuses on doing the same thing for extended periods of time. However, verbal perseverative behaviors are more common than nonverbal ones. With verbal behaviors, the person may change the subject of interest but continue to have difficulties with focusing and social interactions because they stay with the same subject and cannot be redirected.

In the United States, recent changes in the manual used to define psychological disorders show how thinking about autism spectrum disorders has changed. This manual, the *Diagnostic and Statistical Manual of Mental Disorders, 5th Edition* or *DSM-5* (American Psychiatric Association 2013) contains one category called Autism Spectrum Disorder. This is a change from previous editions where autism spectrum disorders had three primary categories (Autistic Disorder, Asperger's Disorder, and Pervasive Developmental Disorder Not Otherwise Specified). This change reflects that all three of these disorders are on the same spectrum rather than being three completely separate conditions. Asperger's Disorder had been a particularly problematic category in this regard as it is typically referred to as "high-functioning autism" but had a name not reflecting any type of autism (often leading to the question, "If it is high-functioning autism then why not just call it high-functioning autism, why call it something completely different?"). Another category of disorder, Social Communication Disorder, was added to the *DSM-5* for individuals who have the social problems associated with autism but do not have the stereotypical or perseverative behaviors (which are now required for the *DSM-5* diagnosis of Autism Spectrum Disorder). This is a very new diagnostic category and it is not yet clear how its development is similar to or different from Autism Spectrum Disorder.

Animal research provides useful information for understanding autism. (*Note:* From now on we will use the term "autism" as an abbreviation for "autism spectrum disorders".) Leekam, Prior, and Uljarevic (2011) reviewed similarities between autism-like behaviors in animals and humans. They reviewed nonhuman primate research and found considerable material for understanding autism in humans. Some of the similarities that they found between humans and other primates, with regard to autism symptoms, include repetitive behaviors, social communication deficits, and compromised ability to follow others' gazes. They also found similar neurological impairments between those primates and humans related to autism symptoms. Impairments in the superior temporal sulcus region of the brain for the nonhuman primates correlate with deficits in responding to social cues. In addition, they found that lesions in the amygdala correlated with alterations in social and emotional behaviors and that "mirror neurons" in the nonhuman primates were also involved with autistic behaviors. These are all physiological factors thought to play significant roles in human autistic disorders.

Autism and genetic functioning

Both animal and human research support that autism most likely develops before or soon after birth. Neonatal developmental issues effecting autism are ones that impact both the immune system and brain development. There are numerous environmental factors that can impact on genetic functioning associated with autistic disorders, and this is one major reason why there is so much symptom variability when it comes to autism. Hsiao and Patterson (2012) addressed these issues and explored how genes, environmental factors, and their interactions impact on autism's development. They reviewed several studies involving rats and mice and concluded that difficulties related to the maternal immune system are likely the principal environmental risk factor for the development of autism. Maternal infection, according to their results, most often precedes the development of autism spectrum disorders. Infections that are most often associated with the development of autism include rubella, cytomegalovirus, and varicella (Brown 2012). Crawley (2012) also reviewed rodent studies and found a significant relationship between genetic mutations associated with maternal infection and the behavioral and biological outcomes related to autism.

In their review of genes and autistic conditions, Faridar *et al.* (2014) found a variety of results related to the development of autism. They initially obtained 40 mice of a certain genetic type ("F2 mice from the cross of BTBR with B6") and selected eight of each who showed extremes of social behaviors. Their results showed that genetic information was significant in terms of determining which mice developed autistic symptoms. Their results also showed a variety of ways that the brain's signaling pathways may be dysregulated in autism and lead to impaired social behaviors. Specifically, they found that disruption in the "extracellular signal regulation kinase" (ERK) was related to the presence of autistic symptoms.

Yoo *et al.* (2014) also provided a review of genetic research involving mice. They focused on the role of the Shank family of proteins in autism but attempted to pull together different genetic research results to help understand autism. They concluded that autism likely develops from a variety of deficits in presynaptic and postsynaptic neural functioning. They also concluded that mouse models of autism are going to be essential for showing how behavioral and physiological deficits associated with autism might be reversed with medical treatment. Specifically, they found that the mutations on what are called "Shank3" proteins are associated with the development of autism and also that these mutations cause impairment in what are called the "glutamatergic synapses." Although defining these genetic terms is beyond the scope of this book, this last term is worth remembering since the authors of this paper concluded that this is likely where the focus of medical treatment for autism will need to be.

Because of the complexity of genetics and neurochemistry involved, developing pharmaceutical approaches to autism presents significant difficulties. There are no medications at this time specifically for treating autism, although there are several that treat some of the specific symptoms (e.g. Ritalin for aggressive behaviors). There have, at this point, been few consistent results when studying drug treatments for autism (Chadman, Guariglia, and Yoo 2012). This is not due to a lack of considerable effort but more to the complications of autism evident in animal research. Autism research focuses primarily on genetic causes and considerable advances in this area have been made over just the past decade or so. But, at the time that we write this book, there is no pharmaceutical treatment for autism. Genetic research is a promising field of research that will likely provide medications, but genetic research presents complications that make finding pharmaceutical treatments difficult. These complications relate primarily to the vast array of different neurological and physiological conditions associated with different types of autism. For example, Ellegood and Crawley (2015) reviewed several animal studies and found at least 19 genetic mutations associated with different types of autism. These genetic and neurological studies involving rodents support the growing understanding of autism being a spectrum of heterogeneous conditions rather than one specific condition.

Social relationships and autism

Autistic spectrum disorders impact social relationships. Individuals with autism have significant social difficulties and are limited in their social connectedness. These problems are due to lack of social comprehension, communication difficulties, and perseveration, all of which interfere significantly with social connectedness. These are the problems that are most likely to present as focal points for treatment. Individuals who cannot connect with others are likely to feel lonely, depressed, anxious, or even angry. They also are likely to raise the concern of parents and other family members that they will become depressed, anxious, or angry if they do not have more social relationships. When treating individuals with autistic conditions, counselors and therapists need to have a solid understanding not only of autistic conditions but also of what aspects of social behaviors need to be addressed.

Social relationships are important for human beings. But the extent to which we understand the types of relationships that are important and which aspects of relationships matter is very limited (Reis and Collins 2004). Perceived or subjective loneliness is an important predictor of psychological functioning and morbidity (Cacioppo and Hawkley 2009). Social relationships are also important for animals, but our understanding of the types of relationships that are important is also limited. For example, Ruan and Wu (2008) studied the lifespan of short-lived *Drosophilia mutant* flies and found that social interactions helped increase their lifespan. Social connectedness was important but there was no specific detail given about the types of social interactions that led to this benefit. These flies showed increased lifespan in response to higher social interactions and it was simply having more social interactions that helped improve mortality of this animal species. There was no clear evidence from the results about what sorts of relationships were necessary for obtaining this benefit, other than just having more social interactions.

Social relationships help decrease the impact of stress. In terms of animal and human physiology, oxytocin is the neurochemical thought to play a significant role in how social relationships reduce stress. Oxytocin reduces stress response in animals and particularly has a significant role in how social relationships lessen this stress (Hostinar, Sullivan, and Gunnar 2014). Liu and Wang (2003) conducted a study of female prairie voles and found both oxytocin and dopamine were essentials for forming social relationships. This is also consistent with the role those neurochemicals play for humans. Oxytocin has been shown to have important roles in several aspects of animals' social relationships (Stavropoulos and Carver 2013), including determining how sheep and male prairie voles choose partners (Young and Wang 2004) and also improving social deficits in mice (Peñagarikano *et al.* 2015).

As social relationships help decrease stress, social isolation tends to increase stress. In a study conducted by Detillion *et al.* (2004), Siberian hamsters showed increased levels of stress neurochemicals and subsequent immobilization stress when socially isolated. This contrasted with hamsters who had frequent positive social interactions and were subsequently less impaired and immobilized by stress associated with wounds. These authors also found that housing the hamsters in social environments provided a buffer against distress and induced activation of the brain pathways that are associated with negative stress response ("hypothalamic–pituitary–adrenocortical" or "HPA" pathway). Their results were consistent with those of Hennessy (1984) and Vogt, Coe, and Levine (1981), who also found that social factors help lessen the impact of stress on the HPA neural pathway.

Detillion *et al.*'s hamster study showed the benefits of social relationships for lessening the impact of stress. But their results also showed how any type of positive social relationship can provide that benefit. There was no indication about the specific types of social relationships that were needed in order to obtain the stress benefits. These were hamsters that had positive interactions with each other and showed some preference to being with each other compared with being alone. There essentially was nothing else noteworthy about the relationships or interactions except that they generally seemed positive in interacting with each other. High levels of positive social interactions were the focus. There was no indication about what type of relationships these hamsters had with each other or even really what was meant by "positive" social interaction. These results essentially showed that any type of social interaction that is generally positive can help reduce stress.

As we move on in this discussion of autism, the issue of which aspects of social relationships provide positive benefits will be important. Individuals with autism have significant problems with social relationships. Poor social comprehension, lack of social skills, impaired communication skills, and repetitive behaviors (which often interfere with establishing social relationships) are essential parts of this diagnosis. So, it is the case that most individuals with autism are going to have social difficulties. These social difficulties may be minor, in the case of less severe autism, but may also be considerable. And it is not always the case that counseling, therapy, or social skills training will help individuals with autism overcome their social deficits enough that they will form strong social relationships, particularly of the type that other people would call "friendships." It is, therefore, essential that counselors and therapists working with individuals who have autism recognize whether it is necessary for individuals with autism to develop social relationships or whether they might be able to still have satisfactory lives if they have social interactions (especially if they are "positive" ones) but do not necessarily develop strong relationships.

Social skills training

Social relationships and skills for developing those relationships are often the focal point of autism treatment. These programs primarily were developed for autism but they follow general steps common to social skills training for other conditions. Counselors or therapists often take on a teaching role in these programs. Escobedo *et al.* (2012) summarized the main steps common to most social skills training programs:

1. Teacher introduces social skill to be learned.

2. Teacher provides visual support material to help with understanding skill (use because autistic individuals often do better with learning visual material).

3. Teacher reads story or scenario to help the student connect the visual support, the social skill, and the social situation.

4. Teacher demonstrates how the skill is used in social contexts.

5. Student rehearses skill (could be in pairs with other students or with the teacher).

6. Student role-plays to produce the skill in different scenarios.

7. Student self-rates performance.

8. Student assigned and encouraged to practice this skill in different real-life scenarios.

Counselors and therapists use these steps to help students develop and use better skills for social interactions. Parental involvement and spousal involvement are also encouraged in these programs to assure that the individual practices skills. Mobile devices, as were used in the Escobedo study, are also used to remind the individual to practice these skills. Reichow, Steiner, and Volkmar (2013) reviewed social skills studies and identified outcomes as improving social competence, improving friendship quality, and improving emotional recognition.

Their review revealed evidence that social skills training resulted in significant progress only for social competence and improving friendship quality. They did not address what goals were initially set for each program and it was not clear whether developing friendships was necessarily the main goal of these programs. It was clear that their evidence did not show friendship quality as the only benefit to these programs. While improving friendship quality was identified as a positive outcome there was no indication that developing friendships was necessary in order for the individuals to gain from the program.

Identifying the goals of social skills training and other interventions is an important matter. What should the goals be for a social skills program? Is improving social competence sufficient? Does making friends really have to be a goal? Is it necessary to make friends or is it sufficient to improve social interactions? What level of relationships have to develop in order for social skills training programs to be worthwhile? What really are clinicians trying to do with skills training programs for autism and what goals are sufficient for helping individuals?

A review of the social skills training literature shows that friendships and the development of friendships are often a major focal point. Rao, Beidel, and Murray (2008) reviewed social skills training programs with a focus on their effects for improving friendships with same-aged peers. Gutstein and Whitney (2002) addressed the importance of social skills programs and improving social reciprocity and development of friendships. Solomon, Goodlin-Jones, and Anders (2004) focused on models for learning friendship skills. There seems to be an assumption that friendships are an essential part of individuals developing social connectedness even though there is no clear evidence to suggest this is the case.

Laugeson *et al.* (2012) developed the PEERS program for teaching social skills to adolescents. This is a well-researched program showing increased interactions resulting from their interventions. Although the goals stated for this program relate to generally improving social skills it is noteworthy that the term "friends" or some variation of this word (e.g. "friendships") appears 41 times throughout the eleven-page article. There is clearly a focus in the program on developing and maintaining friendships for individuals with autism spectrum disorders. Their research review included in the article also shows an emphasis on friendship development in social skills programs throughout the social skills training literature.

Friendships are intimate relationships providing "companionship, mutual support, and affection" (Freeman and Kasari 1998). Developmental theorists posit that friendships develop along a developmental trajectory where children learn skills to make friends (Hartup 1989). Friendships occur throughout the animal kingdom. Animal species developing friendships include horses, elephants, hyenas, dolphins, monkeys, and chimpanzees (Seyfarth and Cheney 2012). These bonds are adaptive for the individuals involved. They improve reproductive success, reduce stress, increase infant survival, and increase longevity. This is consistent with human research showing that friendships reduce mortality rates as individuals get older (Holt-Lunstad, Smith, and Layton 2010). Studies of friendships dominate the literature on social relationships for children with autism (see, for example, Kasari *et al.* 2011). But these rarely address whether friendships are actually necessary for children and what types of friendships (or other types of social relationships) these would need to be. Friendships might be beneficial for humans and nonhumans but are they really necessary?

Social connectedness

Humans are often described as "social animals." But all animals are "social animals" in one way or another. There are no animal species for whom some type of social connectedness is unnecessary. And that social connectedness is an essential part of what distinguishes different species. From an evolutionary perspective social connections meet two needs for humans (Buunk and Dijkstra 2012). One is a sense of belonging and another is a sense of status. This latter need is presented as a striving for positive self-esteem by winning competitions and prestige from others. Social connections help individuals feel safe and accepted. As these authors point out, humans are social animals and have brains that are particularly evolved to deal with living in "large groups." Being a social animal does not emphasize intimate relationships, as beneficial as they might be, but emphasizes more belonging to a large group (e.g. nationality, racial group).

Friendships are not so much the focus of being a "social animal" as is the importance of being a member of a larger social entity.

Sociality provides benefits to animals that include protection, higher quantity and quality of habitats, assistance with raising young, and longevity. But sociality also provides negative aspects that include increased feeding competition, greater likelihood of disease transmission, and loss of reproductive fitness (Hacker, Horback, and Miller 2015). Social behaviors serve particular goals that include finding a suitable mate, and fending off predator attacks, and cooperation in the acquisition of food. These are characteristics of social behaviors essential to species as varied as humans, apes, dolphins, and ants (Miklósi and Gácsi 2012). Székely, Moore, and Komdeur (2010, p.1) defined social behaviors across species as "activities among members of the same species that have fitness consequences for the focal individual and the individuals of the group." But note that few aspects of what makes up social behaviors, based on their definition, require friendships or even (close) relationships. Being part of a large group (e.g. being the citizen of a country or member of a community) for humans could suffice and does not require anything more than that. Friendships, as defined by cultural standards outlined in research, may be helpful but are not necessary.

But these results need to be understood in a fuller context to really grasp their meaning. First, in the Holt-Lunstad *et al.* study there were a variety of different social relationships studied in their meta-analysis. Their results could apply to a variety of types of relationships. It was also not clear what social relationships were left out. There is, for example, no reason to conclude that social relationships maintained primarily online would be less beneficial for longevity than other types of relationships. A second, and possibly more important, aspect of all this research is that it shows that friendships are beneficial but not that they are necessary. Friendships improve longevity and improve reproductive success. But they are not the only entity offering that benefit. Many things offer the same benefit in terms of improving physical health and chance of success. Again, friendships are shown to be beneficial but not necessary.

Yang *et al.* (2011) studied mice who were bred to show multiple social deficits. These mice were split into two groups based on their cage-mates. One group lived with cage-mates who also had social deficits and the others lived with cage-mates who had high social ability. Mice who lived with low sociability cage-mates showed continued low social interactions, while the other group showed high sociability after living with cage-mates who also showed high sociability. This study supports the benefit of having individuals with low sociability interact with individuals with higher sociability. This mouse study results are consistent with studies supporting the benefit of human children being educated around more socially developed peers. These results are also consistent with results showing that higher social environments help improve social behaviors among monkeys (Harlow and Suomi 1971) and mice with low sociability (Branchi 2009). But, again, it is important to note that the results were based on these mice being around peers with higher sociability. There was no clear evidence in this study showing any particular type of social relationships being more beneficial. These lower sociability mice benefited just from having increases in the amount of time they spent around higher sociability peers. There was no indication that these mice benefited based on the types of relationships they developed.

Social species affiliate in an organized way to help them survive, care for offspring, and reproduce. Animal research summarized in Cacioppo *et al.* (2011) show that social isolation heightens sensitivity to social threats and motivates the renewal of social communication. Maintaining social interactions has important benefits for the individuals in social species. Collaborative activities allow access to a range of benefits that would not be accessible if it were not possible to engage in social relationships (Chadman *et al.* 2012). But collaboration is not always a necessity for social species beyond what is necessary for specific tasks. Chimpanzees, for example, are social, but not to the same extent as humans. Chimpanzees are practical when they engage, they are good collaborators for solving problems. Human children, however, show much stronger preferences (even if not a necessity) for working groups to address needs that chimpanzees do not exhibit (Rekers, Haun, and Tomasello 2011). Chimpanzees engage in collaborative activities and engage in behaviors important for collaborative problem-solving. This includes waiting for a partner to approach an apparatus that needs to be pulled and actively recruiting a partner to help pull an apparatus. But chimpanzees will often not attempt to re-engage a partner if a task is interrupted. Human children, by contrast, will attempt to re-engage in these situations (Fletcher, Warneken, and Tomasello 2012). In these tasks, collaboration is the necessity and continuing that collaboration is not necessary, even if it is preferable, beyond what is needed for the task.

Neurodiversity: taking a different view of social connectedness

"Neurodiversity" is a term for an advocacy movement emphasizing that neurological conditions such as autism have their "upsides" along with their weaknesses (Dalton 2013). Individuals with autism, for example, often have above-average attention to details. When you think about autism in terms of possible strength, it is possible to think of how limited interest in social interactions could actually be a benefit. Certainly not being able to make friends could be a weakness, but not having a strong need for friends, or even close personal relationships, could actually be beneficial. Most clinicians could probably think of at least some situations where clients had problems because they were too dependent on friends or concerned too much about whether other people wanted to be friends with them. Having less focus on this could actually be a benefit and could free individuals up to be focused on other things. There is a movement of individuals focused on seeing autism in a way that de-emphasizes the need for being like everybody else, including de-emphasizing the need for social relationships. Having an ability to function socially in such a way that the person gets along with other people, but does not worry about the intensity of those relationships, could be a benefit rather than a weakness.

Individuals with autism who associate with the neurodiversity movement often refer to individuals who do not have autism as "neurotypicals." This emphasizes the view that autism is not necessarily a problem but is more a difference in terms of how the person sees the world. Key among this is recognizing the benefit of having less interest in social relationships and being able to function without the types of intense social relationships that take up many other people's time. One criticism of this approach could be that individuals not concerned about different types of social relationships may miss out on the benefits that those types of relationships provide. But when you look at comparative psychology research, particularly research delving into the benefits of social relationships, you see that there are variety of different social relationships that provide that benefit. There is no clear evidence that having social relationships along the lines of what most people call "friendships" is a necessity for obtaining most of the benefits that social interactions provide. Positive social interactions are important, but they do not necessarily need to be ones that others might consider "close." Social interactions seem to be what provide the benefits rather than social connectedness.

Brownlow *et al.* (2015) and Kasari *et al.* (2011) challenged the dominant understanding of "friendships." Many people with autism develop positive relationships that are of high quality for them even if they are not considered high quality for others (Locke *et al.* 2010). Individuals with autism often have social relationships that are pleasing and beneficial to them but may very well differ from what others are looking for in social relationships. This does not make them "wrong" or even "limited" but just "different." For example, "parallel play" is a characteristic approach to social interactions exhibited by children with autism. It primarily involves the child playing appropriately *around* other children but not interacting *with* other children. Note here that the difference is only that the child is not interacting with other children. Otherwise they are playing fine. This often is referred to as a "symptom" of autism but it really could represent an alternative style of play.

Environmental enrichment

Animal research results support that environmental enrichment can help decrease repetitive behaviors (Lewis *et al.* 2007). Mouse models support that social isolation correlates with increased stereotypical behaviors. Social isolation can be a major self-imposed factor as individuals with autism are often limited in their social interactions. Enriched environments help reduce stereotypical behaviors in minks (Campbell, Dallaire, and Mason 2013). Enriched environments for these animals had two wire mesh towers, a connecting tunnel leading to a larger compartment, and a readily available water drinking bottle.

These results supported the benefits of enriched environments for lessening autistic symptoms. Where these authors went further was to prepare some considerations based on their results for applying these results to human autism treatment. They noted there were difficulties with this process, largely due to determining what constitutes an "enriched environment" for humans compared with what animals in the study received. They defined the term "enriched environment" generally as "increased interaction with the environment" and proposed that interventions for enriching environment should focus on optimizing the functionally intact areas of the brain. They made their proposals based on research that "enriched environments" can help improve the functioning of individuals with neurological damage and applied this to their findings related to the neurological impact of autism. "Enriched environments" need to focus on helping individuals with autism improve in the areas where their functioning is intact along with improving in areas where they have deficits.

Schneider, Turczak, and Przewłocki (2006) also addressed enriched environments and animal studies. But they also went further than other studies by providing specific treatment recommendations based on their findings. In their study, they took a group of rats exposed to valproic acid during gestation, based on research studies showing that rats exposed to this chemical showed behavioral and neurological symptoms similar to those exhibited by humans with autism (including repetitive and stereotypical behaviors and decreased number of social behaviors). They then took a group of these rats, exposed them to an "enriched environment" and compared them with similar rats who were not exposed to such an environment. Their results showed increased social behaviors and lower stereotypic behaviors along with evidence of decreased anxiety and lower sensitivity to non-painful stimuli for rats raised in the "enriched environments."

Environmental enrichment activities that Schneider *et al.* proposed specifically were ones involving behavioral therapy interventions addressing language skills, social behaviors, and cooperative play. When making these recommendations they referenced earlier studies of behavior therapy for autism, including Lovaas (1987), Ozonoff and Cathcart (1998), and McEachin, Smith, and Lovaas (1993). There were no specific types of behavioral interventions consistent across the studies. What distinguished these studies was the intensity of interventions provided several times per week. Parents and spouses were encouraged and helped to continue interventions several more times per week. Intensive interventions were used consistently and frequently throughout each week. All these studies showed intensive behavior therapy interventions increasing the number of children's social interactions. There was no specific focus on relationship quality but, rather, there was a focus on duration and quantity of social relationships. Benefits of these interventions related to their increasing the child's social interactions and doing so in a way matched to the children's developmental levels. Children in the studies not only increased their social relationships but also maintained those increases over time. Increasing the frequency, not quality, of social interactions helped improve their functioning and reduce their autistic symptoms.

In their chapter on environmental enrichment in the book *Zoo Animal Welfare*, Maple and Perdue (2013) addressed several different aspects of environmental enrichment. "Feeding enrichment" addresses types of food and the means by which that food is delivered. "Tactile enrichment" involves providing objects that are physically stimulating for the animal. "Structural enrichment" refers to changes in the animal's physical environment. "Auditory, olfactory, and visual enrichment" involves sounds, smells, and visual cues that improve the animal's environment. "Social enrichment" addresses the animal's social life. "Cognitive enrichment" relates to processes that challenge and stimulate the animal's cognitive abilities. These are all factors that need to be taken into account when taking a comprehensive view of what makes up "environmental enrichment" for any animal. They also show the multi-layered nature of any type of enrichment activities.

Changing goals for autism treatment

We have covered a number of studies in this chapter related to social behaviors and autism. At this point, we should stop and summarize what these animal studies seem to suggest about therapeutic interventions for autism. Our focus here has been more on an understanding of what sorts of goals and outcomes are appropriate for behavioral interventions rather than on the specific types of interventions likely to be helpful. Animal research studies provide clinicians with a good deal to think about when it comes to determining what sorts of goals are necessary when it comes to social interactions. There is reason to consider that the treatment goals often set for autism treatment are not ones likely to be most beneficial.

Comparative psychology research does not show that there is a need for such things as "friendships" when it comes to social interactions. "Friendships" are indeed helpful but are not necessary when it comes to social relationships. If an individual can interact positively with other people but does not necessarily have the skills or interest in developing "friendships," then there is no evidence to suggest that this would impair their ability to benefit from social interactions. Sociality benefits humans and animals in terms of longevity and improved functioning, based on the individual interacting with other people regardless of the level of emotional connectedness evident in those relationships. Parents who take their children with autism to therapy to help them make "friends" may very well be limiting what the child can gain from therapeutic interventions.

Humans are "social animals." There are many other "social animals." Animal research summarized throughout this chapter does not reflect that close relationships are necessary to gain the benefits of being "social." Increasing the frequency and duration with which an individual interacts with other people may in and of itself benefit the individual. This is beneficial to keep in mind when working with individuals with autism, since making "friends" is often difficult and often relies on factors outside the individual's control (e.g. timing, shared interests, maintenance of positive interactions over time). "Friendships" can be beneficial but there is no evidence, based on any research involving "social animals," to suggest they are necessary in order to gain benefits from social interactions.

Treatment goals set for autism do not necessarily have to focus on developing "friendships" or on emotionally intimate relationships. When it comes to benefiting from social relationships there is considerable evidence throughout the comparative psychology research to suggest that the focus can be on "quantity rather than quality" (provided the relationships are positive). "Social animals" benefit from interacting with other individuals of their species in a variety of different ways. Social relationships provide protection and access to potential mates. These are social benefits that humans gain simply from being the members of communities. Humans also benefit from social connectedness through benefits provided to all members of a society. This is done through governmental programs. Many of the things that social research shows are beneficial for social connectedness are ones that are provided to all members of a particular society. Social isolation is a problem to address but can be lessened simply by the person having more positive interactions regardless of how intense those interactions might be. Treatment goals can focus on helping individuals increase the number of social relationships with which they are comfortable. Increasing positive social relationships is a goal that is supported throughout all of the social research contained in this chapter. There is no reason to insist that certain types of relationships must be emphasized more than others.

"Quasi-autism" and Reactive Attachment Disorder

Before moving on to the case study, we discuss here conditions of autistic-like symptoms whose causes are considered to be more psychological than neurological. Autism is considered to be primarily a neurological condition, and research today focuses almost exclusively on physiological factors (e.g. genetics, biochemistry, neurology) when it comes to looking for causes. But this was not always the case. For much of the twentieth century, autism was seen as the result of emotionally distanced mothers and of children raised without any type of consistent emotional support. This is not the way autism is viewed today and, as autism is now seen more as a neurological condition, there has been a need for diagnostic categories explaining conditions where children raised in environments lacking emotional support and devoid of maternal contact develop symptoms similar to autism.

Children raised in emotionally deprived institutions often develop symptoms similar to autism. Rutter *et al.* (2007) called this "quasi-autism" based on their study of 144 children in Romanian orphanages. They found that 16 of these children matched the autism patterns on two major autism assessment instruments (*Autism Diagnostic Interview – Revised* and *Autism Diagnostic Observation Schedule*). These institutionalized children were found to have autistic-like symptoms related to their being raised without emotional support. In more formal diagnostic terms, these children who were described as having "quasi-autism" would be diagnosed with Reactive Attachment Disorder. This is a diagnosis listed in the *International Classification of Diseases* (World Health Organization 1992) and is defined as a condition resulting from extreme conditions of abuse and/or neglect. It has been found both with institutionalized children and maltreated non-institutionalized children (Kay and Green 2013).

When considering this "quasi-autism" condition, it is worth noting that the "Attachment" of Reactive Attachment Disorder is the emotional attachment to material figures described by Harry Harlow and his colleagues (e.g. Harlow and Zimmerman 1959). Harlow's work on monkeys being separated from their mothers set the stage for decades of work, showing the importance of these factors for healthy social and emotional development, prior to when Reactive Attachment Disorder was formally adopted as a diagnosis by the World Health Organization in 1992 (Chaffin *et al.* 2006). This diagnosis was used to distinguish conditions of maternal dis-attachment from autism. This was necessary because autism had mistakenly been considered a result of maternal deprivation and lack of emotional attachment throughout most of the twentieth century. Kanner (1943) was one of the first authors to use the term "autism" and described this condition as resulting from maternal disengagement. Kanner was also one of the first to use the term "refrigerator parent" as a way of describing the emotionally distant (or emotionally "cold") parent who, he said, often raised autistic children.

This was the way autism was treated for several decades. But in the 1980s and 1990s, autism was seen more as a physiological condition with organic causes (Frith 1989; Ridley 1994). Despite autism being seen more and more as a neurological condition during that time, there was still a need for a diagnosis that addressed conditions where autistic-like symptoms arose due to lack of maternal attachment and healthy emotional support. These were not conditions that made up the majority of cases where individuals suffered autistic-like symptoms but did represent some of these cases. This is when the diagnosis Reactive Attachment Disorder started being used. Unfortunately, even at this time, it is not a well-defined condition and is one where the effectiveness of different treatment approaches is not well-supported (Puckering *et al.* 2011).

CASE STUDY

David was a teenage male who presented for outpatient therapy following a neuropsychological evaluation. He was diagnosed with autism about four years earlier at his school and this was confirmed following the neuropsychological evaluation. He presented with significant problems related to social comprehension and reported significant difficulties getting along with peers. He also presented with significant problems communicating his wants and needs effectively. He had a tendency to perseverate on movies and television shows and it was often difficult to redirect him away from those topics. He often had problems completing schoolwork and doing things that he needed to do because he would perseverate on those topics.

David reported that he did not have any friends. His mother brought him to therapy and also reported that David did not have any friends. This had been the situation throughout his life. But there was some discrepancy between David and his mother regarding how significant a problem this represented. David stated that he was comfortable with his positive peer interactions and with his large number of online relationships. He actually described these as online "friendships" even though he did acknowledge that they were different from what other people described as "friendships." David's mother reported considerable anxiety and concern about David because he did not have any friends. She contrasted David's lack of social interactions with his older sister's large number of social relationships. She talked about how David's sister often got invited to parties and social outings and described this as being a major part of his sister's life. She talked about how she was looking for David to have something similar to this and actually presented this as one of the main reasons that she was seeking therapy for David.

During the initial interview David talked at some length about his level of depression and anger regarding the disagreements that he has with his mother about social relationships. He talked at length about how his mother would be very focused on David developing more social relationships and how this became very frustrating and upsetting for him. He described situations where he tried to make friendships but was just not effective. He denied that he was particularly upset about not having more friends at school and reiterated that he was quite satisfied with his online relationships. He reported that other kids made fun of him at times and that this was upsetting for him. He also reported that the frequency with which he was made fun of by other kids made him less desirous of social relationships. His logic in this matter was that if other kids would treat him this way in person he was better off focusing on interacting with others online. He described himself as being much more emotionally distressed about the disagreements that he had with his mother about his lack of friendships than he was by his actual lack of friendships. He also reported that he had come to think of himself as a "failure" because he was not making as many friendships as his sister.

Perseveration was another issue that both David and his mother reported. Therapy sessions allowed for the opportunity to see his poor social skills but even more to see the degree to which perseveration interfered with his functioning. It was difficult during the therapy sessions initially to discuss matters as he would often start to perseverate on movies and television shows. He would also go through "scripting" where he would repeat lines from television shows and movies. This is considered a common behavioral characteristic of autism. His perseveration interfered much more frequently with his functioning during sessions than did his poor social comprehension and poor social skills. Neither David nor his mother identified any definite precipitants to when he showed more problems with perseveration.

David was diagnosed with autism but also with a depressive disorder. He presented with symptoms of depression including sad mood, lack of motivation, and lack of energy. He reported that he often spent time after school in his room because he did not want to interact with other people or do anything. He would watch television or play video games. He talked about being angry at his parents because of the pressure that they put on him to be more like his sister. He also talked about being angry at his parents because he thought they did not treat him very nicely. He exhibited poor self-esteem and described himself in negative terms due primarily to his social difficulties. Further discussion revealed that his poor self-esteem was not due to his actual difficulties getting along with other people but more to his interpretation about those difficulties. He described himself as having a negative view of his abilities due to the strong emphasis that his mother and others put on him developing friendships. He described this is something he felt difficult and saw himself in negative terms because of those difficulties.

David initially was quite resistant to therapy. His resistance lessened when it was made clear that the goal of therapy would not initially be to develop "friendships" but more to get him more comfortable with social interactions. He acknowledged that he would like to at least feel more comfortable interacting with other people even if he did not develop friends. He was quite positive about his frequency of online interactions and also showed less resistance to therapy when it was clear that the goal would not be to stop those interactions. His therapist talked with him about how friendships are often beneficial but not necessary for survival or even for feeling good about oneself. He agreed with his therapist not to take the possibility of developing more "friendships" (as defined by his mother and many other people he knew) off the table provided that this was not set as the initial primary goal of therapy. He and his therapist agreed that the primary goal of therapy would be to help decrease his anxiety level with regard to social interactions and increase the frequency with which he had social interactions that made him feel positive.

Different sets of decision-making steps constituted a large part of David's initial therapy sessions. His therapist worked with David on developing these sets of steps that were called "behavioral scripts." These were specific steps David could take so as to effectively handle social interactions. He responded positively to thinking about these in terms of "scripts" as this related directly to his interest in movies and television. He recognized scripts as specific steps that are laid out for helping individuals decide what to do. His therapist and David developed scripts that he could use for making decisions about different types of social interactions.

Social skills training and shaping were the initial stage of David's therapy. His therapist provided David with some basic social skills to start the discussion and then provided role-playing exercises to help David recognize how to effectively use those skills. He initially utilized those skills in the therapy session with a focus on his therapist helping to shape his affective use of skills when interacting in therapy. His homework assignments were to put some of those skills into use outside of the session and report on progress. Shaping exercises were used to help modify how he implemented those approaches and increase progressively the consistency with which he used effective social skills for dealing with social situations. Problem-solving skills were used in each session to help develop specific ways in which he could use those skills for handling different types of situations. David learned effective skills for dealing with basic social interactions and then also learned behavioral scripts that he could use for deciding how to modify those approaches for implementing effective skills. David had low average intelligence which was sufficient for him to learn basic skills.

Cognitive therapy approaches helped David feel less anxiety and emotional distress about his social behaviors. When his therapist helped him understand that friendships as defined by the general culture were beneficial but not necessary he talked about feeling less pressure to develop friendships. When his therapist explained to him that different types of social interactions can be beneficial he also talked about feeling better about himself. His therapy sessions focused on helping him feel comfortable with the social interactions he had at the present time and also feel comfortable about taking small steps towards developing additional social relationships. Cognitive therapy also helped him feel less emotional distress related to difficulties with other kids picking on him. He was able to develop good decision-making for deciding when to stop attempting social interactions with certain individuals. He developed a series of scripts that helped him make decisions with regard to when he had put enough effort into trying to develop some sort of positive social interactions and terminate the attempts.

Due to his being an older teenager, David's therapy was primarily individual. But his mother was involved for part of each session. His mother's involvement focused on her reporting what she observed about David's behavior and also enlisting her help in making sure David used more effective social skills outside of session. His mother worked on helping make sure David followed the therapist's homework assignments. David's mother initially was not receptive to the discussion of more realistic ways to approach social interactions. She clearly placed a great deal of importance on David developing friendships and was very definite about what she saw as the definition of "friendship." David's therapist presented to her material supporting that friendships could indeed be helpful but were not necessary. The therapist talked about how friendships were necessary neither for survival nor for a happy life. David's mother acknowledged that she knew people who had a variety of different social relationships and often were happy and also that she knew people who had a large number of friendships but were not happy. But she continued to focus on David needing to develop what she and most people she knew saw as "friendships." One reason for her emphasis was because of the benefits David's sister had from those types of friendships. David's mother was not agreeable to the more comprehensive view of positive social relationships until the point that David started talking about feeling better about himself. When she saw that having a different view of social connectedness made David feel better his mother showed less resistance to taking the more global view.

One reason why social skills were emphasized initially in therapy was because of the evidence that decreasing social isolation could decrease perseverative behaviors. This did not mean that David needed to develop close friendships, but more that he would benefit from having more social interactions. This was a goal set early in therapy and David made slow but relatively steady progress in increasing his number of social interactions. As he did this, the severity of his perseverative behaviors seemed to decrease. His therapist also worked with David on skills he could use for decreasing the duration of his perseverative behaviors. Again, as David made progress increasing the duration and frequency of social interactions, the severity of his perseverative behaviors decreased. He continued to make slow but steady progress over the year that he was in therapy. He and his therapist terminated those sessions when David graduated high school and made plans for attending college.

Summary

Autism is a serious neurodevelopmental disorder that impacts millions of individuals throughout the world. There are millions more who are impacted significantly from other types of social communication disorders. These disorders impact significantly on individuals' abilities to interact socially and develop social relationships. There are many types of therapeutic programs used that improve social competence and increase social behaviors. At the present time there are no drug treatments for autism and the process towards developing pharmaceutical treatments is complex. Animal research has contributed significantly to understanding the complexity of autism and the genetic and environmental factors involved. Research studies involving animals support that autism likely incorporates a variety of different conditions rather than one specific condition. This is also the case with social communication disorders.

There are effective social skills programs that counselors and therapists can use. Research shows these to be effective for improving social competence and increasing social behaviors. One essential step needed for programs and often not explored in depth is the goals of these programs. If you are dealing with individuals who have significant social difficulties is it really appropriate to set developing friendships as a goal? Friendships are complex and involve a number of different factors not within the individual's control. There is a great likelihood that counselors and therapists who set developing friendships as a goal for social skills training will be setting individuals up for failure. There is not much that the therapist or individual seeking treatment can do to increase friendships if individuals likely to be their friends are not available.

Developing friendships is often set by clinicians and family members as the goal of therapeutic approaches. And we see through studies covered in this chapter that this goal is unnecessary. There is no clear evidence that friendships or intimate relationships are necessary to gain most of the benefits associated with social interactions. Friendships can increase survival rates over time but there are other things people can do to help themselves live longer. There also is no indication in research on mortality rates that what generally is defined as "friendships" is essential for gaining that benefit. There is, for instance, no evidence that things such as online "friendships" cannot provide the same benefit. What individuals need from social environments is a sense of connectedness. They need to have a sense that there are others who will protect them and will help them gain needed resources. But communities and governments provide those benefits. Individuals need to have social interactions, but these exist even if individuals do not have emotionally intimate relationships with other people.

What we presented throughout this chapter is evidence that being "social animals" does not require emotionally intimate relationships like the ones typically referred to as "friendships." These are nice and can be beneficial but are not necessary for survival in social environments. Social isolation is detrimental but there is a long gap between an individual being socially isolated and having multiple friendships. There really is evidence throughout the literature to suggest that, when it comes to social interactions, quantity surpasses quality in terms of benefits. Individuals who have larger numbers of social interactions do seem to do better regardless of the level or quality of those social relationships. Counselors and therapists working with individuals who have autism or other types of social difficulties can help those individuals best by identifying their comfort level with different relationships and helping to increase the frequency of those relationships. It is increasing the number of social interactions and level of social comfort that is going to help the individual most rather than having a high level of social connectedness or close social relationships.

References

American Psychiatric Association (2013) *Diagnostic and Statistical Manual of Mental Disorders (DSM-5)*. Arlington, VA: APA.

Branchi, I. (2009) 'The mouse communal nest: investigating the epigenetic influences of the early social environment on brain and behavior development.' *Neuroscience and Biobehavioral Reviews 33*, 4, 551–559.

Brookman-Frazee, L., Baker-Ericzén, M., Stadnick, N., and Taylor, R. (2012) 'Parent perspectives on community mental health services for children with autism spectrum disorders.' *Journal of Child and Family Studies 21*, 4, 533–544.

Brown, A.S. (2012) 'Epidemiologic studies of exposure to prenatal infection and risk of schizophrenia and autism.' *Developmental Neurobiology 72*, 10, 1272–1276.

Brownlow, C., Bertilsdotter Rosqvist, H., and O'Dell, L. (2015) 'Exploring the potential for social networking among people with autism: challenging dominant ideas of "friendship".' *Scandinavian Journal of Disability Research 17*, 2, 188–193.

Buunk, A.P. and Dijkstra, P., (2012) 'The Social Animal Within Organizations.' In S.C. Roberts (ed.) *Applied Evolutionary Psychology.* Oxford: Oxford University Press..

Cacioppo, J.T. and Hawkley, L.C. (2009) 'Perceived social isolation and cognition.' *Trends in Cognitive Sciences 13*, 10, 447–454.

Cacioppo, J.T. Hawkley, L.C., Norman, G.J., and Berntson, G.G. (2011) 'Social isolation.' *Annals of the New York Academy of Sciences 1231*, 1, 17–22.

Campbell, D.L., Dallaire, J.A., and Mason, G.J. (2013) 'Environmentally enriched rearing environments reduce repetitive perseveration in caged mink, but increase spontaneous alternation.' *Behavioural Brain Research 239*, 177–187.

Chadman, K.K., Guariglia, S.R., and Yoo, J.H. (2012) 'New directions in the treatment of autism spectrum disorders from animal model research.' *Expert Opinion on Drug Discovery 7*, 5, 407–416.

Chaffin, M., Hanson, R., Saunders, B.E., Nichols, T., *et al.* (2006) 'Report of the APSAC task force on attachment therapy, reactive attachment disorder, and attachment problems.' *Child Maltreatment 11*, 1, 76–89.

Crawley, J.N. (2012) 'Translational animal models of autism and neurodevelopmental disorders.' *Dialogues in Clinical Neuroscience 14*, 3, 293.

Dalton, N.S. (2013, April) 'Neurodiversity and HCI.' *Proceedings CHI'13 Extended Abstracts on Human Factors in Computing Systems.* New York: ACM.

Detillion, C.E., Craft, T.K., Glasper, E.R., Prendergast, B.J., and DeVries, A.C. (2004) 'Social facilitation of wound healing.' *Psychoneuroendocrinology 29*, 8, 1004–1011.

Ellegood, J. and Crawley, J.N. (2015) 'Behavioral and neuroanatomical phenotypes in mouse models of autism.' *Neurotherapeutics 12*, 3, 521–533. 1–13.

Escobedo, L., Nguyen, D.H., Boyd, L., Hirano, S., *et al.* (2012, May) 'MOSOCO: a mobile assistive tool to support children with autism practicing social skills in real-life situations.' *Proceedings of the SIGCHI Conference on Human Factors in Computing Systems.* New York: ACM.

Faridar, A., Jones-Davis, D., Rider, E., Li, J., *et al.* (2014) 'Mapk/Erk activation in an animal model of social deficits; a possible link to autism.' *Mol. Autism 5*, 57.

Fletcher, G.E., Warneken, F., and Tomasello, M. (2012) 'Differences in cognitive processes underlying the collaborative activities of children and chimpanzees.' *Cognitive Development 27*, 2, 136–153.

Freeman, S.F. and Kasari, C. (1998) 'Friendships in children with developmental disabilities.' *Early Education and Development 9*, 4, 341–355.

Frith, U. (1989) *Autism: Explaining the Enigma.* Oxford: Blackwell.

Gadad, B.S., Hewitson, L., Young, K.A., and German, D.C. (2013) 'Neuropathology and animal models of autism: genetic and environmental factors.' *Autism Research and Treatment 2013.* Article 731935.

Gutstein, S.E. and Whitney, T. (2002) 'Asperger syndrome and the development of social competence.' *Focus on Autism and Other Developmental Disabilities 17*, 3, 161–171.

Hacker, C.E., Horback, K.M., and Miller, L.J. (2015) 'GPS technology as a proxy tool for determining relationships in social animals: an example with African elephants.' *Applied Animal Behaviour Science 163*, 175–182.

Harlow, H.F. and Suomi, S.J. (1971) 'Social recovery by isolation-reared monkeys.' *Proceedings of the National Academy of Sciences 68*, 7, 1534–1538.

Harlow, H.F. and Zimmermann, R.R. (1959) 'Affectional responses in the infant monkey.' *Science 130*, 421–432.

Hartup, W.W. (1989) 'Social relationships and their developmental significance.' *American Psychologist 44*, 2, 120–126.

Hennessy, M.B. (1984) 'Presence of companion moderates arousal of monkeys with restricted social experience.' *Physiology and Behavior 33*, 5, 693–698.

Holt-Lunstad, J., Smith, T.B., and Layton, J.B. (2010) 'Social relationships and mortality risk: a meta-analytic review.' *PLoS Medicine 7*, 7, 859.

Hostinar, C.E., Sullivan, R.M., and Gunnar, M.R. (2014) 'Psychobiological mechanisms underlying the social buffering of the hypothalamic–pituitary–adrenocortical axis: a review of animal models and human studies across development.' *Psychological Bulletin 140*, 1, 256.

Hsiao, E.Y. and Patterson, P.H. (2012) 'Immune involvement in Autism Spectrum Disorder as a basis for animal models.' *Autism S1*, 3.

Kanner, L. (1943) 'Autistic disturbances of affective contact.' *Nervous Child 2*, 217–250.

Kasari, C., Locke, J., Gulsrud, A., and Rotheram-Fuller, E. (2011) 'Social networks and friendships at school: comparing children with and without ASD.' *Journal of Autism and Developmental Disorders 41*, 5, 533–544.

Kay, C. and Green, J. (2013) 'Reactive attachment disorder following early maltreatment: systematic evidence beyond the institution.' *Journal of Abnormal Child Psychology 41*, 4, 571–581.

Laugeson, E.A., Frankel, F., Gantman, A., Dillon, A.R., and Mogil, C. (2012) 'Evidence-based social skills training for adolescents with autism spectrum disorders: the UCLA PEERS program.' *Journal of Autism and Developmental Disorders 42*, 6, 1025–1036.

Leekam, S.R., Prior, M.R., and Uljarevic, M. (2011) 'Restricted and repetitive behaviors in autism spectrum disorders: a review of research in the last decade.' *Psychological Bulletin 137*, 4, 562.

Lewis, M.H., Tanimura, Y., Lee, L.W., and Bodfish, J.W. (2007) 'Animal models of restricted repetitive behavior in autism.' *Behavioural Brain Research 176*, 1, 66–74.

Liu Y. and Wang, Z.X. (2003) 'Nucleus accumbens oxytocin and dopamine interact to regulate pair bond formation in female prairie voles.' *Neuroscience 121*, 3, 537–544.

Locke, J., Ishijima, E.H., Kasari, C., and London, N. (2010) 'Loneliness, friendship quality and the social networks of adolescents with high-functioning autism in an inclusive school setting.' *Journal of Research in Special Educational Needs 10*, 2, 74–81.

Lovaas, O.I. (1987) 'Behavioral treatment and normal educational and intellectual functioning in young autistic children.' *Journal of Consulting and Clinical Psychology 55*, 1, 3.

Maple, T.L. and Perdue, B.M. (2013) 'Environmental Enrichment.' In T.L. Maple and B.M. Perdue, *Zoo Animal Welfare*. Berlin: Springer.

McEachin, J.J., Smith, T., and Lovaas, O.I. (1993) 'Long-term outcome for children with autism who received early intensive behavioral treatment.' *American Journal of Mental Retardation 97*, 359–359.

Miklósi, Á. and Gácsi, M. (2012) 'On the utilization of social animals as a model for social robotics.' *Frontiers in Psychology 3*, 75.

Ozonoff, S. and Cathcart, K. (1998) 'Effectiveness of a home program intervention for young children with autism.' *Journal of Autism and Developmental Disorders 28*, 1, 25–32.

Peñagarikano, O., Lázaro, M.T., Lu, X.H., Gordon, A., *et al.* (2015) 'Exogenous and evoked oxytocin restores social behavior in the Cntnap2 mouse model of autism.' *Science Translational Medicine 7*, 271ra8.

Puckering, C., Connolly, B., Werner, C., Toms-Whittle, L., *et al.* (2011) 'Rebuilding' relationships: a pilot study of the effectiveness of the Mellow Parenting Programme for children with Reactive Attachment Disorder.' *Clinical Child Psychology and Psychiatry 16*, 1, 73–87.

Rao, P.A., Beidel, D.C., and Murray, M.J. (2008) 'Social skills interventions for children with Asperger's syndrome or high-functioning autism: a review and recommendations.' *Journal of Autism and Developmental Disorders 38*, 2, 353–361.

Reichow, B., Steiner, A.M., and Volkmar, F. (2013) 'Cochrane review: social skills groups for people aged 6 to 21 with autism spectrum disorders (ASD).' *Evidence-Based Child Health: A Cochrane Review Journal 8*, 2, 266–315.

Reis, H.T. and Collins, W.A. (2004) 'Relationships, human behavior and psychological science.' *Current Directions in Psychological Science 13*, 6, 233–237.

Rekers, Y., Haun, D.B., and Tomasello, M. (2011) 'Children, but not chimpanzees, prefer to collaborate.' *Current Biology 21*, 20, 1756–1758.

Ridley, R.M. (1994) 'The psychology of perseverative and stereotyped behaviour.' *Progress in Neurobiology 44*, 2, 221–231.

Ruan, H. and Wu, C.F. (2008) 'Social interaction-mediated lifespan extension of Drosophila Cu/Zn superoxide dismutase mutants.' *Proceedings of the National Academy of Sciences 105*, 21, 7506–7510.

Rutter, M., Kreppner, J., Croft, C., Murin, M., *et al.* (2007) 'Early adolescent outcomes of institutionally deprived and non-deprived adoptees. III. Quasi-autism.' *Journal of Child Psychology and Psychiatry 48*, 12, 1200–1207.

Schneider, T., Turczak, J., and Przewłocki, R. (2006) 'Environmental enrichment reverses behavioral alterations in rats prenatally exposed to valproic acid: issues for a therapeutic approach in autism.' *Neuropsychopharmacology 31*, 1, 36–46.

Seyfarth, R.M. and Cheney, D.L. (2012) 'The evolutionary origins of friendship.' *Annual Review of Psychology 63*, 153–177.

Solomon, M., Goodlin-Jones, B.L., and Anders, T.F. (2004) 'A social adjustment enhancement intervention for high functioning autism, Asperger's syndrome, and pervasive developmental disorder NOS.' *Journal of Autism and Developmental Disorders 34*, 6, 649–668.

Stavropoulos, K.M. and Carver, L.J. (2013) 'Research review: social motivation and oxytocin in autism – implications for joint attention development and intervention.' *Journal of Child Psychology and Psychiatry 54*, 6, 603–618.

Székely, T., Moore, A.J., and Komdeur, J. (2010) *Social Behaviour: Genes, Ecology and Evolution*. Cambridge: Cambridge University Press.

Vogt, J.L., Coe, C.L., and Levine, S. (1981) 'Behavioral and adrenocorticoid responsiveness of squirrel monkeys to a live snake: is flight necessarily stressful?' *Behavioral and Neural Biology 32*, 4, 391–405.

Wimmer, J.S., Vonk, M.E., and Bordnick, P. (2009) 'A preliminary investigation of the effectiveness of attachment therapy for adopted children with reactive attachment disorder.' *Child and Adolescent Social Work Journal 26*, 4, 351–360.

World Health Organization (1992) *The ICD-10 Classification of Mental and Behavioural Disorders: Clinical Descriptions and Diagnostic Guidelines*. Geneva: World Health Organization.

Yang, M., Perry, K., Weber, M.D., Katz, A.M., and Crawley, J.N. (2011) 'Social peers rescue autism-relevant sociability deficits in adolescent mice.' *Autism Research 4*, 1, 17–27.

Yoo, J., Bakes, J., Bradley, C., Collingridge, G.L., and Kaang, B.K. (2014) 'Shank mutant mice as an animal model of autism.' *Philosophical Transactions of the Royal Society B: Biological Sciences 369*, 1633, 20130143.

Young, L.J. and Wang, Z. (2004) 'The neurobiology of pair bonding.' *Nature Neuroscience 7*, 10, 1048–1054.

Chapter 8

OVEREATING
AND OBESITY

Obesity affects millions of people throughout the industrialized world. It also plays a significant role in most major medical disorders that impact human beings. Obesity impacts on all aspects of physical functioning. When people are obese they are often caught in a circular pattern where poor food choices, and other factors contributing to obesity, impact further on their medical issues. Heart disease, cancer, diabetes, and chronic pain all are impacted significantly in one way or another by obesity. Overeating and lack of exercise are the two most significant behavioral components of this major medical problem.

Overeating and obesity are problems seen by counselors and therapists when patients seek help to decrease the impact of behavioral choices. Psychological counselors and therapists treat obesity and overeating by addressing behavioral and emotional components. Physicians may be the professionals who address medical difficulties caused by obesity, but it is psychological professionals who help break the behavioral patterns. Overeating can be habitual, and psychological professionals often get involved in trying to break the habits. Overeating also often has emotional and stress components that can be treated through psychological interventions. Lack of exercise contributes to obesity and this also involves breaking a behavioral pattern and overcoming emotional obstacles. Decreasing food intake and increasing exercise are often two general treatment plan steps associated with effective interventions for treating obesity and overeating.

There are numerous physiological factors impacting obesity. Genetic factors are the most prominent and likely have much, if not more, impact on obesity than overeating and lack of exercise. And genetic factors make up the majority of animal research on obesity, but that research has minimal use for psychological counselors and therapists. Besides helping patients understand the role their genetics play in their obesity and making appropriate medical referrals, there is nothing else clinical psychology professionals can do to address genetic factors. But counselors and therapists can address the behavioral patterns associated with overeating, food choices, and lack of exercise. And these are factors that can help treat obesity even if they are not the primary causes of a person's obesity. For these reasons, this chapter will focus primarily on overeating, food choices, and exercise.

In this chapter we address comparative psychology research exploring both the behavioral and psychological components of overeating and obesity. We look at how a behavior common and important to every animal species (eating) can become so problematic. We also examine the breakdowns that cause such an essential part of life to become so problematic. Eating is so essential to survival, and so essential to the whole evolutionary process, that it really is remarkable that it can very quickly go awry. We also consider the characteristics of foods and food choices that contribute to increased likelihood of overeating and enumerate environmental factors that help to increase exercise behaviors and decrease food intake.

This is an area where counselors and therapists impact significantly on both the medical and psychological wellbeing of clients. The treatment of obesity and overeating crosses between the areas of medical and emotional health. This is also a subject that gets to the very root of the evolutionary process. Much of what animals, including human animals, do and much of who they are is geared towards the acquisition and maintenance of food sources. This is fundamental to survival and is the basis for all other behavior patterns. Understanding how this then transitions into being a significant problem, one that presents serious dangers for an individual's health, requires us to look at the evolutionary process in its totality.

Animals and obesity

Obesity is not common throughout the animal world; in fact, humans are the only species to have a significant obesity problem (Bartolomucci *et al.* 2012), while domesticated animals are the only other animal population to have obesity to any noteworthy degree. There really are no groups of animals in the wild who suffer problems with obesity. Hibernating and migrating animals are the only other animal populations that have significant weight gain for any extended period of time, but these animals experience that weight gain as a physiological adaptation which is needed because they do not take in food for extended periods of time.

Obesity is also a significant problem for many zoo animals. You find many of the same types of medical issues for zoo animals suffering obesity as you do for humans. Elephants that are overweight cannot deliver their young without human assistance. Male gorillas in zoos who suffer obesity suffer from heart disease in their early twenties and often die young. Zoo animals often suffer from the circular problem of inactivity leading to obesity and then obesity leading to further inactivity. Inactivity is a very serious problem in zoo animals.

We see with all of this that obesity is primarily a human and domesticated animal problem. So, if that is the case, then what can comparative psychology teach us about the factors contributing to obesity? Evolutionary and ethology literature contribute to our understanding of how behavioral factors such as overeating and a sedentary lifestyle came about. Given how different these lifestyle factors are from how animals live in the wild, it is useful to consider what contributed to their development. Comparative psychology research also shows what environmental factors contribute to overeating, and what neurological and biochemical factors contribute to obesity. In addition, animal behavioral research on activity level helps to understand factors contributing to increased likelihood of exercise. All of these are reasons why studying comparative psychology research is important for understanding overeating and obesity.

A review of ethology literature (Wells 2006) documented how humans came to stand out as the only animal species with an obesity problem. There is a pattern of evolutionary demands specific to humans not keeping up with rapid environmental demands.

Humans have developed larger brains through evolution and also live in environments requiring seasonal adaptation. Both of these favor individuals having greater fat accumulation and the ability to store a great deal of energy. And as human development has favored the storage of fat through evolution, so more modern environments have decreased the need for physical work. This is due in large part to more control over the environments leading to decreased energy fluctuations and increased mechanization. This decreased need for physical work has subsequently decreased activity that burned off excess fat storage.

King (2013) presented an evolutionary perspective on obesity. He used the term "obesogenic environment" to describe how humans live in industrialized countries. This term refers to aspects of environments that promote and increase the likelihood of obesity. Evolutionary needs throughout human history strongly supported the need for highly dense foods up until about two hundred years ago. Brain circuitry, developed during that period to meet environment and work demands, overruled the physiology common in most animals that helps to limit meal size and weight gain. Humans and animals needed to keep up nutritional storage for physical demands and facing long periods of time between food source access; physiological and neurological characteristics developed to meet these nutritional and energy needs even as environmental needs changed.

We see that there really is a pattern of physiological needs of humans changing slowly over many centuries but the environmental demands changing much more quickly. Humans developed physiological needs for more dense and higher-fat foods to meet their energy demands, but the rapid pace of technological progress led to less need for the higher energy levels that humans had developed over the centuries. These technological advances include the development of effective tools and farming procedures. Humans developed less of a need for the higher fat and denser food they had relied on because they were able to do what they needed to do without as much energy. It seems now that human beings are still in a transitional stage where they are moving from what they have needed in terms of calories and energy over the centuries to what they currently need. As such, humans still rely in many ways on the types of diet that they needed several hundred years ago even though they do not have a clear need now.

In contrast, consider wild animals. Their environmental needs have not really changed much over the past several centuries. There is still a need for a leopard, lion, gazelle, or gorilla to have as much energy and caloric intake now as was the case several hundred years ago. Conditions in the wild are very similar to what they were during that time. This is, of course, unless humans have brought domestication into the mix. If you have animals who live in the wild but are close enough to wildlife reserves, they are at much higher risk for obesity. Once you bring the human lifestyle into the mix the whole environment changes and the chances for some sort of overeating and/or obesity increase dramatically.

An interesting development over the past several decades is that obesity has risen not just among humans but also among animals living near environments impacted by humans. Klimentidis *et al.* (2011) studied 20,000 animals across 24 populations and found higher levels of obesity among not only domesticated dogs and cats but also primates and rodents living in research colonies and fetal rodents. Given that all of these animals' weight differences were in a positive direction, this supported the finding that factors associated with their similar environments played a significant role. Chemical factors associated with food and common infections associated with these environments were two causes these authors proposed. Changes in medical care and increased availability of food were two additional proposed causes.

Clearly, not every human develops obesity problems. Obesity and overeating do not even consistently occur with every human who you might expect to have weight problems. Anyone walking through a crowded city can see that there are often office workers (who presumably spend much of their time sitting) with no weight problems passing by overweight construction workers (who presumably spend a good deal of time in physical activity). Universities also are full of examples where professors with average BMIs share lecture halls with active students whose BMIs are clearly in the danger range. All of this serves as evidence that overeating and obesity are clearly not due just to reduced demand for physical activity and increased caloric intake. Other factors, such as genetics, clearly play a role. But looking at the evolutionary process shows how the problem of obesity has increased so much over the past several centuries.

Overeating, obesity, and reward properties

Overeating is not the only cause of obesity, but it is a major cause. And overeating often develops from the reward properties of food. Eating is a behavior largely driven by reward motivation. Individuals are driven to eat primarily by the reward potential associated with certain foods, represented by their sensory and physical aspects (Li *et al.* 2013). People seek out food not just for survival but also because of the positive properties associated with food. Seeking and eating food can be triggered by association with both real and anticipated reward values of food. This is often because foods are associated with what are called "hedonistic" properties (see review in Harb *et al.* 2014). There is more to what people find rewarding about food beyond just what it does to meet physiological needs. Pavlovian (conditional) learning often increases this motivation to seek out and eat certain foods even if they are not needed specifically for energy. This is the type of learning that most often leads to overeating and obesity.

Food is a natural reward essential for survival. But many foods also work along similar neurological pathways as drugs of abuse. As such, food is a natural reward that also can become addictive (Hone-Blanchet and Fecteau 2014). Food can also be both a natural reward and a conditioning stimulus. Dopamine plays a major role in the reward aspect of food and in the motivation to seek and eat food (Wise 2006). Animals made obese from consumption of high-fat diets show significant differences in dopamine functioning than non-obese animals. Rada *et al.* (2010) studied groups of "obesity prone" and "obesity resistant" Sprague Dawley rats following five days of a high-fat diet. They found that both rat groups showed increased cellular dopamine following the high-fat diet but only the "obesity prone" rats showed lower dopamine functioning in the neurological area triggering the desire for high-fat food (nucleus accumbens). This reflects that "obesity prone" rats have less neural activity in the area triggering drive for high-fat food in response to eating high-fat foods. These results supported earlier findings in rats by Geiger *et al.* (2009) and Davis *et al.* (2008).

Eating provides reward as it meets an individual's physiological needs. Animals need energy, vitamins, and physiological changes associated with food; and eating provides reward as those needs are met. But many foods provide rewards beyond those physiological demands. Taste, texture, density, and even color are all aspects of food that provide rewards beyond how they meet physiological needs. Foods also provide rewards based on how they make a person feel. Some foods give increased energy and some contribute to a feeling of relaxation. These are direct reward properties of specific foods. But, there also are ways that the ingestion of large quantities of certain foods helps the person feel better. One example of this, and one that is particularly useful for our discussion, relates to "stress eating." This is a behavioral pattern where the person eats large amounts of certain foods that help them feel less stressed. It is not the properties of the specific foods that necessarily help but rather the amounts of food that help the person feel less stressed. It is as if the actual ingestion of large amounts of calories and sugar helps the person feel less stressed. It is not difficult to see how this process of "stress eating" can cause a person significant medical difficulties.

Stress eating

Pool *et al.* (2015) summarized stress eating as it relates to Pavlovian theory. Remember that Pavlov's work is one of the earliest examples of using animal research to understand human behavior and shows a learning system that is present even in the most basic organisms (Amano and Maruyama 2011). As is common with all Pavlovian learning, there is a learned association that develops between a neutral stimulus and a rewarding outcome. This theoretical approach to understanding stress eating posits that high-fat and high-sugar food reduce the discomfort associated with stressful situations. Highly palpable foods are strong reinforcers to animals and often lead to considerable attention and energy being used to obtain those foods. Eating these foods brings about a pleasant experience and reduces the impact of stressful events. Notice that it is not any physiological benefit from the food that is reinforcing, but rather the pleasant experience of eating the food. Stress eating in this way is presented as the result of Pavlovian leaning and forms a type of habit effective for handling stress.

Stress eating is a good example of the way food intake takes on a positive quality not associated in any way with physiological benefits.

Sugary and high-fat foods taste good and have pleasant qualities associated with them. That is what is reinforcing. Stress eating involves the individual taking in that food for the pleasant experience and as a way of reducing the impact of negative experiences associated with stressful situations. Rats often indulge in "comfort foods" during periods of chronic stress, and this ingestion of specific food that is pleasurable has a positive physiological impact. Specifically, the research on rats mentioned earlier shows that elevated stress stimulates the desire for "comfort foods" and the ingestion of such food in turn decreases the negative physiological effects of chronic stressors. These types of foods for rats included dishes of lard along with sugar water. Rats were also more likely to gain weight specifically by eating these foods and then were further likely to gain weight because they ate more of this food under stress.

Rats actually tend to eat less under stress unless the food is highly caloric and/or high in sugar (Bazhan and Zelena 2013). These types of foods (i.e. high in fat and sugar) are often referred to as "highly palpable" foods and they tend to be eaten most under highly stressful situations. They are one of the most positive reinforcers in animals and humans (Berridge 2009; Kringelbach 2004). Animals and humans both tend to eat them more in stressful situations when they are available. And that is where the difference between humans/domesticated animals and wild animals comes into play. Individuals in each of these populations will eat highly palpable foods more in stressful situations but only humans/domesticated animals have those foods readily available. Humans can easily go out and get the foods and domesticated animals often have the foods around them (because the humans with whom they live and count on for survival have them). Wild animals do not often have highly palpable foods readily available. As a result, humans, domesticated animals, and wild animals all will eat highly palpable foods in stressful situations but wild animals will not do this often. This could easily account for one major reason why only humans and domesticated animals have obesity problems.

Liu (2015) studied the effect of a neurochemical associated with increased stress, yohimbine, and found that it also increased overeating in male Sprague Dawley rats. His results showed a strong relationship between overeating and stress levels. When these rats were administered yohimbine, it increased their number of stress level responses significantly regardless of whether they were going after high-fat or standard fat food pellets, but this behavior was significantly more pronounced for the high-fat pellets. These results supported both the effect of stress on overeating and particularly the impact of stress on eating high-fat foods.

Increased preference for sweeteners occurs whether the stress involved is physical or emotional (Pijlman, Wolterink, and Van Ree 2003). These authors studied the impact of physical stress compared with emotional distress by conducting a study on rats in a small open field who were given access to saccharine water. Both types of stress led to an increased intake of the high-sugar water. Physical stress led to a long-term decrease in open field activity and a preference for saccharine water. Emotional stress actually led to an increase in open field activity.

Food deprivation tends to increase the preference for sweeteners and high-fat foods. Rats deprived of food show preferences for sweet-water solutions more than do non-deprived animals (Bacon, Snyder, and Hulse 1962). This is also consistent with food-deprived rats given the choice between standard lab food and food with additional sweetener or fat and showing a consistent preference for the latter (Jacobs and Sharma 1969). Going without food for extended periods of time tends to increase preferences most strongly associated with overeating and obesity.

Highly palpable foods are the foods most likely to lead to obesity. Any change that contributes to increased intake of these foods would therefore also contribute to higher obesity. From the research summarized in the previous paragraphs, we see that stress eating increases the intake of the foods leading to higher obesity. Animal research shows the type of situations and some of the variables that are likely to contribute to increased intake of high-fat and high-sugar foods. Much of the animal research on stress eating is consistent with similar research on humans although, as is often the case, animal research tends to rely more on stricter environmental conditions. From this, we see stronger evidence for the types of factors likely to increase the intake of foods that contribute to obesity.

Food addictions

Animal research on highly palpable foods led to subsequent studies and theoretical papers emphasizing the addictive quality of certain foods. Studies on rats in particular showed the addictive qualities of these foods. When you look at the processes involved with stressful eating it is not difficult to see how those processes are similar to ones associated with addictions. People will often turn to drugs and alcohol as a way of reducing stress and improving how they feel in stressful situations, and many foods have the same neurochemical impact as some addictive drugs. If people use drugs and alcohol to deal with stress then it is not unreasonable to conclude that they may use food for the same reason. In this way the food becomes a source of addiction in much the same way as drugs and alcohol.

Smith and Robbins (2013) provided a summary of the "food addiction" model explaining increased obesity over the past several decades. This theory posits that increased availability of foods high in fat and sugar (what we have been referring to as "highly palpable" foods) also leads to a higher availability of foods that have more of an addictive quality. This leads to obesity being a sort of drug abuse. Individuals become physically and psychologically dependent on these high-fat and high-sugar foods. Addiction to these foods leads to a lack of control over eating, with continued overuse despite severe health, social, and financial difficulties and lack of success in reducing consumption. Withdrawal symptoms are also associated with cutting each of these foods.

Addictive behaviors associated with high-sugar foods are prominent throughout animal research. Avena *et al.* (2008) studied rats and found that they showed anxiety and other withdrawal symptoms after bingeing on sugar water for several days. Colantuoni *et al.* (2001) found neurochemical changes associated with addiction and lack of control over addiction when sugar water was administered excessively to rats over a period of 30 days. Dimitriou, Rice, and Corwin (2000) found that rats who had continuous access to fatty foods would binge on those foods, to the significant detriment to their health, after having limited access for even a short period of time. Levin and Dunn-Meynell (2000) found that rats on high-energy diets will quickly eat enough to return to their initial body weight after a period of caloric restriction.

When you look at the high level of eating high-fat and high-sugar foods you see the basis for developing obesity. This is what makes the possibility of food addiction so important for trying to understand obesity. If there is an addictive nature to eating foods associated with obesity, as the food addiction model would suggest, than this would go a long way to explaining why humans eat so much of a food that clearly is so bad for them. High fat consumption is largely responsible for weight gain while high sugar consumption is often responsible for addictive-like behaviors, including withdrawal symptoms (Davis 2013). Avena (2010) summarized research showing that rats show signs of withdrawal symptoms, similar to the effect of abusing drugs, after a month of bingeing sugar and gaining considerably more weight with daily access to the high-fat sweet foods. Binging on high-sugar foods produces neurochemical changes similar to drugs of abuse and bingeing on high-fat foods more often leads to obesity. This is all evidence supporting that at least considering food addiction as a cause for obesity is worthwhile.

Segni *et al.* (2014) presented considerable evidence regarding the connection between genetic factors and food addictions. They reviewed a number of research studies involving animals and overeating and concluded that compulsive overeating tends to follow access to a highly palpable diet (again usually associated with high-fat and high-energy foods) but only in genetically susceptible individuals. Stressful life events were found to frequently interact with genetic factors to increase the likelihood of food addiction and obesity. This theory has come to be known as the "sugar addiction" theory where some rats showed brain changes similar to drug abuse when given ready access to sugar.

Foods with addictive qualities are also the ones that are most readily available in many industrialized nations. Hebebrand *et al.* (2014) described "obesogenic" environments as ones characterized by energy-dense and inexpensive foods associated with obesity. These are also the types of foods that tend to become addictive. High-fat and sugary food would also fall into that category. Foods like these are more readily available to humans in many societies and this contributes to an addictive cycle. Much like drugs of abuse, foods associated with obesogenic environments are made readily available. This leads to many individuals having access to them, including those with genetic predispositions to food addictions. These individuals then use the ready access to have more of these foods and this then builds on their addiction. If this is accurate, it would explain a good deal of how the pattern of eating highly palpable foods continues for the length of time that it takes to develop obesity problems.

Considering a food addiction model such as the one outlined above also helps to further explain why wild animals do not have obesity problems but humans do. There simply is not ready access to the highly palpable food out in the wild that contributes to food addictions and obesity. Although high-fat and high-sugar foods are used in animal studies involving obesity and overeating, they are not foods that would be as readily available in these animals' natural settings. Experimenters provide foods that are different from ones these animals would seek out or have access to in the wild. Humans and domesticated animals, however, often have ready access to all of the foods associated with "obesogenic" environments.

Animal research and exercise

Research on dogs and cats shows that obese domesticated animals require the same processes to lose weight and reduce obesity as do humans. They include increased physical exercise and decreased calories (Laflamme 2012). Domesticated animals have lower activity levels and increased caloric intake compared with their wild peers and changing that pattern can help with weight loss. Increased protein intake along with reduced caloric intake helps with weight loss for domesticated animals. Limiting snacking to less than ten per cent of calories is also helpful. Domesticated animals gain weight for much the same reasons as humans (i.e. high caloric intake, low exercise level) and can lose that weight also by following the same patterns as humans (i.e. reduce caloric intake, increase exercise level).

When we talk about animal exercising, one clear example for domesticated animals is wheel-running. Hamsters, guinea pigs, and mice will often run for long periods of time on exercise wheels placed in their cages. Researchers often question this as an actual exercise and sometimes describe it as an artifact of captivity. Basically, they argue, this is a behavior in which captive animals engage because they have nothing else to do. Meijer and Robbers (2014) challenged this theory with their study involving wild mice who had access to a running wheel in the wild. They found that not only did the mice use the wheel but they used it for lengths of time comparable to the captive mice.

Questions about wheel-running are interesting here because it is a behavior parallel to exercise behaviors in humans. When you watch an animal run on a wheel it is not difficult to see the similarities to humans running on treadmills or stair-climbers. In addition, animals engage in this type of behavior for its own sake and without any purpose clearly related to survival (as opposed to behaviors such as food searching). Sherwin (1998) conducted a review of wheel-running research in laboratory and domesticated animals and concluded that animals engage in wheel-running for its own sake and often seem to find it "important." It is not clear what the animals see as "important" about it and there are multiple theories for why this occurs. Even if the reason is not clear, what is clear is that animals engage in this type of behavior for its own sake in much the same way that humans see exercise behaviors as important.

Wheel-running gives a more direct view of general activity level than do measures of other activities in the wild. Measures of activities in the wild relate directly to general activity level but also relate to other factors. Many activities that occur out in the wild could be reflective of general activity level but also could be a reflection of anxiety, hunger, and exploratory drive. In their review of the research, Careau *et al.* (2012) identified several factors, including general activity level, space use, dispersion, and attempts to find mates as factors contributing to open-field behaviors. Wheel-running does not tend to be related directly to any of those same outcomes. We can take away from this that wheel-running among animals parallels human exercise behaviors, more than open-field activities, in that it has its own intrinsic importance that is not clearly related to any other factors.

Wheel-running also parallels human exercise behaviors in terms of its physiological effects (Novak, Burghardt, and Levine 2012). Weight loss and neurological benefits are seen in rodents with increased wheel-running and are similar to what is seen in humans with increased exercise. There is, however, less clear evidence that motivation for wheel-running is similar to humans' motivation to exercise. It is not clear whether rodents recognize the potential health benefits that occur along with wheel-running and whether there might be any physiological triggers in rats that help to reinforce this type of exercise behavior. They run on wheels for its own benefits but it is not clear what those specific benefits might be. This limits how much wheel-running research can be applied to understand human exercise, beyond just acknowledging that both animals and humans tend to see this type of exercise behavior as important.

If we see the similarities between wheel-running in animals and exercise behaviors in humans then we would want to see what animal research offers for increasing wheel-running. Both animals and humans show recognition of exercise behaviors as important, but even that does not guarantee that they will engage in the behaviors more often. Exercise is important for weight loss but just recognizing that is not enough. What counselors and therapists need is some insights into what can help individuals exercise more often.

In the animal research summarized so far, accessibility was clearly an important aspect to increasing wheel-running. That is, making sure that the wheel was placed in a way that the animal could get to it. One of the reasons why scientists previously thought that the wheel-running was due to being an artifact of captivity was that accessibility was so prominent. It was hard not to look at a caged hamster or rat and not conclude that they are running on a wheel because it is "right there." But when the wheel was moved out into the wild, accessibility was less but was still compelling. Animals needed to be able to see and have ready access to the wheel if they were going to use it. There was no reason to suspect, and no evidence to support, that they would go looking for the wheel if it was hidden behind a tree or put too far away.

Forty male mice were studied to see if wheel-running experience increased their use of wheel-running when under stress (Sibold, Hammack, and Falls 2011). Rats with wheel-running experience were more likely to choose wheel-running when under stress. These results suggest that familiarity with exercise might increase the likelihood of using exercise when under stress.

Garner *et al.* (1991) found that positive reinforcement using brain self-stimulation increased rats' exercise behaviors. They positioned electrodes on both sides of the ventral tegmental brain areas and provided stimulation when the rats exercised. They found that this process significantly increased exercise behaviors and also did not provide any clear physical and/or mental trauma in the rats.

Exercise is an important aspect of weight loss. Food choices can also help in weight loss. Taking steps to lower sugar and fat intake and so reduce calories works for weight loss in both humans and animals. There is also some evidence to suggest that specific eating patterns might help with weight loss as well. One interesting research finding is that intermittent fasting in Sprague Dawley rats tended to result in reduced caloric intake and reduced body mass gain (Chause *et al.* 2014). This study involved feeding one day and fasting another. Rats involved in the study lost more weight when their feeding patterns were intermittent rather than steady. It is not clear how this would relate directly to human beings, but there are diets produced for humans that follow this schedule and have shown effectiveness for weight loss (e.g. Klempel *et al.* 2012).

CASE STUDY

Vincent was a middle-aged man who entered into counseling to help decrease his problems with overeating. His physician had referred him to counseling because his level of obesity had reached dangerous proportions. He had a BMI of 32.4 and was eating over 3200 calories per day. His physician had run medical tests and determined that there was no specific medical cause for his significant weight problems. Vincent was very open about having a poor diet and talked about doing very little physical exercise throughout each day.

His counselor started Vincent's treatment by having him keep a diary of his food intake and physical activity. Vincent reported that he ate three meals per day and typically ate his meals at about the same time each day. But he also snacked frequently throughout each day. As one might expect, Vincent also reported that his food intake consisted of a large amount of high-fat and high-sugar foods. His counselor even took note that each time Vincent came into session he either was finishing or was looking to throw away a large 20 ounce bottle of a high-sugar and high-caffeine soft drink. What was noteworthy about Vincent's diet history is that even when he tried to change the amount of food that he ate or the type of food that he ate he still would have a significant amount of high-sugar and high-fat foods. For instance, at one point he attempted to cut out starches from his diet as this was part of a very popular diet plan at the time. But even when he cut out breads he still consumed a large amount of meat that was considered to be high fat and also continued to drink sugary soft drinks throughout the day and use condiments such as dressings on his salad that were high in both fat and sugar.

What was evident at the start about Vincent's diet was the degree to which it was consistent with what comparative psychology research has revealed about overeating and obesity. It was relevant to understanding his problems that Vincent had high-sugar and high-fat foods making up large portions of his diet. Even when he cut out carbs or other types of foods that are described as contributing to weight gain he still maintained a lot of high-fat and high-sugar foods. This often seems to be the case with diets in that individuals will cut out certain foods but will have a hard time getting away from foods that are high in fat and high in sugar. Vincent's case is indicative of problems faced by many individuals in industrialized countries who eat large amounts of processed food. There often are hidden sources of fat and sugar in processed foods that are easy to ignore if you are not specifically looking for them.

Vincent's counselor worked with Vincent on identifying ways to decrease the amount of fat and sugar that he had in his diet. His counselor referred Vincent to a dietitian for an evaluation to determine what sorts of foods he should be eating. One reason that dietitians are particularly helpful with this sort of thing is that they can help with identifying the hidden sources of fat and sugar that are part of common foods. Vincent worked with the dietitian for an evaluation and they developed a diet plan together that focused on foods that were limited in terms of fat and sugar.

Once Vincent started identifying the diet that he needed to follow, that was when the counselor had to start working more intensely with him. It was clear that Vincent was not happy with the diet he was given. Many of the foods that he enjoyed were taken out and the diversity of the foods was rather limited. There were quite a lot of salads and vegetables. Vincent did not have a problem with those necessarily, but did have problems with the very limited types of dressing that he could use if he was eating a salad. He also talked about being very surprised at the number of desserts that were taken off the list. He expected cookies and cakes, but was surprised at the types of biscuits and puddings that he thought would still be allowed.

Vincent's counselor not only had to develop a plan for addressing Vincent's frustration with his diet but also worked on a plan that Vincent could follow to help combat the withdrawal symptoms that would likely occur when he cut down on his sugar and fat. As we saw from research reviewed in this chapter, there often are withdrawal symptoms associated when an individual decreases their amount of highly palpable foods. Vincent's dietitian had provided suggestions about what Vincent could do to help minimize the withdrawal symptoms that he ended up experiencing. Vincent's counselor worked with Vincent on overcoming the emotional obstacles that were likely to stand in the way of him putting these plans into place.

What research on overeating and obesity shows is the types of plans that individuals like Vincent need to follow in order to lose weight. But it is often up to the counselor to help the individual stay focused on putting these plans in place. Counselors can learn a great deal from comparative research on what factors contribute to overeating and unhealthy lifestyles but then need to use their clinical skills to work with the individual on overcoming the emotional obstacles that are likely to stand in the way. Supportive therapy in cognitive-behavioral therapy approaches is typically the most effective in helping the person recognize the types of approaches that they can use for keeping these obstacles from standing in their way.

Vincent's counselor also worked with Vincent on an exercise program. Vincent had a treadmill and also had a relatively nice area in which to take walks every day. But the counselor had to work with Vincent on behavioral steps to help increase the likelihood that he would utilize these activities. One step that Vincent took with the counselor's recommendation was to put the treadmill in an area where he would see it multiple times throughout every day. This increased the accessibility of the exercise equipment. Vincent's counselor also worked with Vincent on a number of reinforcements that Vincent could apply when he participated in exercise. This was done to help increase the likelihood that Vincent would experience the neurochemical effects associated with reward when he exercised, and this would in turn increase the likelihood that he would continue exercising. His counselor worked with Vincent a great deal on exercise specifically during the first several sessions after the exercise plan was introduced. This was to help increase Vincent's experience with exercise behaviors. Once he was in a pattern where he had exercised on a fairly regular basis for several weeks, the experience itself seem to prompt him into exercising on a more consistent basis.

Vincent stayed in counseling for six months and ended up reaching a pattern of healthy eating and exercising that stayed in effect for the last two months of therapy. By that point Vincent had lost 30 pounds and had cut his caloric intake to 1800 calories per day. He was also exercising five out of seven days per week. When counseling terminated, both Vincent and his counselor agreed that Vincent was on a good path to continue losing weight and maintaining his healthy lifestyle.

Summary

Research primarily involving rats has shown a great deal about factors contributing to overeating and obesity. High-fat and high-sugar foods are considered "highly palpable" foods and a heavy intake of these foods is likely to cause obesity. There are a number of genetic factors and environmental factors that also play a role but a diet high in sugar and fat is often a common denominator in overeating and obesity. These are foods that are not readily available to animals in the wild and this could explain why there really is not an obesity problem for wild animals. Domesticated animals do have more of an obesity problem and this is likely due to their lifestyle patterns being similar to those of the humans that take care of them. High-sugar and high-fat foods also often have addictive qualities to them and this is one of the reasons why the concept of "food addiction" has been discussed prominently in the obesity literature. There is considerable animal research to support that highly palpable foods do have addictive qualities and that animals who stop taking these foods after taking them regularly for long periods of time often suffer withdrawal symptoms.

Animal research supports the common understanding that weight loss often involves decreased caloric intake and increased exercise. Decreasing the amount of sugar and fat is often difficult due to their addictive qualities. Sometimes all the counselor can do is make sure the individual is preparing to experience those withdrawal symptoms once they make significant changes in their diet. There is some evidence from animal research that intermittent eating (e.g. eating only every other day) can be helpful for weight loss. There are diets that follow this pattern of intermittent eating and they have shown some effectiveness for weight loss. Exercise is also a very important aspect of weight loss. Wheel-running research involving animals has shown that having accessibility to exercise equipment is important. Animals will run on wheels even out in the wild provided they are accessible. Animal research also supports that having experience with exercising can help to increase future exercise behaviors.

References

Amano, H. and Maruyama, I.N. (2011) 'Aversive olfactory learning and associative long-term memory in Caenorhabditis elegans.' *Learning and Memory 18*, 10, 654–665.

Avena, N.M. (2010) 'The study of food addiction using animal models of binge eating.' *Appetite 55*, 3, 734–737.

Avena, N.M., Bocarsly, M.E., Rada, P., Kim, A., and Hoebel, B.G. (2008) 'After daily bingeing on a sucrose solution, food deprivation induces anxiety and accumbens dopamine/acetylcholine imbalance.' *Physiology and Behavior 94*, 3, 309–315.

Bacon, W.E., Snyder, H.L., and Hulse, S.H. (1962) 'Saccharine preference in satiated and deprived rats.' Journal of Comparative and Physiological Psychology 55, 1, 112.

Bartolomucci, A., Parmigiani, S., Rodgers, R.J., Vidal-Puig, A., Allan, S.E., and Siegel, V. (2012) 'The Obese Species: a special issue on obesity and metabolic disorders.' *Disease Models and Mechanisms 5*, 5, 563–564.

Bazhan, N. and Zelena, D. (2013) 'Food-intake regulation during stress by the hypothalamo-pituitary-adrenal axis.' *Brain Research Bulletin 95*, 46–53.

Berridge, K.C. (2009) '"Liking" and "wanting" food rewards: brain substrates and roles in eating disorders.' *Physiology and Behavior 97*, 5, 537–550.

Careau, V., Bininda-Emonds, O.R., Ordonez, G., and Garland Jr, T. (2012) 'Are voluntary wheel running and open-field behavior correlated in mice? Different answers from comparative and artificial selection approaches.' *Behavior Genetics 42*, 5, 830–844.

Chausse, B., Solon, C., Caldeira da Silva, C.C., Masselli dos Reis, I.G., *et al.* (2014) 'Intermittent fasting induces hypothalamic modifications resulting in low feeding efficiency, low body mass and overeating.' *Endocrinology 155*, 7, 2456–2466.

Colantuoni, C., Schwenker, J., McCarthy, J., Rada, P., *et al.* (2001) 'Excessive sugar intake alters binding to dopamine and mu-opioid receptors in the brain.' *Neuroreport 12*, 16, 3549–3552.

Davis, C. (2013) 'From passive overeating to "food addiction": a spectrum of compulsion and severity.' *ISRN Obesity 2013.*

Davis, J.F., Tracy, A.L., Schurdak, J.D., Tschöp, M. H., et al. (2008) 'Exposure to elevated levels of dietary fat attenuates psychostimulant reward and mesolimbic dopamine turnover in the rat.' *Behavioral Neuroscience 122,* 6, 1257.

Dimitriou, S.G., Rice, H.B., and Corwin, R.L. (2000) 'Effects of limited access to a fat option on food intake and body composition in female rats.' *International Journal of Eating Disorders 28,* 4, 436–445.

Garner, R.P., Terracio, L., Borg, T.K., and Buggy, J. (1991) 'Intracranial self-stimulation motivates weight-lifting exercise in rats.' *Journal of Applied Physiology 71,* 4, 1627–1631.

Geiger, B.M ., Haburcak, M., Avena, N.M., Moyer, M.C., Hoebel, B.G., and Pothos, E.N. (2009) 'Deficits of mesolimbic dopamine neurotransmission in rat dietary obesity.' *Neuroscience 259,* 4, 1193–1199.

Harb, M.R., Sousa, N., Zihl, J., and Almeida, O.F. (2014) 'Reward components of feeding behavior are preserved during mouse aging.' *Frontiers in Aging Neuroscience 6,* 242.

Hebebrand, J., Albayrak, Ö., Adan, R., Antel, J., et al. (2014) '"Eating addiction", rather than "food addiction", better captures addictive-like eating behavior.' *Neuroscience and Biobehavioral Reviews 47,* 295–306.

Hone-Blanchet, A. and Fecteau, S. (2014) 'Overlap of food addiction and substance use disorders definitions: analysis of animal and human studies.' *Neuropharmacology 85,* 81-90.

Jacobs, H.L. and Sharma, K.N. (1969) 'Taste versus calories: sensory and metabolic signals in the control of food intake.' *Annals of the New York Academy of Sciences 157,* 2, 1084–1125.

King, B.M. (2013) 'The modern obesity epidemic, ancestral hunter-gatherers, and the sensory/reward control of food intake.' *American Psychologist 68,* 2, 88.

Klempel, M.C., Kroeger, C.M., Bhutani, S., Trepanowski, J F., and Varady, K.A. (2012) 'Intermittent fasting combined with calorie restriction is effective for weight loss and cardio-protection in obese women.' *Nutrition Journal 11,* 98, 4.

Klimentidis, Y.C., Beasley, T.M., Lin, H.Y., Murati, G., et al. (2011) 'Canaries in the coal mine: a cross-species analysis of the plurality of obesity epidemics.' *Proceedings of the Royal Society of London B: Biological Sciences 278,* 1712, 1626–1632.

Kringelbach, M.L. (2004) 'Food for thought: hedonic experience beyond homeostasis in the human brain.' *Neuroscience 126,* 4, 807–819.

Laflamme, D.P. (2012) 'Companion Animals Symposium: obesity in dogs and cats: what is wrong with being fat?' *Journal of Animal Science 90,* 5, 1653–1662.

Levin, B.E. and Dunn-Meynell, A.A. (2000) 'Defense of body weight against chronic caloric restriction in obesity-prone and -resistant rats.' *American Journal of Physiology – Regulatory, Integrative and Comparative Physiology 278,* 1, R231– R237.

Li, J. X., Yoshida, T., Monk, K.J., and Katz, D.B. (2013) 'Lateral hypothalamus contains two types of palatability-related taste responses with distinct dynamics.' *Journal of Neuroscience 33*, 22, 9462–9473.

Liu, X. (2015) 'Enhanced motivation for food reward induced by stress and attenuation by corticotrophin-releasing factor receptor antagonism in rats: implications for overeating and obesity.' *Psychopharmacology 232*, 12, 2049–2060.

Meijer, J.H. and Robbers, Y. (2014) 'Wheel running in the wild.' *Proceedings of the Royal Society of London B: Biological Sciences 281*, 1786, 20140210.

Novak, C.M., Burghardt, P.R., and Levine, J.A. (2012) 'The use of a running wheel to measure activity in rodents: relationship to energy balance, general activity, and reward.' *Neuroscience and Biobehavioral Reviews 36*, 3, 1001–1014.

Pijlman, F.T., Wolterink, G., and Van Ree, J.M. (2003) 'Physical and emotional stress have differential effects on preference for saccharine and open field behaviour in rats.' *Behavioural Brain Research 139*, 1, 131–138.

Pool, E., Delplanque, S., Coppin, G., and Sander, D. (2015) 'Is comfort food really comforting? Mechanisms underlying stress-induced eating.' *Food Research International 76*, 207–215.

Rada, P., Bocarsly, M.E., Barson, J.R., Hoebel, B.G., and Leibowitz, S.F. (2010) 'Reduced accumbens dopamine in Sprague–Dawley rats prone to overeating a fat-rich diet.' *Physiology and Behavior 101*, 3, 394–400.

Segni, M.D., Patrono, E., Patella, L., Puglisi-Allegra, S., and Ventura, R. (2014) 'Animal models of compulsive eating behavior.' *Nutrients 6*, 10, 4591–4609.

Sherwin, C.M. (1998) 'Voluntary wheel running: a review and novel interpretation.' *Animal Behaviour 56*, 1, 11–27.

Sibold, J.S., Hammack, S.E., and Falls, W.A. (2011) 'C57 mice increase wheel-running behavior following stress: preliminary findings 1, 2.' *Perceptual and Motor Skills 113*, 2, 605–618.

Smith, D.G. and Robbins, T.W. (2013) 'The neurobiological underpinnings of obesity and binge eating: a rationale for adopting the food addiction model.' *Biological Psychiatry 73*, 9, 804–810.

Wells, J.C. (2006) 'The evolution of human fatness and susceptibility to obesity: an ethological approach.' *Biological Reviews 81*, 02, 183–205.

Wise, R.A. (2006) 'Role of brain dopamine in food reward and reinforcement.' *Philosophical Transactions of the Royal Society of London B: Biological Sciences 361*, 1471, 1149–1158.

HOW A CLINICAL PSYCHOLOGIST AND A COMPARATIVE PSYCHOLOGIST SEE THE WORLD

How a clinical psychologist sees the world

Dr. Daniel Marston

I have been a practicing clinical psychologist for over 20 years and have worked with many patients across the spectrum of age and backgrounds in a number of different settings over the years. I teach and write but the bulk of my work has been in clinical practice. These experiences have allowed me to develop a worldview based on essential questions psychologists often ask. These include questions like, "Why do people do the things they do?" and "How do we get people to change?"

Theoretical perspectives

When you are a psychologist interested in comparative psychology, and particularly evolutionary theory, you are often directed towards Freudian psychology. In my opinion, Sigmund Freud was the first, and still the most prominent, psychological theorist to emphasize evolution in his theories. In part because of their similar timelines,

Freud made quite a bit of reference to Darwin with references in several of his major theories to evolutionary concepts and particularly to the behaviors and development of primates. His concept of the id referenced the behaviors of primates and his concept of the superego referenced the group authority primates developed throughout primate evolution. Deference to group norms, again a necessity that develops for individuals throughout evolutionary processes, also necessitates the suppression of sexual urges that is at the base of the famous oedipal complex theory.

But Freudian theory also, in my opinion, makes too many assumptions about evolution and animal behaviors. After reading a good deal of modern comparative psychology research, I found it difficult to give much weight to any psychoanalytic theorist, Freud or others, and to the evolutionary and animal psychology concepts they address. There was just too much of a generalization of concepts. Evolutionary processes and animal psychology topics were addressed as if they were the same across different species and for different individuals within those species. When Freud writes about the behaviors of apes, as a way of trying to illustrate the oedipal complex theory, I am left asking, "What type of apes?" and "What type of environment?" This is also true of other psychoanalytic authors who make reference to evolutionary concepts. There is just not enough focus in these theories on different, individualized factors to allow for drawing parallels between animal psychology and human psychology.

For me, behavior theory provides a much more practical view of how comparative psychology research and evolutionary theory can help us understand human functioning. This is because behavior theory provides much more of an emphasis on the interactions between behaviors and environment. There is much more of an opportunity to take into account individual factors rather than see human behaviors as the result of one general evolutionary process. In my opinion, behavior theory takes into consideration many more different factors that could account for why different individuals respond to similar events in different ways. When you review the different types of animals studied in comparative psychology, this is in line with the realities of animal behaviors. Different species respond to the same types of situations in different ways, and different animals within same species respond in different ways depending on environment and experiential factors. Evolution plays a role for the species, but then those more individualized factors enter into the equation as well. Understanding human actions from a behavioral perspective provides, for me, a much more complicated and inter-related view of human behaviors than I have seen anywhere else.

Cognitive theory also played a significant role in my understanding of human behaviors. There is a wide range of cognitive theories associated with comparative psychology as well, and this adds another level of complexity to understanding human and animal behaviors. There is no need to think of the brain, mind, consciousness or any other aspect of mental processes as a "black box" where there is no understanding of what happens once a human or nonhuman animal has an experience, where sensory material is taken in and then the individual processes that material. And, like behavioral aspects, these cognitive processes have a large number of individual factors that enter into their influences. Even though there is a different understanding of these cognitive processes for human and nonhuman animals there still is evidence of the intersection between environmental, evolutionary, and individual factors that enter into understanding what happens on cognitive and behavioral levels. Interventions used to address behaviors can focus on making changes on both of these levels.

Cognitive–behavioural therapy

My primary focus throughout my years of practice has been in cognitive-behavioral therapy interventions. This approach is one that incorporates how a person thinks and behaves. It is the therapist's job to help the patient see the unhealthy patterns of thinking and behaviors and then to help them to learn and use healthier ones. Thinking/behavioral patterns that are unhealthy are mainly ones that are focused too much on the negative and/or are unrealistic. Actually, being overly negative is equivalent to being unrealistic from a cognitive-behavioral perspective. People suffer from clinical disorders often not because they see negative aspects to the world (that would be realistic) but when they see primarily negative aspects. One thing I often tell patients who are depressed is that the opposite of "depressed" is not "happy" but rather "balanced." Having a balanced view that allows one to see both the positive and negative aspects of their lives is one characteristic of a psychologically healthy approach to the world. Helping people see and accept the good and bad is one of the major goals of cognitive-behavioral therapy as a way of helping people become more psychologically healthy.

Identifying the behavioral and thinking patterns contributing to a psychologically unhealthy approach to life is one of the first jobs of a clinical professional. When helping patients I look for the purpose of their behaviors and thinking styles. In this way, the word "purpose" serves a primary role in what I look for when helping people to change their thinking and behavioral styles. My experience has been that every person has a reason for doing what they do. They have a reason (or "purpose") even if that reason does not make sense to other people. Whether the term is "purpose," "reason," or "function" (as in the case of functional behavioral analysis), the emphasis is always on trying to figure out what sort of outcomes the person wants and how the behaviors they use help them reach those outcomes. We are all trying to get somewhere in our lives and psychological counselors and therapists often provide direction or guidance to help people find healthy paths to their goals.

When I was in graduate school I was first exposed to the work of Albert Ellis. I actually heard quite a bit about him during my early graduate training when he came to lecture at the South Florida campus where I attended graduate school. Albert Ellis had a reputation for being rather blunt and, when he was at my campus, he did not disappoint. He was very blunt when explaining his therapy approach and his general view of the world. His cognitive-behavioral therapy approaches emphasized the need to help patients recognize and accept that there is no such thing as "have to" or "should" when it comes to behaviors. You may not like the outcomes of your behaviors but it is not correct to say that your behaviors "have to" or "should" be a certain way. As the theory goes, if you recognize that there is no one way your behavior has to be then you can become more comfortable with yourself and your choices. You have control over your behaviors and ways of thinking. People tend to feel less distressed about their behaviors when they accept that those behaviors result from choices they make rather than something forced upon them.

Ellis's work added an important component to my view of the world and, specifically, my view of human behavior. I recognized up until that point that behaviors had a purpose even if it was not always clear to the individual what that purpose might be. Certainly Freud's work emphasized that behaviors had purposes and meaning even if the individual was not conscious of what they were. In psychoanalytic theory, unconscious processes often direct individuals towards goals about which they are often unaware. This is an example of how purpose is a major factor when considering behaviors for all major psychological theories. Ellis's work really emphasized the importance of helping people recognize they are often making choices in their behaviors and that they do not have to make only certain choices. People have the freedom to make their own choices but they also have to deal with the consequences of those choices. This is an important part of helping patients change their lives in more psychologically healthy directions.

Purposeful behaviors

Behaviors have purposes. That is the way the world works. There are consequences resulting from behaviors and people have to deal with those consequences. What often tends to create emotional distress is when people expect that their behaviors have to turn out a certain way. When people expect that the outcomes of their behaviors are required to be a certain way they tend to develop anger, depression, anxiety, or general feelings of emotional distress. These are all factors that contribute to significant mental health issues. When the prevalence of mental health problems increases, this tends to reflect an increase in expectations that people have to act a certain way or that their decisions must lead to definite results. When people are given the freedom to make their own choices about how they want their lives to turn out, they tend to have less emotional distress. This helps them deal more effectively with the unpredictability of life. You have an easier time accepting that you often cannot control what happens in life when you also accept that you can modify your choices as situations dictate. You are not required to make certain choices in every situation. Or, put another way, there are very few "have to's" and "shoulds" that are locked in for every individual in every situation. This is my general worldview of how the world works and tends to be in line with many cognitive and behavioral theories.

Patients often present to therapy with feelings of being unwell due in large part to their expectations that their lives should be different from how they are turning out or how they have turned out. People often present to therapy expecting that they will be told exactly what they should do to make their lives turn out the way that they should. One thing that most surprises people in therapy is when I present to them the concept that it is entirely up to them how they want their lives to turn out. It is not that what they have done is necessarily acceptable but, rather, that an outcome is not necessarily unacceptable just because situations did not turn out a certain way. When people are faced with the reality that there are a number of different options for how their lives turn out this is often not a viewpoint that is easy to accept. People often want to believe that situations have to turn out a certain way even if it means that they punish themselves for not taking their lives in that direction. Therapy often presents them with the necessity of deciding how they want their lives to turn out, even if that decision is different from what others might expect should be the case. What makes that decision tougher is that they also are required to accept that there will be consequences they have to accept for their decisions leading to certain outcomes. Patients often have faced few situations where they have allowed themselves to accept that their lives do not necessarily have to turn out a certain way.

But what leads people to decide how they want their lives to turn out? They may not have to be locked in to what they or others expect things "should" or "have to" be, but there may not be clarity in what direction they want to follow. Patients often turn to therapists and counselors, once they have established that there are few "have to's" in this world, to help them decide what direction they really want to choose for their lives. They want to find ways to make their lives feel important. They also want to find ways to make their lives meaningful.

In my opinion, people primarily look for meaning in their lives. Often times when people expect that their lives need to go in a certain direction it is because they have come to expect that this is where they will find meaning. One important step for people I work with in therapy is helping them decide how they will bring meaning into their lives. This is more complicated that it first appears to many people because it often involves stepping over what they had come to expect should be where they find meaning. Again, you can see here the complicated nature of the word "should" when it comes to human behavior. People often put themselves down because they are not taking their lives in the directions that others have told them should be the case. When individuals learn how to find where they truly expect to find meaning, they find a path to decrease their level of dissatisfaction. They decrease their dissatisfaction with themselves and with their lives. This is not to say that they will not choose the same path to meaning that important people have told them is important. It is just that the whole process becomes healthier when it is the individual making clear they are choosing the path to meaning on their own rather than choosing a path just because someone else told them that they should.

Eclectic view of therapy

It is not difficult to see that the view of human behavior I have presented so far is one that combines cognitive, behavioral, dynamic, and existential approaches. It is an eclectic mix of the different major psychotherapy approaches. A combination of all these approaches is important as it takes the different aspects of their worldviews into a more comprehensive view of how people act and how people change. Helping people change starts with an understanding of how they likely view the world, and specifically how they view their place in the world. People want to find meaning but are often stuck in their expectations that their lives should start off in a different direction. Their behaviors serve the purpose of reaching goals but can become problematic when the goals are ones that others set for them. People very often do not even recognize how they are being influenced by what others have said and done because they are not still conscious of the impact of others on their behaviors. Behaviors serve the goal of heading a person in a certain direction but they often are not aware of what direction they are heading. They also may not even be aware of why they chose that particular direction in the first place. Psychotherapy offers them the opportunity to become more aware of where they are heading, why they are heading that way, and what they can do to make course corrections.

Psychological therapy and psychological counseling help people find meaningful directions in their lives and understand the "purpose" of their behaviors. Finding a way of directing people in meaningful ways is helped considerably, in my opinion, by comparative psychology research. Humans and animals are similar in having "purpose," however one chooses to define that term, in their lives and in their behaviors. Human behaviors serve a purpose in the same way that animal behaviors serve a purpose. Animals also are not necessarily aware (although they may be) of why they are heading in a certain direction or what purposes their behaviors serve. There is a function to all behaviors; and individuals, whether they are human or nonhuman animals, function best when their behaviors head them towards beneficial and meaningful goals. Animals and humans are all trying to bring meaning into their lives even if the meaning is related exclusively to survival.

To understand behaviors in a global worldview it is important to note that "survival," as described in evolutionary theory, is not necessarily survival of the individual. When animals seek the opportunity to reproduce, this reproduction does not mean that they survive as individuals. Their search for reproduction opportunities comes from a goal of survival of the species. When you look at behaviors in this way, you see that human and nonhuman animals have similar desires for meaningful behaviors. They are both looking to reach goals outside of themselves. They are not just looking for something that will benefit them, but are looking often for goals that will impact others. Both human and nonhuman animals seek behaviors that not only serve specific goals but also serve meaningful goals. Survival of the species, which benefits the species rather than the individual, is important both for human and nonhuman animals.

Behaviors serve the purpose of helping individuals reach meaningful goals. This is true both for human and nonhuman animals. To me, a global worldview is one that takes into account that all creatures seek to reach goals that are meaningful to them. And, in many ways, those goals relate to the survival of their species. Humans may not always describe it in this way, but they do often describe their search for meaning as being one that involves finding benefits not only for themselves but also for their children and their children's children. Human beings seek to do things that can make the world a better place for themselves and their offspring. This is something that is also true of animals, although they are not able to verbalize this way of thinking. But their behaviors show that their goals are ones that benefit not only themselves but also their families and other members of their species.

When you look at behaviors serving the function of helping individuals reach meaningful goals then the purpose of therapeutic interventions becomes clearer. As a therapist I am trying to help individuals work towards identified goals that are meaningful to them but also help them verbalize to themselves why these goals are meaningful. This helps the person not only to learn from the experience of trying to develop purposeful goals but also to develop the skills to help them develop additional goals for their lives. And then this allows the individual to look at their behaviors in the context of what sorts of goals they are trying to reach. When they are trying to move in a positive direction then having meaningful goals presents a useful context for analyzing their behaviors. This also allows for discussion about how an individual does not necessarily need to take the definition of what is meaningful from other people. Individuals can take input from others but tend to function at their best when they are making their own decisions about what is meaningful for them.

I find it interesting that there are more individual differences throughout the animal kingdom than might be initially apparent. Animal psychology has often been presented over the centuries as being very mechanical, where all members of the species are following the same pattern and dealing with the same environmental factors. But when you review the animal literature it is much more apparent that there is a considerable amount of individuality in how specific animals are dealing with situations. I particularly found it interesting to read some of the evolutionary material about depression and find that there are times where individual animals may determine that a fight is not worthwhile. What was particularly noteworthy about this to me was that animals are not necessarily correct when making decisions about whether a fight is worthwhile. Just because the animal reaches a conclusion to not continue with the fight does not mean that they could not have won that confrontation. There are a considerable amount of individual factors that enter into whether the animal decides it is time to fight. There also are a number of different factors that balance out the likelihood that the animal will determine that a fight is not worthwhile and the likelihood that the animal could actually have won that fight.

So, all over the world there are individuals of different species who are trying to make their way. They are trying to find the most effective ways to bring meaning into their lives and to do things that they deem important. They are making their individual decisions and finding their own ways to accomplish goals. These may be goals of which they are aware or they may be goals that are directing them on some other level. Call it survival instinct. Call it unconscious. Or just call it motivation. These are the forces that direct individuals through their lives. Human and nonhuman animals follow these forces in a way that directs their behaviors. Many times individuals have some sense of success in where these forces take them, but often times they do not lead them in an effective direction. There are obstacles that stand in the way that may relate to individual characteristics or environmental factors. For humans this could be emotional immaturity, intellectual disability, physical limitations, or poor motivation. For nonhuman animals this could be physical weakness, poor instinct, limited intelligence, or sensory impairment. All of these are factors that can stand in the way of individuals finding their way towards the goals they set.

Meaningfulness in human and nonhuman animals

My view of the world is one where people are trying the best ways to make their lives meaningful. They may find meaning in advancing their own interests or in helping their families. Usually what they find meaningful is helping themselves, their families, and their communities. This is where I see the most similarity with animal behaviors. That may be surprising to some because many people do not think of animal behavior as meaningful. But their behaviors, even if they seem basic and simplistic to humans, are clearly meaningful to the animals themselves. Because animals seek to do what they find meaningful just as much as humans do. Their definition of "meaning" may reflect primarily survival instinct but that does not make it any less meaningful. Humans also have goals they find meaningful that other humans may find too basic. Just because the goals for meaning are simplistic does not make them any less important.

When we look at animals working for the survival of themselves and their species we are looking at the search for meaning. And that is where the behavioral and cognitive aspects of those behaviors really come to light. Throughout this book we have looked at different behaviors and behavioral goals. None of these would make any sense if the animals were not looking to do something they find meaningful. It would just be random behaviors with no particular direction if meaningful goals, developed over centuries of evolution, were not at the heart of those behaviors. There is a direct goal to animal behaviors and human behaviors. We seek to head in a meaningful direction that brings purpose to ourselves and to others. That is the focus of how I see the world and the focus of my clinical work.

On a side note, psychologists also look for meaning. We look for meaning in our work in terms of helping others and advancing the profession. Our search for meaning in our work often involves trying to find ways to make the best use of what we do. I know that my hope for this book is that it will provide a way to advance the work of both comparative psychologists and clinical professionals. Comparative psychologists, by allowing another way to show why their work is important. Clinical professionals, by providing another resource for understanding behavioral process and behavioral change. This follows from a view of the world where the most important work is that which advances understanding and helps people help others. This is what we are looking to do with this book.

How a comparative psychologist sees the world
Dr. Terry Maple

As a comparative psychologist who specializes in the behavior of exotic wildlife, I've lived in two distinct worlds: the academic world as a professor in the School of Psychology at the Georgia Institute of Technology; and in the zoo world as the chief executive of two zoological parks in Atlanta and West Palm Beach, Florida. In many ways I have functioned as an applied psychologist as I have always been interested in the helping professions. As a graduate student I worked in state hospitals and studied behavior modification principles under the tutelage of clinical psychologists who specialized in behavior therapies. My principal interest in those days was human aggression and war; mankind's irrational inhumanity to others. As I studied this issue, I was equally influenced by Skinnerian psychology and ethology. Even today, I find these schools of thought to be complementary and synergistic.

As I began to specialize in nonhuman primate behavior at the California Primate Research Center, I conducted my doctoral research on attachment, separation, and social deprivation. The work we carried out in Davis, California, was shaped by my graduate mentor's apprenticeship with the iconic Harry F. Harlow at the University of Wisconsin. As a young member of Harlow's national network in developmental psychobiology (and his academic grandson), I worked on projects utilizing monkey models of mental health. In fact, our research, in collaboration with specialists at the UC Davis Medical School, was supported by grants from the National Institute of Mental Health. All of us enjoyed a deep sense of purpose in our work. We knew that the objective study of animals would generate insights into the greater complexity of human behavior. We aimed to contribute to a kinder, gentler world. In fact, there are many generalizations from the study of monkeys and apes that help us understand human nature, but I soon discovered that behavior pathology in primates was so widespread in primate centers and zoos that many of my observations and ideas could be applied to create a better life for the animals themselves.

A Darwinian perspective

The ideas of Charles Darwin have broad application in all of psychology, not just clinical psychology. In his published work Darwin made extensive use of observations from his corresponding collaborators. He had little experience observing primates, but took notice of their behavior in the many citations in *The Descent of Man* (1871) and *Expression of the Emotions in Man and Animals* (1872). His illustrations of primate facial expressions are still accurate today, but his interpretations were flawed. For example, the primate facial grimace (indicating fear) was interpreted as a joyful grin. Many of my colleagues regard Darwin as the starting point of comparative psychology, as he demonstrated a keen interest in animal behavior and found many similarities in human and animal behavior. In my primate professional network, we try to celebrate Darwin's birthday every year. He was born on the same day (February 12) and in the same year (1809) as Abraham Lincoln. Entire books have celebrated the enduring influence of his ideas (Ekman 1982). Both ontogenetic and phylogenetic history shape our behavior and these forces are often better studied by observing animals. Homologous behavior reflects linkage to a common ancestor. For example, human facial expressions and bodily postures are highly similar to those of our close phylogenetic relatives the great apes. The threatening stare common to gorillas and people is an example of homology. In the ape taxon (*Pongidae*), however, there are also unique specializations. Gorillas, but not chimpanzees or orangutans, beat their chests as an aggressive display. When humans do this in combat sports it is an example of imitation. The study of emotional expression in nonhuman primates has important implications for our understanding of human emotions.

European ethology

During the 1960s, students of my generation were fired up about the Vietnam war. If you were in college at the time you couldn't avoid heated discussions about the folly of war. I kept looking for answers in textbooks on history, sociology, and political theory but nothing seemed to explain human warfare. Finally, in my first course on animal behavior I learned about the work of the European ethologists. *On Aggression*, a book written by Konrad Lorenz, caught my eye and I couldn't put it down. One of Lorenz' key discoveries was the finding that fighting between members of the same species rarely ended in death. Venomous snakes did not use their venom on a conspecific combatant. Wolves never bite the necks of another wolf; in fact defeated wolves present their neck and the victor stops the attack. Animals recognize signals of appeasement and settle their disputes without the use of their lethal weapons. People are different. Fighters are trained to fight to the death and our big brains help us to develop technology that keeps us from ever getting a close look at our adversary. Bombs from a long distance kill as if there were no human beings where the bombs fell. In the end, we are defeated by our big brains. There are submissive gestures that ought to work to inhibit attack by other humans, but we ignore them or overcome them. The ethologists concluded that human beings are the most dangerous species on the earth. Clinical psychologists with a knowledge of human expression are able to detect deficiencies in such emotions as empathy. Deficits in nonverbal communication may be an indication of behavioral pathology (Ekman and Friesen 1974).

Human facial expressions are universal. The scientist best known for his lifelong study of nonverbal communication is clinical psychologist Paul Ekman (1993). Ekman demonstrated the universality of expression in his studies of a Stone Age culture in New Guinea. He developed a tool (Ekman and Friesen 1971) for measuring facial movement known as the Facial Action Coding System (FACS). Computer-based software has enabled business and clinical applications of this system. Ekman's studies of deception have helped to detect strong negative feelings associated with suicidal tendencies in patients trying to hide them. Ekman and his group have enjoyed some success training others to use specialized technology to detect micro-expressions. I first met Ekman in 1974 at the Langley Porter Institute in San Francisco when I lectured there on interspecific communication in macaques and baboons. His evolutionary approach to human communication required that he keep up with the literature on primate behavior. Thus animal studies continue to be relevant to Ekman's clinical and neuropsychology research. Ekman's career is a fine example of the deep synergy between comparative and clinical psychology.

Environmental psychology

One of my mentors in graduate school, Robert Sommer, introduced me to the field of environmental psychology. He coined the terms hard and soft architecture to describe how the structural environment influenced behavior. Some of the hard environments he studied were airports, mental hospitals, prisons, and zoos. In an important paper published in the magazine *Natural History* he asked the question, "What do we learn at the zoo?" Sommer (1974) According to Sommer, visitors to zoos were exposed to abnormally behaving animals that were psychologically damaged by isolating, inflexible, inappropriate, concrete and steel cages that produced stereotyped behavior and other deprivation acts including catatonia, repetitive rocking, self-injurious behavior, and hyper-aggression. These were the worst kind of lessons for zoo visitors as wild animals do not behave this way. By extension, Sommer had determined that hard architecture was hard on people and animals. My exposure to Sommer's research led me to focus on zoos as institutions that needed reform. After a career in which I advocated soft architecture and other conversions to naturalistic exhibition, I did my best to introduce revolutionary change in zoos and aquariums.

In 1989 when Sommer looked back on the fifteen years since the publication of his book *Tight Spaces* (1974), he observed that of all the hard institutions he studied, only zoos had significantly improved. He attributed these improvements to the willingness of zoo managements to apply the findings of behavioral scientists. Given that environmental psychology is largely focused on human environments, it is fascinating that this field had such profound effects on quality of life for animals. In this case, it was a human model that contributed so much to advancing animal welfare.

Flight from the animal laboratory

When I was in graduate school, radical behaviorism dominated academic psychology. Every graduate program offered an experimental laboratory where students trained rodents or pigeons on learning tasks. This was a fundamental rite of passage for students of psychology. Even clinical psychologists studied Skinner and many clinicians were trained in Skinnerian behavior modification. However, the *zeitgeist* began to shift in the 1970s when cognitive psychology began to dominate. Behaviorism was criticized by proponents of cognitive psychology and ethology because it could not explain many complex behaviors, including language. Ethologists discovered biological constraints on learning that defied the laws of behavior as defined by Skinner and his collaborators. For example, animals were wired to learn according to innate tendencies. Two of Skinner's students, Marian and Keller Breland (Breland and Breland 19611), learned about this phenomenon when they tried to train domestic animals on operant tasks that were easy for pigeons but harder for pigs and chickens. When pigs were trained to place a token in a slot, they resisted the task because they were inclined to root the token. The Brelands had to find tasks that were appropriate to the biology of the subjects they selected. As psychology shifted its interests and the federal government began to shift its funding, other factors forced changes in college curricula. Concern about animal rights and the increased cost of facilities' improvements and security made animal labs too costly to maintain. When animal psychologists began to retire, they were not replaced and animal programs began to disappear in America. This trend and the shift from macro- to microbiology produced a generation of students who rarely encountered an intact, living laboratory animal. It is unusual for biology departments to offer courses or labs in herpetology, mammalogy, or ornithology today.

Applied behavior analysis in the zoo

During my first two years in graduate school I worked in the California state hospital system for clinicians with backgrounds in behavior modification. I saw firsthand the value of operant conditioning in settings where patients were severely impaired. My clinical advisor was an expert in the "conditioned emotional response" and I found this to be a useful construct in dealing with fear and aggression. In fact, as a college baseball player, I applied the CER paradigm in attempting to understand my own behavior when I entered a hitting slump. Somehow fear was generated when I came up to bat and my emotional response was interfering with my ability to hit. I had to learn to manage fear by visualizing success. This was the beginning of my interest in behavior change. My graduate advisor at the time took an interest in the student athletes he mentored and he eventually became a sports psychologist working with the U.S. Women's Olympic Volleyball program. Had the field been fully developed when I was a student I might have gone in this direction, but I have retained a strong interest in the field. At Georgia Tech I taught an occasional class on the subject to prominent student athletes including Nomar Garciaparra, Jason Varitek, John Salley, David Duval, and Kim Whisenhunt, each of whom went on to achieve great success in professional sports. In these classes I always stressed the importance of conditioned fear and visualization.

A young colleague of mine, Valerie Segura, whom I first met while lecturing on the west coast, began to collaborate with me in 2013. She is a certified behavior analyst who worked with developmentally disabled populations and contacted me to explore opportunities in zoos. Our discussions led to a paper that we co-authored for the journal *The Behavior Analyst* (Maple and Segura 2015). In this paper we made the case for upgrading training in zoos and aquariums through the application of applied behavior analytic techniques. We observed that zoos and aquariums were more dependent on training than at any other time in the history of these institutions. However, the commitment to training arrived at a time when only a few behavior analysts were working in these settings. Thus, training was left to trainers who learned from other trainers. Without academic background in behavior analysis, training lacks the sophistication necessary to refine schedules of reinforcement and rarely are training regimes evaluated or published. In our publication we argued that it is necessary to build partnerships between academic behavior analysts, their students, zoo biologists, veterinarians, and other members of the animal care team. Veterinarians are drawn to training because it enables them to avoid the dangers of chemical immobilization. Large animals can now be trained to give blood, endure the tightness of a blood pressure cuff, accept ultrasound examinations, and present body parts for medical or dental inspections. Our ability to medically intervene with captive wildlife is vastly improved due to the efficacy of operant conditioning methods. I believe we are opening doors for students who want to work with animals to study and treat both wild and captive animals that are suffering. Applied behavior analysis may also be useful in promoting social cohesion and promoting social development in a variety of species. Applied behavior analysis is a promising tool for the advancement of psychological wellbeing in people and animals.

The empirical zoo

As a psychologist with an interest in zoo animals, I discovered that many decisions were made without a shred of evidence to guide the decision. Zoos too often relied on traditional practices and not necessarily best practices to manage animals. Although a few zoos hired specialists with scientific training, it seemed to me that a scientific foundation would lead to better decisions and a better quality of life for all animals. In graduate school I learned about the pioneering career of Dr. Heini Hediger, who served as director of three Swiss zoos while simultaneously working as a professor of ethology. I visited Hediger in Zurich in 1988 and interviewed him on videotape (Maple 2014). He described his lifelong interest in the psychology of zoo animals and his belief that zoos should be fundamentally objective. He published more than any other zoo director and wrote some important books that still resonate today (Hediger 1950, 1969). I admired Hediger's approach so much that I organized a task force to study scientific zoo biology when I served as President of the Association of Zoos and Aquariums in 1999. The contributed papers were published together in the journal *Zoo Biology* (Maple and Lindburg 2008). In my administrative career at Zoo Atlanta and the Palm Beach Zoo, spanning twenty-four years, I strongly advocated scientific institutional management and evidence-based planning and continue to mentor other zoo directors who see the value in this approach.

Wildlife wellness

Harlow's pioneering studies of socially deprived monkeys led to discoveries about the nature of love. As an experimental psychologist he was unique in turning animal models on their head. He once said that he never studied a phenomenon in monkeys that wasn't based on human research. Although he has been vilified for the suffering he inflicted on monkeys, his findings actually led to extensive reforms in zoos. Harlow's monkey research also contributed to a theory of parenting known as "attachment parenting," demonstrating the importance of close contact between mother and offspring. My wife and I raised our three daughters based on these principles (I called it "natural parenting" as discussed in Maple and Warren-Leubecker 1983). I've met many other parents with backgrounds in primatology and anthropology who were similarly guided by these ideas.

Harlow's first graduate student at Wisconsin was Abraham Maslow, better known for his role in the founding of humanistic psychology. According to Clara Harlow (personal communication), who knew him in graduate school at Wisconsin, Maslow didn't want to carry out an experimental dissertation. Instead, Maslow saw an opportunity to conduct an observational study since Harlow wasn't provided a lab in his early years in Madison. Harlow and Maslow conducted their research on a group of rhesus monkeys at the Vilas Park Zoo, and

Maslow later published research on his studies of monkeys at Vilas Park Zoo and the Bronx Zoo in New York City (Maslow 1940). Maslow's intellectual focus on the hierarchy of needs was shaped by his early research on nonhuman primates. A comparative psychologist trained by C.P. Stone at Stanford, Harlow succeeded in mentoring Maslow on empirical methods and this is revealed in Maslow's future publications. Maslow's clinical interests were greatly influenced by his formative exposure to comparative psychology. For example, in 1942 he published a paper in the journal *Psychiatry* entitled "A comparative approach to the problem of destructiveness." Maslow's successful career (he was elected President of the American Psychological Association in 1968) demonstrates the value of an empirical foundation for the practice of clinical psychology. Furthermore, his work with Harlow is a good example of how comparative psychology provides deep insight into the most complex forms of human behavior.

Maslow's contributions to the field of humanistic psychology were useful in formulating the construct of wellness, which I have characterized as an expansion of animal welfare. Humanistic psychology was also known as the "human potential movement" and it sought to elevate people to attain optimal levels of mental, physical, and spiritual health embodied in Maslow's construct of self-actualization. Such people don't just cope with life; they thrive. My recent work in zoos and aquariums attempts to find ways for animals to reach a state of optimal welfare or wellness. Wildlife wellness is based on our knowledge of human wellness so the human model is once again successfully applied to animals. The fundamental difference between welfare and wellness is that welfare is minimal and regulatory, while wellness is optimal and aspirational. There are no limits to our aspirations for personal wellness. This is a new way of thinking about animals living in zoos and aquariums.

Teaching animal behavior

Teaching animal behavior to psychology undergraduates provides a deeper understanding of human behavior. One of my most popular lectures was built around nonverbal behavior. I reproduced a collection of images showing the evolution of primate facial expressions including illustrations from Darwin's classic *Expression of the Emotions in Man and Animals* (1872). To render this talk even more compelling I found photographs of athletes expressing what I call "the thrill of victory, and the agony of defeat." These images illustrate human emotional displays in an entertaining context and introduce students to the emerging field of evolutionary psychology. Because monkeys and apes are fellow members of the primate order, students who major in the helping professions, medicine, nursing, or counseling and clinical psychology usually find it useful to learn as much as possible about the biological underpinnings of human emotions. Recognizing and deciphering nonverbal behavior is also instructive to young people who must negotiate tricky social relationships. Clinical psychology can also be taught from a comparative perspective, and the observation skills cultivated through the study of animals make us keen observers of our own kind. The best therapists are perceptive to a fault, and these attributes are sharpened through systematic observation of another species. Careful studies of chimpanzees and gorillas have demonstrated that these close relatives of human beings are capable of self-awareness and empathy. Other species such as elephants and orcas have also exhibited emotions akin to empathy in responding to injured conspecifics. We no longer underestimate wildlife, who are more similar to humans than we ever imagined.

Why I chose animals

When I was in high school I was elected to serve as student body president. As I endured the slings and arrows of adolescent politics, I began to think that I was more of a statesman than a politician. In college I dreamed about entering the Foreign Service so I could become an ambassador for my country. My disappointment in humanity in the turbulent 1960s led me to investigate the science of psychobiology and by focusing on animal behavior it could be argued that I ultimately became an ambassador for wildlife. Although my mentors recognized my potential as a clinician, I was drawn to the science rather than the practice of psychology. My innate people skills have actually helped me to solve complex environmental problems. Most animal problems can be solved, but people inadvertently or purposefully get in the way of workable solutions, so training in psychology is an appropriate background for individuals who enter the field of wildlife conservation.

Looking at the planet from a distance, I see a fully integrated natural world where humankind is part of nature and the one being with the capacity to protect all others. With this in mind, I will continue to use the comprehensive tools of psychological science and practice to build a better world for every living thing. I am a comparative psychologist with the compassion of a clinician.

References

Breland, K. and Breland, M. (1961) 'The misbehavior of organisms.' *American Psychologist 16*, 681–684.

Ekman, P. (1982) 'Methods for Measuring Facial Action.' In K.R. Scherer and P. Ekman (eds) *Handbook of Methods in Nonverbal Behavior Research*. New York: Cambridge University Press.

Ekman, P. (1993 'Facial expression and emotion.' *American Psychologist 48*, 4, 384–392.

Ekman, P. and Friesen, W.V. (1971) 'Constants among cultures in the face and emotion.' *Journal of Personality and Social Psychology 17*, 2, 124–129.

Ekman, P. and Friesen, W.V. (1974) 'Detecting deception from the body or face.' *Journal of Personality and Social Psychology 29*, 3, 288–298.

Hediger, H. (1950) *Wild Animals in Captivity*. London: Butterworth.

Hediger, H. (1969) *Man and Animal in the Zoo*. London: Routledge and Kegan Paul.

Maple, T.L. (2014) 'Commentary: Elevating the priority of zoo animal welfare – the chief executive as an agent of reform.' *Zoo Biology 33*, 1, 1–7.

Maple, T.L. and Lindburg, D.G. (2008) 'Empirical zoo: opportunities and challenges to research in zoos and aquariums.' *Special Issue of Zoo Biology 27*, 6, 431–504.

Maple, T.L. and Segura, V. (2015) 'Advancing behavior analysis in zoos and aquariums.' *The Behavior Analyst 38*, 1, 77–91.

Maple, T.L. and Warren-Leubecker, A. (1983) 'Variability in the Parental Conduct of Captive Great Apes.' In M.D. Reite and N.G. Caine (eds) *Child Abuse: The Nonhuman Primate Data*. New York: Alan R. Liss, Inc.

Maslow, A.H. (1940) 'Dominance-quality and social behavior in infra-human primates.' *Journal of Social Psychology 11*, 313–324.

Maslow, A.H. (1942) 'A comparative approach to the problem of destructiveness.' *Psychiatry 5*, 517–522.

Sommer, R. (1974) *Tight Spaces*. Englewood Cliffs, NJ: Prentice-Hall.

Chapter 10

CONCLUSION

In this final chapter we look at the future of comparative psychology. We address four of the main comparative psychology areas covered in modern scholarship: group dynamics, behavioral analysis, cognitive neuroscience, and evolutionary psychology. These are areas that are likely to continue making up major proportions of research studies and academic publications over the next several decades. We summarize recent research studies (all within a few years of this book's publication) and then look at what their findings might mean for clinicians. These are research studies that did not necessarily fit into any of the specific psychological areas discussed in previous chapters. And we cannot say for sure that our conclusions about what these findings might mean for clinicians will end up being accurate as more studies are conducted. What we can say is that these studies provide some interesting insights into where comparative psychology is going and some interesting things to consider with regard to what the field might offer clinicians in the future.

Group dynamics

In their article on group fairness, Santos *et al.* (2015) stated that human beings "...are truly singular in the extent to which they resort to collective action." Collective action is evident throughout the animal world but is seen in more prominent and more complex ways among humans. This level of complexity is due primarily to the wide variety of situations where group action is involved. Comparative psychology research provides material important for understanding group dynamics among species. A review of comparative psychology research shows that group dynamics is important for all species and that there do seem to be similarities in terms of how groups work across many different species. As the field of comparative psychology becomes even more complex (in terms of addressing many more species) and more detailed (in terms of addressing many more different types of social behaviors) we find more material that can help understand group dynamics across different species. Looking at different species in different ways helps us to understand the complexities of how social behaviors work.

In this section we look at studies providing a view of how group dynamics has been addressed recently across comparative psychology scholars. This material is of potential interest to clinicians because it addresses a topic that is fundamental to understanding families, friendships, peer groups, and work environments. Many clinical issues become prominent only when seen in the context of group situations. For example, individuals who have problems with anger management certainly may cause difficulties for themselves when they are aggressive alone, but tend to have even more significant difficulties related to anger when they act out in group situations. It is that social aspect of aggression that tends to makes the behaviors stand out. Understanding group dynamics is essential in order for clinicians to be prepared for understanding how to help people address problems. We are looking in this section at material not covered in previous chapters, in part because it does not relate specifically to any particular condition. But group dynamics relates to the totality of contexts in which any of the clinical problems discussed throughout this book arise.

Strandburg-Peshkin *et al.* (2015) studied group dynamics in baboons so as to understand processes by which group consensus is reached. This is an essential part of group dynamics in terms of addressing how groups reach important decisions. Studying baboons has particular importance for understanding humans because baboons, much like humans, form stable groups with stratified social standings. They have the types of social complications that are common among humans and other primates. There are many types of different social groupings throughout the animal world but the social systems used by baboons are very similar to those used by humans. These authors specifically looked at how groups of baboons reached a consensus about moving in certain directions. They found that the ways in which baboon groups moved depended largely on how much difference existed between two choices. Specifically, if there was more than a 90 degree angle between the two directions that group directors were trying to move groups in then the baboons tended to choose one specific choice over another. But if there was less than a 90 degree difference between the choices then the baboons in the group tended to compromise and follow what was pretty much the average between the two choices.

It is interesting to put this information into the context of human decision-making. There are many examples of how humans seem much more rigid and definite in their choices when there are more differences between the choices. For example, political decision-making among humans particularly comes to mind. Political parties are often accused of trying to emphasize differences between groups as a way of forcing people to choose one over the other. This research on baboons supports that this is an effective strategy for primates. Trying to bring groups closer together tends to increase the likelihood that the groups will compromise. This is also research that could be useful when considering family issues or school programs. If there is a tendency for individuals to be more willing to compromise when there are less clear differences between groups, then bringing choices the groups face closer together is likely to be more effective in terms of getting those groups to reach some sort of compromise.

Chivers and Ferrari (2015) provided an interesting study on how group size relates to what tadpoles learn about predators from other tadpoles. Tadpoles are not animals with much similarity to humans but it is interesting to note how even tadpoles depend a great deal on environmental factors and group factors for improving the likelihood that they will learn important information. Specifically, this research showed that group size does not influence learning much but that the ratio of instructors to learners (called "tutors to observers" in this study) was very important. Tadpoles tended to learn this new and important information more readily when the ratio of instructors to learners was smaller. Notice how similar this finding is to educational research showing that students tend to learn better when class sizes are smaller.

Griffin and Guez (2015) studied group dynamics as it related to problem-solving. They hypothesized that animal groups tend to be better than individual animals at handling problems. Two reasons for this are that groups as a whole are more vigilant (because members can share time they look out for predators) and larger groups are more likely to have individuals with needed expertise. They specifically studied situations where animals needed to look out for and fight predators. They found that groups tend to be better than individual animals for solving problems and that vigilance and expertise are two of the main reasons why. Keeping focused and handling more complex tasks are two benefits groups provide over individuals. Results like these can help with insights about how to strengthen the benefits group membership provides.

When looking at group dynamics, the experience of being outside groups (loneliness) is also worth exploring. Cacioppo *et al.* (2015) looked at loneliness as a construct across different animal species. Group belonging, these authors propose, developed importance across evolution as a way of promoting survival and reproduction. Being alone can be dangerous for animals out in the world. This evolutionary preference for being part of the group developed along with the neurological processes for increasing vigilance and increasing psycho-motor readiness when alone. Depressive symptomology also accompanies being alone as a way of nonverbally signaling the need for support and connection. Human and nonhuman animals develop loneliness as a separate physiological and emotional state as a way of preparing for dangers associated with being alone.

This material on loneliness provides probably one of the best examples of how psycho-educational methods can be useful when incorporating comparative psychology research into clinical work. Loneliness may have developed as a protection against predators, but this does not mean that it is a protection needed these days. Notice how this material on loneliness relates to the material we discussed in the chapter on autism. Once again, we see here the emphasis on group belonging as beneficial, even if it is not actually a definite need. This also fits in with the discussions we had throughout this book about how evolutionary adaptations are not always the most beneficial for certain environments. Being alone may trigger feelings of needing to be hypervigilant and work towards group involvement, but this is not actually something that is necessary. Comparative psychology research we reviewed in the autism chapter does not support that group belonging is actually a modern human necessity, even if humans still have physiological responses when alone, triggered by a feeling of possible danger. Loneliness is not the same liability for humans as it is for animals out in the wild. Individuals who do not belong to groups can function quite well in modern society where there are private businesses (e.g. grocery stores) to provide food and public resources (e.g. police forces, fire stations) to provide safety. Educating clients on the evolutionary purpose of feelings of loneliness can provide some useful insights to help them more realistically interpret their negative feelings when they have limited group belonging.

Behavioral research with animals has shown similarities between humans and animals when it comes to addressing conflicts and problem situations. When engaged in conflicts, animals will often use different types of communication with their audience. Fedurek, Slocombe, and Zuberbühler (2015) studied chimpanzees and found that victims of aggressive acts will use two types of communication with audiences surrounding their conflicts. They will use screams and also what the authors called "waa" barks. Screams are used to try and get bystanders, usually adults or late adolescent males, to provide support while the "waa" barks are used to show a willingness to retaliate. This is similar to how humans often will respond when faced with conflicts; they will often use some way of communicating that they are willing to get into a fight and may also try to find some ways of getting people around them involved in providing support. It is interesting to note here how chimpanzees handle conflicts similarly to humans; and what will be particularly interesting in the future is to see if research supports that either of these types of approach are more effective than other types of approaches for handling conflicts.

Animals suffer many of the same effects of social conflicts as humans. Kamphuis et al. (2015) studied the impact of social conflicts on how well rats sleep. They did this to assess the impact of social conflict on sleeping patterns. Past research had shown that social defeat stress (where one animal is attacked and defeated by another animal) has a significant impact on sleep but that research was not conclusive on what caused that effect. In the Kamphuis study, NREM sleep for losers of social conflict was significantly increased following the conflict but not the NREM sleep for the winners. This increased amount of sleep was directly related to the physiological impact of losing the social conflict. Notice how this would also be consistent with what you would expect when you address that "social defeat" is one theory of depression discussed earlier in this book.

Although the Kamphuis study is not directly applicable to humans it does bring up an interesting possibility. Notice, in that study, how the impact on rats' sleep was significant after losing a conflict but that increased sleep related directly to the conflict itself. There was no intermediate factor such as feeling upset or being emotionally distraught about losing the conflict that impacted on sleep. Humans who engage in social conflicts with other humans will often suffer the same effect in terms of having increased sleep. This is often interpreted as a symptom of "feeling depressed" and explained in terms of the person withdrawing after losing a conflict. Individuals who lose conflicts are often described as "feeling depressed" and may be seen as increasing sleep as a way of dealing with that the stress.

But what if the increased sleep is not due to any sort of emotional factor but is instead due to the physiological response to losing a conflict? This would offer a different way of interpreting how people are acting following a conflict and could be significant for helping individuals bounce back after significant interpersonal difficulties. Helping individuals see that their wanting to sleep more is not necessarily some sort of negative emotional response to a conflict but is more a natural physiological reaction to the conflict itself could be helpful for clients who are trying to move their lives forward following a conflict. Again, it is too early to say from one study how this might apply to humans but it does offer a possibility of alternative ways of helping clients understand their feelings and reactions following disagreements and conflicts.

When you look at the research on animal group behaviors you do see different ways of interpreting what happens in social behaviors. Social behaviors that humans interpret as emotional responses to interactions may be more natural physiological responses triggered by social events. Feelings such as loneliness may be more of a previously necessary, but presently unnecessary, physiological response to potential dangers when apart from groups. This is the type of response that would be important for animals who live out in the wild but not necessarily important for human animals who live in domestic settings. And group membership itself may be overemphasized more than is actually necessary for humans. Helping human clients interpret their responses differently may be one of the most important benefits comparative psychology research on social behaviors offers clinicians.

Behavioral analysis

In this book's earlier chapters we looked at the history of behavior analysis as it related to comparative psychology. These fields are closely related as animals were used in large numbers of studies making up the early field of behavioral analysis. We looked at several journals that specifically addressed behavioral analysis as it applied to animals and also as it applied to direct human interventions. Behavioral analysis is interesting in that it is a field that is very complex but often in the more common application it gets rather simplified. Schools, support agencies, and treatment facilities often refer to behavior analysis primarily when talking about things such as reinforcement and punishment. There often is a rather simplistic view of what makes up behavioral interventions and this more simplified view can make behavioral interventions ineffective. Because behavior analysis is a very detailed process, there is a number of different factors to consider. When you look at recent comparative psychology research that would fit in the category of behavior analysis you see that there are a lot of different complex issues being studied. These are issues that are important for clinicians to consider so that they can give a full range of insight when providing behavioral interventions based on applied behavioral analysis.

Recent research into behavior analysis using animals has even looked into the detailed aspect of the type of materials used to measure behaviors. Cunningham, Kuhn, and Reilly (2015) looked at this issue relative to how impulsivity is measured. They specifically looked at the issue of impulsivity as measured in rats and found that the type of apparatus matters significantly when studying this issue. Two common instruments used for studying animals' impulsivity are the two-lever chamber and the T-maze. The first is an apparatus where the subject chooses one of two levers to push for reinforcement and the other is a maze where the animal subject reaches a point when they have to choose one of two directions (they reach a point shaped like a "T"). These authors found that, when used with rats, the T-maze takes longer to yield impulse choice data. This could influence significantly the outcome of studies related to impulsivity as using this measure would likely result in longer response times. There was no reason identified for why this might occur but this research shows the need for looking at whether different behavioral analysis methods might yield different results.

When you consider this study it may be that there is no clear reason why it would matter to clinicians. But we included this study as a way of looking at how even today there is still a lot of consideration about whether methods that have been used for years are the most effective means of assessing behavior. There have been many different types of measures used throughout the years for addressing different aspects of behaviors which, initially, were accepted as a way of yielding useful information. But, once methods have been in place for years, it is often important to look again at whether what they are supposed to measure is actually being measured. This allows professionals using research to make more informed decisions about the authors' findings. It also brings up interesting areas of study that can yield even more detailed information about different behavioral constructs. In the research outlined in the previous paragraph it will be interesting to see in the future why the T-maze yields such different results from the lever system.

Recent animal research has shown specifics about not only the types of apparatus used for measuring behavioral factors but, also, what factors associated with reinforcement schedules are most effective. Bensemann *et al.* (2015) studied six pigeons to determine how preferences change when the rate of reinforcer changes. Most introductory behavioral courses address the different fixed interval and variable interval reinforcement behavioral schedules. But there are vast numbers of variable intervals that can be used and there are considerable unknowns about how changing intervals impacts reinforcement strengths. Pigeons in this experiment changed where they looked for reinforcement next when they recognized that the reinforcement schedule changed. These pigeons were subject to different reinforcement schedules that were changing and the authors were looking at what sort of factors influenced where they looked for the next reinforcement. Pigeons learned where they were most likely to find the next reinforcer, based on different reinforcement cues showing where the next reinforcer might be, rather than keeping their focus on where they had just received reinforcement. This is an example of studies addressing the complexities related to how different types of reinforcement schedules impact behaviors and, more generally, complexities associated with behavior analysis.

Counselors working with parents who are trying to use effective behavior approaches for children can see the benefit to research addressing how reinforcement changes impact behavior. Behavioral programs tend to break down quickly when used with children and reinforcers often lose their impact as children get bored and look for reinforcement elsewhere. It is useful to consider where an individual might look for different sources of reinforcement when the impact of previous reinforcement and reinforcement schedules change. When reinforcement schedules change there is a tendency for individuals to look for signals about where they are most likely to find reinforcement next. This is the type of thing that was addressed in the study outlined in the previous paragraph. Parents need to monitor behavioral progress frequently and make sure that they are showing continued interest so that the child receives the reinforcement they want. Otherwise, children are likely to look for reinforcement elsewhere and not be consistent with a program used for too long.

"Resistance to extinction" is an important component for clinicians implementing behavioral interventions. This is the issue of how strongly subjects will respond to reinforcers over time. When reinforcement schedules have been in place for a time there is a strong tendency for reinforcement strength to lessen. Craig, Cunningham, and Shahan (2015) discussed their study of pigeons who received reinforcers through pecking behaviors. They found that, with these pigeons, their pecking rates were at high levels when the rates of reinforcement were higher. They also kept their pecking rate rather high only when a fixed rate of reinforcement was used for several days prior to any change. This type of study shows the need to keep reinforcement patterns consistent at the beginning of the treatment program and then keep the rate high, on average, even after switching to a variable rate. When changing the schedule of reinforcement, individuals running behavioral programs might also prefer to change how often the person receives reinforcement. This is not likely to be the most effective approach and, as this study suggests, it would probably be best to keep the total amount of reinforcement the same right after changing to a variable schedule and then wait to change the total amount of reinforcement until the variable schedule has been in place for some time.

Behavior analysis research over the past decade has shown the complexity of behavioral interventions, and in this chapter we have looked at just some examples of the complexity addressed in behavioral analysis research involving animals. A further example is in the study conducted by Trask and Bouton (2015) on the subject of reinforcers and extinction. They studied what happens during the extinction of the behavior and what can help increase the behavior again following extinction. They studied situations where rats learned to press levers for reinforcement, extinguished that behavior by stopping the reinforcers, and then taught the rat to show that behavior again. This is known as the "renewal effect." They found that reinforcers that were present separately when the behavior was being extinguished helped to increase the renewal effect when that reinforcer was also present during the target behavior being reinforced again. This would be applicable, for example, if a parent was using a sticker chart for a child to address behaviors but wanted to phase it out. So, the parent might start using praise instead of stickers for addressing the target behaviors that would be worked on next. If the parent then wanted to start using the sticker chart again, implementing praise as a reinforcer while also implementing the sticker chart might, according to this research, be a positive and effective approach. This is because the praise was a reinforcer used previously when the sticker chart was being phased out.

Trask and Bouton's paper shows the kind of multi-level research characteristic of behavior analysis research these days. This is a particularly useful type of research for clinicians to consider because it shows the complexity of behavioral interventions. Many professionals seem to see behavioral interventions as rather basic and involving only stimulus–reward patterns and secondary reinforcers. However, the comparative psychology reviewed in this chapter shows the breadth and complexity that behavioral analysis provides. Being familiar with this complexity can be helpful when clinicians work with families and/or other professionals who take more basic approaches to behavioral interventions.

Clinical therapists and counselors should consider that expectations of what behavior analysis can offer have been rather limited in recent decades. Beyond its contributions to treating autism and other developmental disorders, there really are few areas, clinical and otherwise, where behavior analysis is seriously discussed as a viable option for addressing behavior change. Maple and Segura (2014) discussed this issue in their article on behavior analysis in zoos. There is actually very limited use of behavioral analysis in zoos, as opposed to the use of animal trainers, despite the continuous emphasis on animal behavior in behavior analysis publications over the past 80 years. Martin (2015) addressed the potential contributions behavioral analysts can make to clinical psychology as well as addiction treatment, job safety measures, sports training, and education. And, towards the end of his career, B.F. Skinner (1987) addressed what behavioral analysis has to offer on a global scale for making the world better. Poling (2010) addressed this more specifically, citing global problems, including overpopulation, global warming, and famine, where behavioral analysis can make a major contribution.

Cognitive neuroscience

Recent cognitive neuroscience research shows how different technological advances help in studying neural mechanisms more intensely. There are a number of major neurological areas that cannot be studied because aspects of different technologies stand in the way. One example is that some neural connections can be difficult to study in rats because anesthesia, which is difficult to administer to small animals, is needed for MRI scans. Li *et al.* (2015) studied a method where carbon paste electrodes were implemented in rats and could be used to study neural connections without the use of anesthesia. They implanted these electrodes into the rats' brains and were able to use them while the rats moved around frequently. Their conclusion was that this method was effective for addressing the neural connections that otherwise could not be studied without the use of anesthesia.

Veyrac *et al.* (2015) presented in their research a new, more complex method for studying episodic recollection. This is the type of memory that involves a combination of what happened, where it happened, and the context in which it happened. It is a complex form of memory and studying it in rats is seen as an early stage for understanding it better in humans. It has been known about for decades but has been very difficult to study. Veyrac *et al.* developed a method in which rats had to remember the odor–drink associations that were provided in different locations, in different environments, and in different contexts. Use of this study method with cellular imagery showed that a specific network in the hippocampal–prefrontal cortex is involved with episodic memory recollection.

Animal cognition research also points to how cognitive systems develop. As this research area advances, there are more opportunities to look deeper into where cognitive systems start and how they develop from the earliest stages of life. Goldman and Wood (2015) studied newly hatched chicks with regard to determining whether they could recognize movements that had been in their living chambers since birth. This was a controlled environment where the object repeatedly performed three movements. Their results showed that the chicks had visually encoded the object's movements starting as soon as they developed vision and could recognize its movements in their second week of life. These results suggest the possibility that newborn visual systems can learn and recognize visual movements starting when the individual first develops visual abilities.

Haller *et al.* (2015) conducted a review of cognitive neuroscience research involving rats to understand how to help adolescents with poor social skills. They studied the impact of social contact on physiological pituitary gland–adrenocortical stress responses and found that this response was lessened in adulthood when adolescent rats were raised around more socially dominant rats. These findings support that less socially skilled adolescents were helped when they were around more socially skilled peer rats. This is the type of intervention that could be applied directly when clinicians are trying to help less socially skilled human adolescents.

Neuroscience research involving animals has often set the stage for more recent human neuroscience research. This is particularly the case with autism research, given the degree to which human autism research, particularly neuroscience research, has expanded in recent years. One example of this type of research involves cortisol levels and their relationship to stereotypic (repetitive) behaviors (Bitsika *et al.* 2015). High cortisol levels in humans with autism correlate with higher frequencies of stereotypic behaviors (Lydon *et al.* 2015). This is consistent with animal research on cortisol behaviors that has been carried out over the past decade, including research on elephants (Wilson, Bloomsmith, and Maple 2004), rhesus monkeys (Feng *et al.* 2011) and pandas (Liu *et al.* 2006).

Animal research shows the individual differences that impact behavioral processes. These differences are often assumed to be neurochemical, although much of this research has not identified specific causes. Reznikov *et al.* (2015) provided a different way of looking at PTSD through the impact of behavioral extinction. They studied the individual differences that impact on extinction, specifically extinction of anxiety responses. They looked at individual variations in anxiety responses among Sprague Dawley rats and found a subpopulation of these rats (about 25% of their sample) showing low extinction rates. This meant that these rats took significantly longer to extinguish anxiety responses than did other rats. They also found that these rats showed their weak extinction rates in stressful situations but not in nonstressful situations. These weak extinction responses were shown across different anxiety tests (open-field test, novelty-suppressed feeding, and elevated-plus maze).

Urakawa *et al.* (2013) earlier studied anxiety responses and found that neurochemical and environmental factors could help explain these individual differences. They also looked specifically at what caused some rats to hold on to anxiety longer than other rats (i.e. what caused some rats to extinguish anxiety responses more slowly than other rats). They found that specific neurons (parvalbumin-expressing neurons) were associated with rats being more anxiety-resistant. This was the neurochemistry part of the explanation for what might cause these differences. They also found that enriched environments (specifically involving ladders, blocks, a bridge, and a maze in their cages) led to rats having significantly more of these neurons and significantly stronger extinction responses. Animal research here shows not only the individual differences but offers insights into the neurochemical and environmental factors associated with those differences.

Animal cognition research shows how different types of cognitive systems work for different species. Despite vast amounts of memory research in recent decades, there is still much to learn about how different types of memory work. This is true of both human and nonhuman primates. Neurological research shows how memory works on a minuscule level but there also is research needed on the macro-level for understanding how memory works when individuals are faced with problems. Animal research allows for more opportunity than human research to study individuals in their natural environments, or close to their natural environments, and to see how individuals use different types of memory and cognitive processes. Noser and Byrne (2015) spent weeks observing a wild male chacma baboon who faced the need to both protect his group from aggressive males and look for food. These observers watched as the baboon made effective use of his time away from his group. It was his memory, for things such as where he previously looked for food and where he found food, that helped him maximize his food gathering while minimizing his time away from his group. Their study showed much more detail of how a primate, in this case a baboon, uses memory than would be the case in human memory research.

And this last study provides an example of where animal research provides benefits that human research does not provide. In many ways it brings us back to issues we discussed at the very beginning of this book. Even in these days of modern electronic equipment for viewing all different areas of the brain, animal research still provides benefit by simply allowing for more detailed observations of individuals in their natural environments. Researchers can attach all sorts of electronic gadgets to animals and can measure all different parts of their brain and neurological systems. But they also can spend days, weeks, and even months studying their behaviors in all different types of settings. They can observe in detail how animals make use of their cognitive systems and how they try to maximize the benefits of their cognitive abilities. Observing animals over time helps us understand more about what these animals do to make the most of what they are able to do. And this sort of observation can also help us understand ways in which humans can make effective use of the same cognitive systems.

Evolutionary psychology

Evolutionary psychology is the branch of psychology that looks at behaviors, cognitive processes, and emotions from the perspective of evolution. This is not a field that always involves animals, but makes use of principles evident through and supported by animal research. It involves the application of Darwinian principles to human and nonhuman behaviors. There is a consistent focus in evolutionary psychology on how behaviors seen in laboratories function when out in the natural environment. When we look at behaviors from this direction we get to see the real function of those behaviors. Also, when considering behaviors from an evolutionary perspective we look not only at how the behaviors serve a function in the present environment but also how they have served functions throughout large spans of time. We see behaviors through the purposes that they serve and the natural goals that they help individuals reach.

Evolutionary psychology involves the application of evolutionary principles to understanding human and nonhuman behaviors. It is not a branch of comparative psychology per se but animal research does play a significant role in its development. It emphasizes evolutionary constructs and these constructs rely heavily on animal research. This approach to understanding behavior draws heavily on such animal-focused fields as zoology, ethology, evolutionary biology, and social biology. It emphasizes the functions of behaviors and psychological processes that develop as a result of natural selection.

Evolutionary psychology has become a more prominent field within psychology over the past twenty years. It started primarily as a subfield of comparative psychology but has branched out into other areas of psychology. With its emphasis on functional aspects of behaviors it often seems aligned with behavioral theory, but that does not adequately account for evolutionary psychology's emphasis on function as it applies to natural selection. Basically, evolutionary psychology addresses what function behaviors and other psychological processes serve as related to the survival of the individual and species.

This global approach to understanding behaviors, not only in their immediate functions but also in their functions throughout a species, offers a more comprehensive theoretical approach than other theories. Evolutionary psychology provides a way of understanding behaviors that addresses function over time and also function in the immediate environment. Humans and all animals with nervous systems developed different parts of their brains that allowed them to adapt to their environments. They dealt with changes in the environment and what those changes meant for what they needed to do. This is a process that involves addressing a number of different abilities over time. But this process is not quick and it does not change rapidly. Evolution is a process that is not necessarily clean and definitely not without complications. As a result, evolutionary psychology becomes a theoretical process to understand not only how behaviors change (slowly) over time but also how individuals must change (quickly) in order to adapt successfully to more immediate environmental changes.

We saw this complicated process previously in the chapter on overeating. Human obesity likely increased when physiological changes suited for heavy labor and physical exertion, including the need for high levels of calories to produce energy, were no longer needed given technological advances. Tools for farming and hunting made it less necessary for humans to exert large amounts of energy. Those physiological changes developed over many centuries but the environmental changes developed only over two hundred years or so. And a significant amount of those technological changes accrued over the past few decades. Humans became more obese in larger numbers as the technological advances outpaced their need for physical exertion. Domesticated animals face the same consequences as they no longer need to exert physiological energy to obtain food. Combating obesity is in many ways a method of finding some way to adapt quickly to environmental changes that outpace evolutionary changes.

Evolutionary psychology often emphasizes problem-solving as an important developmental concept. Individuals must develop effective problem-solving abilities to help them adapt to environmental factors. Even if evolution limits them on how they adapt to their environment, humans and other primates have the ability (and ability also developed through evolution) to problem-solve ways around and beyond those limits.

Seyfarth and Cheney (2015) looked at evolutionary processes as they apply to infants. Here we can see the very heart of what evolution produces, an ability to start an individual off successfully to interact with the world. Three core systems exist for human infants to prepare them to interact with the world: causal and spatial recognition among objects; numbers and recognition of individual agents' goals; and attentional states and causal mechanisms. These are all factors that start infants off as they enter the world and prepare them for interacting with the world. There is also research to support that many other types of animal species enter into the world with these same types of traits. From an evolutionary perspective, having these skills from birth would strengthen individuals', humans and nonhumans, likelihood of survival by preparing the individuals to recognize others' social attributes and use that recognition when interacting with them. Recognizing who is friendly and supportive and who is not would be essential from the start if one is likely to survive.

Looking at counseling and therapy from an evolutionary psychology perspective we see how much of counseling and psychological theories focuses on ways that individuals adapt to their own environments. Pavlovian and Skinnerian conditioning are both ways of building on primary needs and drives to develop new behaviors allowing us to adapt differently to our environments. "Differently" is the key word here because the ways patients learn on their own to adapt is not always effective or beneficial. Counseling and therapy often serve the role of helping individuals use conditioning techniques and learn to adapt in ways that are more beneficial and effective.

Understanding where psychology and counseling can fit in this process requires understanding one part of evolution and behaviors that often gets passed over. Just because animals learn that different behavioral and cognitive processes fit in with their survival instincts does not mean that what they learn is accurate. Animals learn all the time behavioral patterns that are ineffective and even harmful. We have discussed this throughout this book and emphasized it particularly in the chapters on depression and substance abuse. Behavioral patterns learned through conditioning are not always effective even if they developed through processes meant to aid in survival.

Hayes and Sanford (2015) provided a summary of the main contributions evolutionary psychology offers in the understanding of psychotherapy. They take a quote directly from a text on ethology (a branch of comparative psychology discussed throughout this book) when suggesting that psychology therapy can focus on the "...functions, mechanisms, development, and history of a phenomenon..." (Tinbergen 1963). This is, as the authors suggest, not a typical way of thinking about psychotherapy. As the authors state: "Most behavioral and life scientists are used to thinking about genetics in such a way but not behaviors or cognitions." Evolutionary theory presents a different way for clinicians to view behavior and behavior change; that is, a multi-level way of looking at behaviors where the important functions are not only immediate but also historical. Evolutionary theory addresses behavioral patterns that the person develops in their own life and also looks at what has been passed on to them from previous generations. This might involve learning and genetic information. Evolutionary theory provides a way of looking at behaviors from all different perspectives and addresses behaviors in more long-term ways than is the case with other theories.

With their focus on using evolutionary theory to understand psychopathology, Hayes and Sanford present a view of how the general fields of comparative psychology and clinical psychology merge. Psychological symptoms, this theory posits, arise from rigid behavioral patterns that arise from problematic criteria used to select behaviors. Individuals often avoid situations that would give them exposure to successful use of alternative behaviors and this limits their ability to develop new patterns. Individuals also have a tendency to recall behavioral patterns that reduce negative thoughts or feelings and this often leads to unhealthy patterns that are not effective long-term but bring about only temporary relief from different thoughts and feelings.

Notice here how the pattern for unhealthy psychological processes fits into the evolutionary patterns discussed throughout this book. Animals, human and nonhuman, are hard-wired neurologically for certain goals that increase the likelihood that they and their species will survive. Whether their emphasis is on individual or species survival continues to be an issue addressed through comparative psychology research. But the emphasis is, first and foremost, on survival. Pavlovian and Skinnerian conditioning are two prominent processes in psychology that explain how animals build on their natural instincts, again developed through centuries of evolution, to also rely on cognitive and behavioral patterns that parallel their instincts for survival. Animals, human and nonhuman alike, learn and retain behavioral and cognitive patterns that help direct them towards survival.

Evolution is not a flawless process. Behavioral patterns are not always effective. Human and nonhuman animals learn behavioral and cognitive approaches that are not the most effective. Entire species die out because their evolutionary processes did not lead to physiological or cognitive processes that actually aid in their survival. Human and nonhuman animals develop skills and abilities that are poor fits for their environments. And environmental changes often develop so quickly that they outpace any changes individuals make to help them function optimally. Evolution is an efficient and nonjudgmental process that emphasizes survival on a large scale but may cause difficulties on the more individual level. And those differences on the more individual level are the bulk of the difficulties counselors and therapists face.

This approach to understanding how evolutionary theory can impact psychotherapy's emphasis has undergone significant changes recently. In their book *Evolution in Four Dimensions*, Jablonka, Lamb, and Zeligowski (2014) note that the biological and genetic emphasis in evolutionary theory has changed over the years to take into account behavioral and learning processes. This is a significant change from Darwin's original position that evolutionary adaption occurs only through natural selection of random genetic variations. Some evolution, this new way of thinking goes, can be nonrandom and passed on through language and behavioral processes. This is not likely to be a revolutionary concept to therapists and counselors but over the years it was considered revolutionary within comparative psychology.

Evolutionary theory has supported various major therapy approaches over the past century and has also supported "up and coming" theoretical approaches for therapy. One example is compassion-focused therapy as summarized in Leaviss and Uttley (2015). This therapy approach focuses on self-assessment with particular emphasis on addressing shame and self-criticism. Compassion, as discussed in this approach, is conceptualized from an evolutionary perspective in terms of addressing the benefit that compassion has for aiding in survival. Compassion is the individual's motivation to try and alleviate suffering in an individual and others. It is also the motivation to try to know and prevent suffering in themselves and other individuals. This sensitivity developed throughout evolution for humans and animals as a way of aiding in the survival of their species. This helps towards those goals due to its ability to strengthen social bonding and feelings of contentment. These authors studied the effectiveness of compassion-focused therapy and found it effective for helping people who were high in self-criticism.

Evolutionary psychology might very well represent where comparative psychology is most likely to have benefits for clinical and counseling psychology. Comparative psychology research provides findings that benefit the understanding of animals and, in this way, has benefit even if the findings have no direct relationship to understanding humans. But the theoretical aspects of understanding the functions of behaviors and mental processes across different animal species can go a long way to more fully understanding why humans, as members of an animal species, do the things they do. There is more of an emphasis here on theoretical understanding of the functions behaviors and mental processes serve rather than understanding how specific processes work. Looking at these processes across different animal species, identifying their similarities, and determining what role their development serves in aiding survival and reproduction offers long-term benefits for understanding more comprehensively the function of different psychological processes.

References

Bensemann, J., Lobb, B., Podlesnik, C.A., and Elliffe, D. (2015) 'Steady-state choice between four alternatives obeys the constant-ratio rule.' *Journal of the Experimental Analysis of Behavior 104*, 1, 7–19.

Bitsika, V., Sharpley, C.F., Agnew, L.L., and Andronicos, N.M. (2015) 'Age-related differences in the association between stereotypic behaviour and salivary cortisol in young males with an Autism Spectrum Disorder.' *Physiology and Behavior 152*, 238–243.

Cacioppo, J.T., Cacioppo, S., Cole, S.W., Capitanio, J.P., Goossens, L., and Boomsma, D.I. (2015) 'Loneliness across phylogeny and a call for comparative studies and animal models.' *Perspectives on Psychological Science 10*, 2, 202–212.

Chivers, D.P. and Ferrari, M.C. (2015) 'The effect of group size and tutor-to-observer ratio on socially learned antipredator responses in woodfrog tadpoles.' *Animal Behaviour 104*, 25–29.

Craig, A.R., Cunningham, P.J., and Shahan, T.A. (2015) 'Behavioral momentum and accumulation of mass in multiple schedules.' *Journal of the Experimental Analysis of Behavior 103*, 3, 437–449.

Cunningham, P.J., Kuhn, R., and Reilly, M.P. (2015) 'A within-subject between-apparatus comparison of impulsive choice: T-maze and two-lever chamber.' *Journal of the Experimental Analysis of Behavior 104*, 1, 20–29.

Fedurek, P., Slocombe, K.E., and Zuberbühler, K. (2015) 'Chimpanzees communicate to two different audiences during aggressive interactions.' *Animal Behaviour 110*, 21–28.

Feng, X., Wang, L., Yang, S., Qin, D., *et al.* (2011) 'Maternal separation produces lasting changes in cortisol and behavior in rhesus monkeys.' *Proceedings of the National Academy of Sciences 108*, 34, 14312–14317.

Goldman, J.G. and Wood, J.N. (2015) 'An automated controlled-rearing method for studying the origins of movement recognition in newly hatched chicks.' *Animal Cognition 18*, 3, 723–731.

Griffin, A.S. and Guez, D. (2015) 'Innovative problem solving in nonhuman animals: the effects of group size revisited.' *Behavioral Ecology 26*, 3, 722–734.

Haller, S.P., Kadosh, K.C., Scerif, G., and Lau, J.Y. (2015) 'Social anxiety disorder in adolescence: how developmental cognitive neuroscience findings may shape understanding and interventions for psychopathology.' *Developmental Cognitive Neuroscience 13*, 11–20.

Hayes, S.C. and Sanford, B.T. (2015) 'Modern psychotherapy as a multidimensional multilevel evolutionary process.' *Current Opinion in Psychology 2*, 16–20.

Jablonka, E., Lamb, M.J., and Zeligowski, A. (2014) *Evolution in Four Dimensions (Revised edition): Genetic, Epigenetic, Behavioral, and Symbolic Variation in the History of Life*. Cambridge, MA: MIT Press.

Kamphuis, J., Lancel, M., Koolhaas, J.M., and Meerlo, P. (2015) 'Deep sleep after social stress: NREM sleep slow-wave activity is enhanced in both winners and losers of a conflict.' *Brain, Behavior, and Immunity 47*, 149–154.

Leaviss, J. and Uttley, L. (2015) 'Psychotherapeutic benefits of compassion-focused therapy: an early systematic review.' *Psychological Medicine 45*, 5, 927–945.

Li, J., Martin, S., Tricklebank, M.D., Schwarz, A.J., and Gilmour, G. (2015) 'Task-induced modulation of intrinsic functional connectivity networks in the behaving rat.' *Journal of Neuroscience 35*, 2, 658–665.

Liu, J., Chen, Y., Guo, L., Gu, B., *et al.* (2006) 'Stereotypic behavior and fecal cortisol level in captive giant pandas in relation to environmental enrichment.' *Zoo Biology 25*, 6, 445–460.

Lydon, S., Healy, O., Roche, M., Henry, R., Mulhern, T., and Hughes, B.M. (2015) 'Salivary cortisol levels and challenging behavior in children with autism spectrum disorder.' *Research in Autism Spectrum Disorders 10*, 78–92.

Maple, T.L. and Segura, V.D. (2014) 'Advancing behavior analysis in zoos and aquariums.' *The Behavior Analyst 38*, 1, 77–91.

Martin, A.L. (2015) 'The primatologist as a behavioral engineer.' *American Journal of Primatology 77*, 1, 2–10.

Noser, R. and Byrne, R.W. (2015) 'Wild chacma baboons (Papio ursinus) remember single foraging episodes.' *Animal Cognition 18*, 4, 921–929.

Poling, A. (2010) 'Looking to the future: will behavior analysis survive and prosper?' *The Behavior Analyst 33*, 1, 7–17.

Reznikov, R., Diwan, M., Nobrega, J.N., and Hamani, C. (2015) 'Towards a better preclinical model of PTSD: characterizing animals with weak extinction, maladaptive stress responses and low plasma corticosterone.' *Journal of Psychiatric Research 61*, 158–165.

Santos, F.P., Santos, F.C., Paiva, A., and Pacheco, J.M. (2015) 'Evolutionary dynamics of group fairness.' *Journal of Theoretical Biology 378*, 96–102.

Seyfarth, R.M., and Cheney, D.L. (2015) 'The Evolution of Concepts about Agents: Or, What do Animals Recognize when they Recognize an Individual?' In E. Margolis and S. Laurence (eds) *The Conceptual Mind: New Directions in the Study of Concepts*. Cambridge, MA: MIT Press.

Skinner, B.F. (1987) 'Why We Are Not Acting to Save the World.' In B.F. Skinner *Upon Further Reflection*. Englewood Cliffs, NJ: Prentice-Hall.

Strandburg-Peshkin, A., Farine, D.R., Couzin, I.D., and Crofoot, M. C. (2015) 'Shared decision-making drives collective movement in wild baboons.' *Science 348*, 6241, 1358–1361.

Tinbergen, N. (1963) 'On aims and methods of ethology.' *Zeitschrift für Tierpsychologie 20*, 4, 410–433.

Trask, S. and Bouton, M.E. (2015) 'Discriminative properties of the reinforcer can be used to attenuate the renewal of extinguished operant behavior.' *Learning and Behavior*, 1–11. DOI: 10.3758 s13420-015-0195-9

Urakawa, S., Takamoto, K., Hori, E., Sakai, N., Ono, T., and Nishijo, H. (2013) 'Rearing in enriched environment increases parvalbumin-positive small neurons in the amygdala and decreases anxiety-like behavior of male rats.' *BMC Neuroscience 14*, 1, 13.

Veyrac, A., Allerborn, M., Gros, A., Michon, F., *et al.* (2015) 'Memory of occasional events in rats: individual episodic memory profiles, flexibility, and neural substrate.' *Journal of Neuroscience 35*, 19, 7575–7586.

Wilson, M.L., Bloomsmith, M.A., and Maple, T.L. (2004) 'Stereotypic swaying and serum cortisol concentrations in three captive African elephants (Loxodonta africana).' *Animal Welfare 13*, 1, 39–43.

SUBJECT INDEX

addiction *see* food
   addictions; gambling
   problems; substance
   abuse
adolescents
   aggression 91
   substance abuse 111–3
aerobic exercises 36
aggression
   in adolescents 91
   always serves a function
      78–9, 86, 92
   anger and 78, 95
   animal research 79–81,
      86–91
   assertiveness training
      and 100
   case study 97–101
   clinical applications of
      animal research
      92–6
   cognitive-behavioral
      therapy for 94–5
   competition and 83–6
   conciliatory behaviors
      90, 214
   cost-benefit ratio 80–1
   costly to the individual
      80
   domesticated animals
      79, 89
   Functional Analytic
   Therapy 96

functional behavioral
   assessment 92–3
and group formation
   86–9
legal outcomes of 94
object relations therapy
   96
operant conditioning
   and 29
overview of 78–9
perception role in 85–6
in play 90–1
proactive 84–5
reactive 84–5
recalibration theory
   82–3
sexual 87–8
sleep and 96
Stress Inoculation
   Therapy 94
testosterone and 91–2
weapons and 81–2, 214
welfare-tradeoff ratios
   82–3
Ainsworth, Mary 18–9
alcohol *see* substance abuse
Analysis of Receiver
   Operating
   Characteristics (ROC)
   32
Animal Intelligence 12

antidepressant medication,
   research into 65–6,
   68–71
anxiety 235
Aristotle 13
Asperger's Disorder 152–3
associative learning 27–30
attachment theory 18–9,
   21, 168–9
autistic spectrum disorders
   case study 170–4
   diagnosis 152
   environmental
      enrichment
      research 164–6
   friendships 159–60, 161,
      164, 167–8
   genetic factors 153–5
   maternal infection 154
   neuroscience research
      234–5
   no medication
      specifically for 155
   overview of 151–2
   "quasi-autism" 168
   Reactive Attachment
      Disorder 168–9
   social interaction needs
      155–8, 163–4,
      226–7
   social skills training
      158–60

behavior theory 203–4,
      205–6, 229–33
behavior therapy 39
behaviorism 16–7, 20–1,
      216
Bowlby, John 18–9

capital punishment 29
case studies
      aggression 97–101
      autistic spectrum
            disorders 170–4
      depression 71–3
      gambling problems
            144–7
      overeating and obesity
            195–8
      substance abuse 120–4
causal illusion 34
causal reasoning 34
classical conditioning 27,
      40–1
coalitions 86–9
cognitive neuroscience
      233–6
cognitive rehabilitation 45
cognitive theory 204
cognitive-behavioral
      therapy
      for aggression 94–5
      cognitive impairment
            and 45
      history of 20–1
      need for significant
            stimulus 41
      purpose of behavior and
            41, 204–6
      for substance abuse 116,
            118
comparative psychology
      and clinical psychology
            240, 242
      criticism of 11
      definition of 9–10
      history of 12–4
      and psychotherapy 14–5,
            209–12

compassion 241–2
competition
      and aggression 83–6
      social competition
            theory 58–61
conciliatory behaviors 90,
      214
conditioned fear 217
Conditioned Reflexes and
      Psychiatry 14
conditioning
      classical 27, 40–1
      operant 27–30, 40–1,
            217–8
construct validity 53
contextual processing
      gambling problems
            137–8
      substance abuse 109–10,
            111
counseling see
      psychotherapy

Darwin, Charles 12, 13,
      213–4
de-escalation strategies
      59–60, 61–2
decision-making
      and gambling problems
            131–2, 136–8, 143
      and group dynamics 225
declarative memory 42
dementia 37–8
depression
      "affect" 52
      as an adaptation 63, 65
      antidepressant
            medication
            research 65–6,
            68–71
      case study 71–3
      chronic stress and 64
      clinical interventions for
            64–8
      ethological observation
            methods 55

evolutionary perspective
      61–3, 66–7
genetic predisposition
      to 63–4
Harlow's model 54–6
interpersonal loss and 62
learned helplessness
      56–7, 70–1
methods used to test
      models 52–4
mindfulness for 67
"mood" 52
overview of 51–2
and perceptions of likely
      outcomes 66–7
problem-solving therapy
      67
psychotic symptoms
      54–5
social competition
      theory 58–61
social defeat theory
      57–61, 227–8
validity of models 53–7
Descartes 11
Descent of Man, The 12,
      213
Determinants of Infant
      Behavior 18–9
domesticated animals
      aggression 79, 89
      overeating and obesity
            192–3
drugs see antidepressant
      medication; substance
      abuse

eating see overeating and
      obesity
Ekman, Paul 215
Ellis, Albert 205
enriched environments
      autistic spectrum
            disorders 164–6
      learning and memory
            35–6

environmental psychology
215–6
environmental stability 44
episodic memory 233–4
ethology 14, 19–20, 55
*Evolution in Four
Dimensions* 241
evolutionary psychology
237–42
evolutionary theory 12,
213–4, 241–2
exercise research 36, 192–5
*Expression of the Emotions
in Man and Animals*
213, 220–1
extinction
gambling problems
143–4
resistance to 231–2
Eysenck, Hans 15

face validity 53
Facial Action Coding
System (FACS) 215
facial expressions 215,
220–1
family therapy 68
Flourens, Pierre 12–3
food addictions 190–2
see also overeating and
obesity
Freud, Sigmund 8, 202–3
Freudian instinct theory 19
friendship 159–60, 161,
164, 167–8
Functional Analytic
Therapy 96

gambling problems
animal research 129–31
case study 144–7
clinical interventions for
139–44
contextual processing
and 137–8
decision-making and
131–2, 136–8, 143

evolutionary theory and
138–9
extinction techniques
143–4
functional analytic
therapy for 143
impulsivity and 134–5,
139–40
motivational
interviewing 140
neurochemical factors
135–6
overview of 128–9
reinforcers and 131–5,
138, 143–4
self-monitoring
techniques 140–3
understanding benefits
to individual 140–1
group dynamics 86–7,
223–9

habituation 26
hard architecture 215–6
Harlow, Harry 12, 54–6,
213, 219
Hediger, Heini 218–9
hierarchy of needs 220
hippocampus 36–7
history of comparative
psychology 12–4
humanistic psychology 220
Huntington's Disease 38

impulsivity
and gambling problems
134–5, 139–40
measurement of 229–30
and substance abuse
110–3, 117–9
instrumental aggression
84–5
Istradefylline 70

*Journal of Applied Behavior
Analysis* 17

*Journal of the Experimental
Analysis of Behavior*
17

Kohler, Wolfgang 12

learned helplessness 56–7,
70–1
learning
aerobic exercise and 36
aging and 37
associative 27–30
as change in mechanism
of behavior 26
definition of 25–6
enriched environments
35–6
environmental stability
and 44
hippocampus role 36–7
improving in
psychotherapy 43–6
neurobiological factors
35–8
non-associative 26–7
predictability and 44
in psychotherapy 38–46
similarities across
species 33–4
social 30–1
loneliness 226–7
see also friendship; social
interaction
Lorenz, Konrad 14, 19, 214
*Love at Goon Park: Harry
Harlow and the
Science of Affection* 56

Maslow, Abraham 219–20
meaningfulness 207–12
memory
aerobic exercise and 36
aging and 37
Analysis of Receiver
Operating
Characteristics
(ROC) 32

memory *cont.*
  declarative 42
  definition of 31
  dementia 37–8
  for emotional events
      43–4
  enriched environments
      35–6
  environmental stability
      and 44
  episodic 233–4
  hippocampus role 36–7
  improving in
      psychotherapy 43–6
  neurobiological factors
      35–8
  predictability and 44
  procedural 42
  in psychotherapy 38–43
  reconsolidation of 45–6
  research methods 32,
      236
  similarities across
      species 33–4
mindfulness 67
Minocycline 70–1
motivational interviewing
  gambling 140
  substance abuse 116–7

negative punishment 29
negative reinforcement
    28–9
neurobiological factors
  cognitive neuroscience
      233–6
  gambling problems
      135–6
  learning and memory
      35–8
non-associative learning
    26–7

obesity *see* overeating and
    obesity
object relations therapy 96
On Aggression 214

operant conditioning
    27–30, 40–1, 217–8
Origin of Species, The 12
overeating and obesity
  animal research
      (exercise) 192–5
  case study 195–8
  domesticated animals
      192–3
  evolutionary perspective
      183–5
  food addictions 190–2
  genetic factors 182, 191
  not found in animals in
      wild 183, 192
  and reward properties
      186–7
  stress eating 187–9
  zoo animals 193

Parkinson's Disease 70
pathological validity 53
Pavlov, Ivan 12, 14
pharmacological validity
    53
Plutarch 13
positive reinforcement 28
positive punishment 29–30
predictability 44
primary reinforcers 130
proactive aggression 84–5
problem-solving 67, 225–6
procedural memory 42
psychoanalysis 15, 42–3
  see also Freud, Sigmund
Psychologie Comparée 12
psychotherapy
  comparative psychology
      and 14–5, 209–12
  learning and memory in
      38–46
PTSD 235
punishment 29–30
purposeful behaviors
    204–12

reactive aggression 84–5

Reactive Attachment
    Disorder 168–9
recalibration theory of
    aggression 82–3
reconsolidation, memory
    45–6
reinforcement
  and gambling problems
      131–5, 138, 143–4
  and learning 27–9
  schedules of 40, 133,
      230–2
risk *see* gambling problems
Romanes, George John
    12–3

*Science and Human
    Behavior* 16
secondary reinforcers 130
self-actualization 220
self-monitoring techniques
    140–3
sensitization 26–7
sexual aggression 87–8
skills training
  autistic spectrum
      disorders 158–60
  substance abuse 116,
      118–9
Skinner, B.F. 12, 16–7, 216
sleep
  and aggression 96
  and social conflict 227–8
Social Communication
    Disorder 153
social competition theory
    58–61
social defeat theory 57–61,
    227–8
social interaction
  autistic spectrum
      disorders 155–8,
      163–4, 226–7
  friendships 159–60, 161,
      164, 167–8
  neurodiversity and 163

social connectedness
160–4
social skills training 116,
118–9, 234
social learning 30–1
social skills training 116,
118–9, 234
Society for the
Experimental Analysis
of Behavior 17
soft architecture 215–6
spanking 29–30
SSRIs 68–9
stress eating 187–9
Stress Inoculation Therapy
94
subordination 58–60
see also social defeat
theory
substance abuse
adolescents 111–3
animal studies vs.
human studies
119–20
case study 120–4
clinical applications of
research 115–9
cognitive-behavioral
therapy 116, 118
contextual processing
and 109–10, 111
costs/benefits of 114–6
definition of 105–6
distraction-based
strategies 118
evolutionary factors
113–5
functional analysis of
115
impulsivity and 110–3,
117–9
isolation and 111–2
motivational
interviewing 116–7
rats primary in research
106

reward processing and
108–10
skills training 116, 118–9
use vs. addiction 107–8

Tavistock Study Group 18
teaching by animals 34
teenagers *see* adolescents
Thorndike, Edward 12
Tight Spaces 216
Tinbergen, Nikolaas 14
Tolman, Edward 12
training animals 217–8

"uniqueness" of humans 11

validity of depression
models 53–7
von Frisch, Karl 14

wellness, animal 220
wheel-running 192–4
Witmer, Lightner 13
Wolpe, Joseph 14–5

Zoo Animal Welfare 166
zoos
applied behavior analysis
in 217–8
Harlow's work and 55
obesity in zoo animals
193
structural environment
in 215–6

AUTHOR INDEX

Abbé, A. 66
Adriani, W. 112
Aharonovich, E. 45
Ahmed, S.H. 106, 107, 137
Ainsworth, M.S. 11, 18, 19
Allan, S. 61
Altman, J. 112
Amano, H. 187
American Psychiatric
    Association 152
Anders, T.F. 159
Angell, M. 66
Anselme, P. 137, 138
Anthony, J.C. 108
Arakawa, S. 70
Avena, N.M. 190, 191
Averill, J.R. 82
Azrin, N.H. 29

Bacon, W.E. 189
Bartolomucci, A. 183
Baumeister, R.F. 130
Bazhan, N. 188
Beck, R. 94
Beidel, D.C. 159
Bell, R.L. 106
Benjamin Jr, L.T. 15
Bensemann, J. 230
Berridge, K.C. 137, 188
Bertram, S.M. 80
Bitsika, V. 235
Bizon, J.L. 37
Blase, S.L. 15

Blaszczynski, A. 128
Bloomsmith, M.A. 235
Blum, D. 55
Boesch, C. 11
Bohnert, K.M. 108
Boileau, I. 136
Bouton, M.E. 232
Bowlby, J. 18, 19
Brake, S.C. 112
Branchi, I. 162
Breland, K. 216
Breland, M. 216
Bretherton, I. 18
Brezis, M. 65
Brookman-Frazee, L. 151
Brown, A.S. 154
Brownlow, C. 164
Burghardt, P.R. 193
Buss, D.M. 83
Buunk, A.P. 160
Byrne, R.W. 236

Cabeza, R. 43
Cacioppo, J.T. 156, 162, 226
Campbell, D.L. 164
Camus, S.M. 55
Careau, V. 193
Carr, G.V. 68
Carré, J.M. 84
Carroll, K.M. 115
Carroll, M.E. 113
Carvalho, S. 60
Carver, L.J. 156

Cassel, R. 42
Cathcart, K. 165
Chadman, K.K. 155, 162
Chaffin, M. 169
Chambers, R.A. 112
Chang, Q. 43
Chase, H.W. 134
Chausse, B. 195
Chen, M.K. 136
Cheney, D.L. 160, 238
Chiarotti, F. 112
Chivers, D.P. 225
Chomsky, N. 20
Claidiere, N. 11
Clark, L. 134, 135, 136
Clyman, R.B. 43
Coccaro, E.F. 83
Coe, C.L. 157
Colantuoni, C. 190
Collins, W.A. 156
Cooper, M.A. 57
Coppens, C.M. 91
Corwin, R.L. 190
Courtney, K.E. 113
Craig, A.R. 231
Crawley, J.N. 154, 155
Cunningham, P.J. 229, 231
Curlik, D.M. 43

Dallaire, J.A. 164
Dalley, J.W. 110
Dalton, N.S. 163
Daly, M. 11

Daoura, L. 112
Darwin, C. 10, 12, 213, 220
Davis, C. 191
Davis, J.F. 186
Davis, R.L. 35
DeFazio, R.A. 37
Degenhardt, L. 108
Del Vecchio, T. 95
Dellu-Hagedorn, F. 137
Detillion, C.E. 156
Dewsbury, D.A. 19
Dijkstra, P. 160
Dimitriou, S.G. 190
Ding, Y. 112
Dolcos, F. 43
Domjan, M. 25
Drury, J.P. 85
Dunn-Meynell, A.A. 190

Edwards, T.C. 17
Ekman, P. 214, 215
Ellegood, J. 155
Ellis, B.J. 84
Engh, A.L. 88
Erikson, K.I. 36
Escobedo, L. 158
Evenden, J.L. 110
Everitt, B.J. 107, 110
Every-Palmer, S. 66
Ewan, E.E. 133
Eysenck, H.J. 39

Falls, W.A. 194
Faridar, A. 154
Fecteau, S. 186
Fedurek, P. 227
Feng, X. 235
Fernandez, E. 94
Fernando, A.B. 110
Ferrari, M.C. 225
Finnie, P.S. 45
Fletcher, G.E. 163
Flinn, M.V. 90
Flourens, P. 12
Foss, B. 19
Foster, T.C. 37
Fournier, M.A. 61

Freeman, S.F. 160
Friesen, W.V. 215
Frith, U. 169
Fruth, B. 88
Fuchs, T. 42

Gácsi, M. 161
Gadad, B.S. 151
Gage, F.H. 35
Galef, B.G. 11
Gardner, H. 20
Garner, R.P. 194
Gass, P. 56
Geary, D.C. 86
Geiger, B.M. 186
Gilbert, P. 61
Glickman, S.E. 139
Gold, P.E. 43
Goldman, J.G. 234
Goldman-Rakic, P.S. 113
Goodlin-Jones, B.L. 159
Gosling, S. 12
Graham, P. 33
Green, J. 169
Greene, R. 86
Griffin, A.S. 225
Guariglia, S.R. 155
Guez, D. 225
Gunnar, M.R. 156
Gutstein, S.E. 159

Haaker, J. 112
Hacker, C.E. 161
Haller, S.P. 234
Hammack, S.E. 57, 194
Harb, M.R. 186
Hare, B. 87, 88
Hariri, A.R. 84
Harlow, H.F. 18, 54, 162, 169
Harper, D. 134
Hartup, W.W. 160
Hasin, D. 45
Hauber, M.E. 80
Haun, D.B. 162
Hawkley, L.C. 156
Hawley, P.H. 92

Hayden, B.Y. 132
Hayes, C. 13
Hayes, K.J. 13
Hayes, S.C. 21, 239
Hebebrand, J. 191
Hediger, H. 219
Heilbronner, S.R. 132
Hennessy, M.B. 157
Hernstein, R.J. 20
Highfield, R. 11
Hikosaka, O. 70
Hillman, C.H. 36
Himmler, B.T. 91
Hofmann, S.G. 67, 95
Hohmann, G. 88, 91
Holt-Lunstad, J. 160
Hone-Blanchet, A. 186
Horback, K.M. 161
Horner, V. 30, 31
Horton, B.M. 80
Hostinar, C.E. 156
Howick, J. 66
Hsiao, E.Y. 153
Huhman, K.L. 57
Hulse, S.H. 189
Hunt, M. 134
Hutchinson, R.R. 29

Iaria, G. 43
Irish, M. 38
Irwin, M.R. 62

Jablonka, E. 241
Jaccard, J. 52
Jacobs, H.L. 189
Jacoby, J. 52

Kamin, L.J. 40
Kamphuis, J. 96, 227
Kandel, E. 42
Kanner, L. 169
Kar, S. 15
Kasari, C. 160, 164
Kassinove, J.I. 134
Kawecki, T.J. 35
Kay, C. 169
Kazdin, A.E. 15

Kempermann, G. 35
Kessler, R.C. 51
Kharlamova, A. 89
King, B.M. 184
Kirch, R.D. 38
Kleine-Budde, K. 51
Klempel, M.C. 195
Klimentidis, Y.C. 185
Koen, J.D. 32
Kohlenberg, R.J. 21
Komdeur, J. 161
Koob, G.F. 109
Kramer, A.F. 36
Kreek, M.J. 113
Krimer, L.S. 113
Kringelbach, M.L. 188
Krishnan, V. 64
Kuhn, R. 229
Künzl, C. 89
Kurz, A. 45

Laflamme, D.P. 192
Lagorio, C.H. 133
Lakshminarayanan, V. 136
Laland, K.N. 11
Lamb, M.J. 241
Lambe, E.K. 113
Laugeson, E.A. 159
Laviola, G. 112
Lawrence, A.J. 135
Layton, J.B. 160
Leach, H. 89
Leaviss, J. 241
LeBar, K. 43
Lecourtier, L. 42
Leekam, S.R. 153
Lennings, C.J. 96
Levin, B.E. 190
Levine, J.A. 193
Levine, S. 157
Levy, K.N. 21
Lewis, M.H. 164
Lezak, K.R. 57
Li, B. 70
Li, J. 186, 233
Li, T.K. 106
Liberzon, I. 109

Lindburg, D.G. 219
Liotti, G. 21
Lipska, B.K. 112
Liu, J. 235
Liu, X. 188
Liu Y. 156
Lobo, D.S.S. 136
Locke, J. 164
Lorenz, K. 18
Lovaas, O.I. 165
Lucki, I. 68
Luigjes, J. 108
Lum, J. 42
Lydon, S. 235
Lynch, W.J. 106

Ma, D. 33
Maas, J. 140
McBride, W.J. 106
McCormick, C.M. 84
McDonald, M.M. 79
McEachin, J.J. 165
McIntyre, S.H. 26
MacKillop, J. 118
McLaughlin, R. 29
MacLeon, E.L. 10, 33
McTighe, S.M. 38
Madden, G.J. 133
Maestripieri, D. 10
Maier, S.F. 56, 57
Maney, D.L. 80
Maple, T.L. 166, 218, 219, 233, 235
Maren, S. 109
Marshall, A.J. 91
Martin, A.L. 233
Maruyama, I.N. 187
Maslow, A.H. 220
Mason, G.J. 164
Matsumoto, M. 70
Meijer, J.H. 192
Mery, F. 35, 44
Miklósi, Á. 161
Miller, L.J. 161
Miller, R.R. 31
Mirrione, M.M. 70
Moeller 110

Molander, A.C. 135
Moore, A.J. 161
Morey, D.F. 89
Morris, E. 17, 85
Moussavi, S. 51, 66
Muehlenbein, M.P. 90
Munson, J.M. 26
Murphy, C.M. 118
Murray, M.J. 159

Nader, K. 45
Navarrete, C.D. 79
Neisewander, J.L. 112
Nesse, R.M. 62, 113
Nestler, E.J. 64
Nielsen, M. 31
Nobel Prize in Physiology
   or Medicine 14
Noser, R. 236
Novak, C.M. 193
Novotny, C. 8
Nowak, M. 11
Nower, L. 128
Nunes, E. 45
Nylander, I. 112

O'Leary, K.D. 95
Onken, L.S. 115
Oskina, I. 89
Ozonoff, S. 165

Packard, M.G. 37
Papachristou, H. 111
Papini, M. 13
Pascucci, T. 112
Pate, J.L. 27
Patterson, P.H. 153
Pavlov, I.P. 14, 27
Peartree, N.A. 112
Peñagarikano, O. 156
Pentkowski, N.S. 112
Perdue, B.M. 166
Perry, J.L. 113
Peters, H. 134
Phan, K.L. 109
Pieretti, S. 112
Pijlman, F.T. 189

Pinker, S. 82
Platt, M.L. 132
Poldrack, R.A. 36, 37
Poling, A. 17, 233
Ponzi, D. 90
Pool, E. 187
Potenza, M.N. 112
Premack, D. 34
Price, J. 58
Prior, M.R. 153
Pruessner, J. C. 45
Pryor, K. 28
Przewlocki, R. 165
Puckering, C. 169

Rada, P. 186
Rampon, C. 35
Rao, P.A. 159
Ravaud, P. 66
Reichow, B. 158
Reilly, M.P. 229
Reis, H.T. 156
Rekers, Y. 162
Reznikov, R. 235
Rice, H.B. 190
Richards, D. 51
Ridley, R.M. 169
Riley, W.T. 78
Rivalan, M. 137
Robbers, Y. 192
Robbins, T.W. 107, 110, 129, 190
Robinson, M.J. 137
Rogers, R. 110
Romanes, G.J. 12
Roney, J.R. 10
Rosen, A.C. 45
Ruan, H. 156
Rumbaugh, D.M. 27
Rutter, M. 168

Sado, M. 51
Sanford, B.T. 239
Santos, F.P. 223
Santos, L.R. 136
Savage, S. 33
Schare, M.L. 134

Schildberger, K. 80
Schneider, S. 17
Schneider, T. 165
Schwabe, L. 36, 45
Segni, M.D. 191
Segura, V. 218, 233
Seligman, M.E. 56
Sell, A.N. 82
Seyfarth, R.M. 160, 238
Shackelford, T.K. 83
Shahan, T.A. 231
Sharma, K.N. 189
Sherwin, C.M. 193
Shors, T.J. 43
Sibold, J.S. 194
Skinner, B.F. 16, 17, 21, 233
Slavich, G.M. 62
Slocombe, K.E. 227
Smid, H.M. 44
Smith, D.G. 190
Smith, M.T. 96
Smith, T. 160, 165
Snyder, H.L. 189
Solomon, M. 159
Sommer, R. 215, 216
Spear, L.P. 112
Spear, N.E. 31
Stavropoulos, K.M. 156
Steiner, A.M. 158
Stevenson, P.A. 80
Strandburg-Peshkin, A. 224
Sullivan, R.M. 156
Suomi, S.J. 54, 162
Székely, T. 161

Takács, Á. 140
Taylor, J.R. 112
Teasdale, J.D. 67
Terrace, H.S. 42
Thierry, B. 90
Thomas, H. 13
Thompson-Brenner, H. 8
Tinbergen, N. 240
Tomasello, M. 162, 163
Tooby, J. 82
Trask, S. 232

Treiber, F.A. 78
Trinquart, L. 66
Trut, L. 89
Tsai, M. 21
Turczak, J. 165

Uljarevic, M. 153
Ullman, M.T. 42
Urakawa, S. 235
Uttley, L. 241

van den Bos, R. 135
Van Praag, H. 35
Van Ree, J.M. 189
Van Vugt, M. 79
Vanderschuren, L.J. 106
Venzala, E. 58
Verdejo-García, A. 135
Veyrac, A. 233
Vezina, P. 109
Vitacco, M.J. 110
Voermans, N.C. 37
Vogt, J.L. 157
Vohs, K.D. 130
Volkmar, F. 158
Vollmayr, B. 56
vom Scheidt, J. 114

Wang, Z. 156
Warneken, F. 163
Warren-Leubecker, A. 219
Watson, R.I. 15
Wells, J.C. 183
Wen, J.Y. 35
Westen, D. 8
Whiten, A. 11, 31
Whitney, T. 159
Wilson, M. 11
Wilson, M.K. 18
Wilson, M.L. 79, 235
Wilson, W.J. 25
Winstanley, C.A. 129, 135
Wise, R.A. 186
Wobber, V. 88
Wolf, M. 17
Wolpe, J. 15
Wolterink, G. 189

Wood, J.N. 234
Woods, M.G. 78
World Health Organization
    169
Wrangham, R. 79, 88, 89
Wu, C.F. 156
Wystrach, A. 33

Yamada, K. 70
Yang, M. 161
Yang, Z. 56
Yonelinas, A.P. 32
Yoo, J. 154, 155
Young, L.J. 156

Zeeb, F.D. 129
Zelena, D. 188
Zeligowski, A. 241
Zentall, T.R. 133
Zimmermann, R.R. 18,
    54, 169
Zuberbühler, K. 227